Philosophy, Politics, and Society, Sixth Series

Philosophy, Politics, and Society, Sixth Series

Justice between
Age Groups and Generations

PETER LASLETT & JAMES S. FISHKIN

EDITORS

Yale University Press   New Haven & London

Designed by Sonia Scanlon.

Set in Galliard type by Rainsford Type.

Printed in the United States of America by
BookCrafters, Inc., Chelsea, Michigan.

Library of Congress Cataloging-in-Publication Data

Philosophy, politics, and society, sixth series :
justice between age groups and generations /
Peter Laslett and James S. Fishkin, editors.

p.   cm.

Includes bibliographical references.

ISBN 0-300-05073-9 (alk paper)

1. Distributive justice. 2. Justice.

3. Intergenerational relations. I. Laslett, Peter.

II. Fishkin, James S.

JC578.P45   1992

320'.01'1—dc20   91-40658

CIP

1007549 S52 1

The paper in this book meets the guidelines for permanence
and durability of the Committee on Production Guidelines for
Book Longevity of the Council on Library Resources.

10 9 8 7 6 5 4 3 2 1

Contents

Preface

The series entitled *Philosophy, Politics, and Society* began in 1956 and its fifth number was issued in 1979, under the editorship of Peter Laslett, the initiator of the series, and James Fishkin. Until this number, occasional replacements of editors have been the only changes in the format of these collections, whose sole object and function have been the publication of the most significant contributions to the area of reflection, inquiry, and theoretical generalization current at the time each volume was assembled. The volumes were not organized around a particular theme, being simply collections of what the editors judged to be important.

With this collection there has been a change. For the first time a theme has been followed in choosing the contributions, one that was adopted for a conference held at the University of Texas at Austin in October 1988 under the auspices of the Liberty Fund. Deliberate choice has been exercised in three directions: in the determination of the theme of the meeting, in the choice of the people who were asked to contribute papers at the conference, and in the selection of contributions to appear in this volume, from those papers and from other sources. George Sher, for example, did not attend the conference; his chapter has been in print for some years. Tyler Cowen, Derek Parfit, and Larry Temkin attended the meeting but wrote their contributions later, stimulated by the dialogue begun at the conference.

We have departed from the established pattern of thirty-five years for two reasons. The theme of justice over time, between age groups and between generations, seemed to us to be an issue of overriding significance in the 1990s, not only to scholars and to the highly educated generally but also to people throughout the world. In addition, because justice over time has not been sufficiently discussed by philosophers, political theorists, or social scientists, we felt that we should commission papers on the topic.

We discovered to our surprise, moreover, that in Western thought this theme is of extremely recent origin. These points are covered in our extended Introduction, another innovation in the *Philosophy, Politics, and*

Society series, and we have decided to explore the issue further, perhaps in a joint book, perhaps in two individual volumes.

Peter Laslett
James S. Fishkin

Introduction: Processional Justice

PETER LASLETT AND

JAMES S. FISHKIN

Political Theory and the Passage of Time

The revival of political theory over the past three decades has taken place within the grossly simplifying assumptions of a largely timeless world. It is a world limited, at most, to the horizons of a single generation who make binding choices, for all time, for all successor generations. Although such recent theorists of justice as Rawls, Nozick, and Ackerman and recent advocates of utilitarianism all gesture toward taking time into account, the problems detailed in this volume demonstrate that their efforts should be considered to be no more than gestures.

Over significant periods of time, new issues arise that cannot easily be assimilated into current patterns of analysis. Principles of justice, equality, and utility that yield reasonable conclusions for fixed population sizes over short periods begin to produce bizarre results once cohort sizes or total population sizes or both vary over time. The implicit contractual relations among generations fail for the same reason. Our ordinary notions of benefits and harm lose their effectiveness because they are tied to notions of identity that give way when choices involving future possible people must be made. Over long periods of time the standard practice of discounting leads us to value one life now more than millions in the distant future—even when we can be quite sure of the danger posed by nuclear wastes, for example, to lives in the distant future. In general, time produces crucial theoretical impediments to the kind of systematic theory that has motivated the recent revival of political philosophy. Those impediments are the focus of this volume.

The moral notions embedded in our actual practices are

no more adequate than our political theories to deal with justice over time. The modern welfare state is commonly said to be founded on a kind of intergenerational contract. During its productive years, each generation pays to support those who are dependent on it, assuming that when its own dependent phases come, it will be supported in turn by successor generations. If this kind of intergenerational contract were viable, it would resolve many of the moral relations among generations. Issues of distributive justice and mutual obligation would be viewed as settled by a continuing implicit agreement.

Let us say that a strong version of the generational social contract argument would apply if the contract settled, in a determinate manner, the sufficient conditions for obligations among generations. There are, however, reasons to be skeptical that any strong version of a social contract argument can apply across generations. If we think of a contract among contemporaries, it would be reasonable to stipulate that either of two conditions apply: (1) that the comparability of benefits and burdens undertaken by the parties be reasonably foreseeable, or when (1) does not apply, (2) that there be some possibility of redress among the relevant parties for gross unforeseen inequities undermining (1). If a contract is to settle things, people should be able to rely on some account of what to expect and what will be expected of them. If, however, things turn out otherwise, there should be some possibility of redressing any inequities among the parties.

In fact, the relations among generations routinely undermine both of these conditions. As David Thomson, Peter Laslett, James Fishkin, and others argue in this volume, variations in cohort sizes and in political decisions about the character and destination of welfare flows produce conditions that undermine (1), while the temporal asymmetry of the parties undermines (2).

To take a simplified example of the effect of differential cohort sizes, the junior editor of this series is a member of the so-called Baby Boom generation. His children are members of a much smaller cohort. During their adulthood, his children will be required to contribute to the support of an elderly population vastly increased in size over that of the present in the United States. Yet their prospects of receiving similar treatment in their later years will depend to a considerable extent on the relative size of the cohorts, as yet unborn, who will be adults during those years. Given the processional character of generational relations, A (the current Baby Boom generation) will find itself supported by B and B in turn by C. If A is much larger than B and the size of C is at present unknowable, the per capita sacrifice of the Bs may be far greater than anything the As had to pay, but their prospects of receiving any comparable benefits are completely uncertain given the unknowable character of C. Furthermore, by the time the Cs come along, the As will be disappearing. There will be no possibility of redress because the previous beneficiaries will have passed away in the interim. The temporal asymmetry of the parties involves disappearing beneficiaries and unknowable per person sacrifices.

David Braybrooke shows how these problems are only increased over longer time periods. The benefits and burdens of any social contract become totally unforeseeable and the possibility of redress among the relevant parties is only made more difficult when the time periods for which a contract might hold are increased. Braybrooke takes the position that only revisable contracts, continually open to renegotiation, could be of any use in intergenerational issues. But such a weak concept of contract is far, indeed, from the strong contract that would settle things in a determinate manner.

Conditions routinely apply that would invalidate any strong version of the generational contract argument across generations. This does not mean that there may not be some room for weaker versions of the contract metaphor (as Fishkin suggests at the end of his chapter), but the basic issues ought not to be viewed as already determined by an agreement. The lack of a strong generational contract should, however, be viewed as the beginning of the debate and not the end of it. For without a strong version of the generational contract argument, we face many substantive issues about the consequences of one policy or another across generations. Even if our obligations are not settled by a contract, we still must consider the effects of our actions (and inactions) on subsequent generations.

Or need we? Richard Epstein takes the position that we should simply leave these issues to the market because our efforts to do otherwise will only make things worse. This view is extremely controversial, however, as shown by the debate between Epstein and Braybrooke. Braybrooke argues that single-minded reliance on markets risks consigning some of our successors to effective slavery. How could we regard such a bargain as binding on our posterity? Yet a total commitment to market relations may have this result.

But the other possibility—that of considering the substantive effects of policies across generations—requires some conceptual framework. The contributions to this volume focus on a number of issues that pertain to common principles across the generational boundaries; variations in population and birth cohort size and the problems of personal identity and discounting deserve special mention. Our substantive moral principles have not usually been refined to deal with variations of this character. Classical utilitarianism will tell us that a society is better off even when people far less happy than the average are added—because they raise the total. Average utilitarianism, on the other hand, is completely insensitive to numbers. Suppose human history really did start with a supremely happy Adam and Eve. According to average utilitarianism, the entire history of the world since then would be a violation of the principle.

These difficulties with utilitarian views are well known, especially since the work of Derek Parfit. Larry Temkin shows how puzzles of the same kind arise for equality, and by implication for many other nonutilitarian substantive principles. If we judge equality proportionately, we can find ourselves approving changes that increase the number of the worst off in the name of equality. We may also sanction changes that have no effect on the worst off but in the name of equality increase the percentage of those near the median. Are the poor better off merely because there are more middle-class people and the worst placed therefore constitute a lower percentage of the whole? If our interest in equality is motivated by a concern for the interests of the less fortunate, then it is muddled by variations in the size of birth cohorts.

The contingencies of personal identity also complicate the assessment of human interests across generational boundaries. We would ordinarily assume that a person can be harmed only by being made worse off than that person would otherwise be. But when we deal with the interests of future possible people this assumption breaks down, for many of the actions that would apparently produce harms also affect whether a person will come into existence at all. We can no longer say about the apparently harmful action that the persons harmed are worse off than they otherwise would have been. Had the harmful action not occurred, the persons in question would never have come into existence.

Our notions of how to assess human interests seem to break down for intergenerational cases. These difficulties are examined by Jonathan Glover for individual choice, by James Fishkin for social justice, and by George Sher for compensatory justice.

Sher argues that members of a present generation can owe compensation for past injustices. He is raising an issue outside the simplified, timeless world of contemporary theories of justice. These have commonly provided a clean slate for applications of principle unencumbered by history. Yet the real world is inescapably constituted by the effects of past injustice. Sher argues that we should attempt to rectify the past to varying degrees depending on remoteness in time. In putting forward such a claim he must confront the identity problem—that were it not for the injustices in question, the persons demanding compensation would not exist. Laslett argues that such efforts are inconsistent with the intergenerational tricontract, which he expounds in his chapter, and are necessarily selective and hence tied up with new injustices. He contends that bending current theories of justice to the demands of the past would distort them beyond recognition. In effect our duties go forward, not backward in time. Yet this position will seem insensitive to demands for compensation and rectification that have become commonplace, particularly in the United States.

The arguments of Derek Parfit and Tyler Cowen against discounting are a frontal assault on the way economists, utilitarians, and public policy makers have conventionally taken time into account. They point out that with a social discount rate of 5 percent, one statistical death next year is the equivalent of a billion deaths in four hundred years. Given the time periods for which some toxic wastes must be safeguarded, such issues arise for real public policy problems. Cowen and Parfit argue that none of the arguments for discounting justify pure time preference of the sort commonly employed. Those arguments might justify discounting for probabilities but not for time per se. There are effects in the remote future that we should be highly confident about (for example, the dangers of nuclear waste) and there are proximate effects (for example, global warming) whose assessment is highly risky. Possible events in the remote future can be discounted for their likelihood, but not for their remoteness. If these arguments are correct, we will have to rethink radically how we assess the consequences for future generations of all public policies, from decisions for capital expenditures for dams and highways to the disposal of nuclear waste.

The vitality of the debates in the six volumes of this series demonstrates how a new generation of political theorists has developed over the past three decades. Yet this generation of revival thrived within the crucial simplifying assumption that the barriers between generations—and the enormous complexities they produce for moral discussion—need not be crossed. The essays published here are intended to foster a second generation of contemporary theories about justice, property rights, liberty, equality, utility, and other principles. These new formulations are distinctive in that they are capable of being applied to a world where cohorts of people die and others are born. As shown by this volume, the results are strikingly different from those which are now familiar to us, and which fail to take account of duration. Just as social contract arguments must be tested by unforeseen complexities arising in later generations, earlier discussions of principle must now be tested by the complexities presented in this volume.

Obstacles to the Understanding and Analysis of Justice over Time

It has never been usual, and it is certainly not easy, to think in terms of duration when considering issues of ethical and political theory. Paradox, or even absurdity, is never far beneath the surface. The demonstration of this not very convenient fact is important to the subject of this book since it raises a number of the issues with which our contributors are concerned. Let us start with what looks to be the core of a defensible principle of justice over time, certainly with respect to the environment. This principle states that every member of every generation must have equal access to the resources of the world, quite irrespective of the generation into which he or she was, is, or will be born. We find, however, that a limit has to be set to the number of generations that we can take into account, because if we allow the series to be open-ended and therefore potentially infinite, we meet with absurdity forthwith. This is because the resources of the human world, social, political, and material, cannot themselves possibly be infinite, even if it is uncertain how large they are in fact and how far technical ingenuity could spread them out. Now a finite quantity divided by an infinite number must have a zero result— no one gets anything at any time. Here political theorists encounter a circumstance notorious to mathematicians and statisticians, that infinity is a fundamentally elusive concept.

Unfortunately, however, there seems to be little or nothing in the previous studies of political theorists that would help decide how to limit the series of generations over which justice is to be secured.[1] Nor is there much to indicate where the series should begin and end, though our predisposition in favor of ourselves suggests that we begin in our time and go backward and forward through a considerable but indefinite number of generations, indefinite but necessarily having an end in both directions because of the paradox of infinity. The initial and final positions, however, have implications for generational justice that give it an unexpected, multidirectional character: it points two ways at once, forward and backward.

For the putative first generation, justice is entirely prospective, sharing equally with all generations to come. Symmetrically, for the last generation, justice is exclusively retrospective, directed toward all preceding generations. For all other generations, justice must go both ways, prospectively and retrospectively. If we abandon our intuitive prejudice in favor of our own generation as the beginning, and place as we should that present we inhabit at a random point along the series, then temporal justice for us as for all our predecessors and successors, except the first and the last, goes in both directions, toward the future and toward the past.

This is surely appropriate, but it brings up the difficulty about reciprocity that every student of justice over time has encountered. Individuals are in reciprocal relationship with their contemporaries, but with their contemporaries only. They can affect their successors in the future, who come behind them in time, indeed affect them to such an extent that they can decide who shall be and who might but will not be present among their successors. This recurrent theme in discussions of justice over time appears in this volume on several occasions. But future successors can do nothing to affect present people, ourselves that is, and although past people obviously have affected us, indeed have determined our identities and our general position to a considerable extent, we cannot affect them at all. Though we seem to be obliged to act justly with respect to past people as much as to future people, we can do nothing about it.

Past and future people here mean those belonging to completely removed generations, those whose lifetimes never overlap the lifetimes of those in our or other generations. There can evidently be partially as well as totally removed generations. Members of partially removed generations share a present with one another, so that they can interact. But this overlap, and the concept of generation itself, raises other issues that we shall come to in due course.

Insofar as justice over time proceeds from, and requires, reciprocal interaction it can scarcely apply between removed generations. This must mean that rules of justice resting on agreement, on contract, on a system in which "a right legitimately claimed is to be met, and cancelled, by a duty correctly performed"[2] can be only hypothetical between removed generations. It is not difficult to show, moreover, that even the case of overlapping generations, where contemporaries interact with contemporaries and justice could proceed from reciprocity, can look equivocal once considerations of duration are taken into account.

Contemporaneity, for one thing, lacks duration, and no undertaking can strictly speaking be fulfilled in the present, since by the time it is acted on the future will have arrived. This is only occasionally important in individual experience, because individuals spend long periods of their lives in reciprocal association with other individuals, so that agreed undertakings can be, and normally are, carried through during what is perceived to be present time. We all occasionally face problems arising from the death of persons with whom we have been dealing, and may also find ourselves arranging matters for persons not yet born. We proceed under these circumstances as far as possible as if the parties were still or already are in existence: we act as if they were notional contemporaries. But what satisfies us in individual relations of this kind operating within our own lifetime cannot be easily or convincingly extended to collections of individuals, say generations, even to partially overlapping generations.

Sir Robert Filmer, who until recently was regarded as the most obscurantist, irrational, and reactionary thinker in the Western record, wrote of the people: "The people, to speak truly and properly, is a thing or body in continual alteration and change, it never continues one minute the same, being composed of a multitude of parts, whereof divers continually decay and perish, and others renew and succeed in their places. They which are the people this minute, are not the people the next minute."[3] Filmer's point was that since the people have no durational existence, they cannot enter as a collective body into any political arrangement, and furthermore they cannot have a representative.

If generations are thought of as cohorts, all those born between two specified dates, they seem to possess greater stability over time than the people described by Filmer. Although members of a generation are perpetually disappearing over time, turning the original cohort into a remnant, no one new is appearing. The problem of representation nevertheless remains. A remnant is hardly a just representative of the original collection, especially after the passage of time has reduced it to an ever-diminishing minority. If that remnant elects delegates, the body that results, itself perpetually losing members, has an even smaller claim to represent the original cohort. A more telling point is that the choice of birth dates to determine a cohort's membership is entirely arbitrary: a cohort can be of any size and be recruited at any time and over any period of time.

In the face of such uncertainty, the tendency is indeed to appeal to the individual, and to the individual's generative or kin relationships. Hence the term *generation* itself: brothers, sisters, and cousins of the individual are the present generation and stand for a whole societywide order of contemporary persons: children, nephews, and nieces stand for the next generation, parents and grandparents for the two previous ones, and grandchildren and great-grandchildren those coming after the next generation, and so on. This disposition to use generative relationships to give structure to the order of succession in a population over time extends to the content of the relationships in society at large. Brotherhood symbolizes, even denotes, the relationship of common membership in the present generation of people in the entire population, parenthood the relationship of the present generation with its successor, and similarly up and down the kin network, backward and forward in time. Arguing symbolically or analogously from generative links to political links, lateral and vertical, is commonplace among contemporary philosophers and political theorists analyzing justice over time, as is shown in this volume, for instance in Laslett's chapter. The habits and the vocabulary are well nigh universal among politicians, administrators, journalists, and the public at large.

But once we look critically at this confounding of cohort with generation, its inadequacy stares us in the face. The generations perceived individually by a particular ego are manifestly different from cohorts, different in logic and different in fact. They are not even necessarily in proper order of succession over time, since aunts and uncles can be younger than nieces and nephews. As for taking our relationships with our kin as representative of relationships between all other persons in current, preceding, or succeeding generations, we know that we treat those allied to us by kin ties with a consistent preference. The closer the tie, the stronger the preference, whereas we tend to treat all nonkin indifferently. Geneticists have demonstrated that we are programmed to behave in this differential fashion, and Epstein makes confident use of the circumstance in his chapter, "Justice across the Generations." The commonsense assumptions of personal individual experience, not even entirely consistent in their individual personal contexts, are once more simply inadequate when it comes to collectivities and collective experience.

When he described the people as he did, Sir Robert Filmer did not have generations in mind, but presumably everyone (except those he defined as natural rulers) alive at a particular present, elusive as we have already seen the concept of present to be. By discussing generations in accordance with Filmer's critique, however, we have seen how jumbled and confusing an assemblage of contemporaries inhabiting a present time turns out to be, especially in terms of duration and securing justice between age groups and generations, given how equivocal the term *generation* has shown itself to be. From one point of view the assemblage of all contemporary persons can be, and indeed usually is, regarded as the current generation by its members and is assumed to be structured, if rather loosely, on the kinship analogy that we have found faulty. From another point of view it comprises an entirely indefinite number of cohorts, or rather remnants of cohorts, and the longer the present is taken to last, the more of a remnant each becomes. A further complication is that new cohorts are appearing in that present all the time and immediately start to diminish.

These overlapping cohorts consist of individuals who are contemporaries, at least for some fraction of the lives of each. Overlapping cohorts are distinct from removed generations, in that reciprocal interaction between them is possible, though the character of that interaction is somewhat complicated. As for the length of time the overlap will last, it may differ for each dyad of individuals from overlapping generations. In practice, however, one-half of a present seems to go by for a given generation while it overlaps with a preceding generation, or set of generations, and the rest of a present seems to elapse while the current generation overlaps with the succeeding generation, or set of generations. Under these circumstances, and perhaps generally, a present seems to last for about the lifetime of the average member of the current generation, itself evidently an indefinite period of time.

It must be apparent how arbitrary the suppositions that we have been describing really are, and how intricate the problem of giving an objective meaning to the concept of generation and so setting about the questions we have to answer. But this does not seem to have worried political theorists. Filmer's radical skepticism about "the people" based on considerations of duration and contemporaneity did not prevent the phrase "the people" from entering into the whole gamut of radical and contractarian political thinking that came after he published his objections. John Locke, the most distinguished of Filmer's critics, never as much as referred to his durational critique of the concept of the people in the famous *Two Treatises of Government,* published in 1689–1690, which succeeded admirably in its aim "to justifie to the World the People of England."[4]

"The present" has been accepted as the arena of the behavior and relationships that political theorists study, seemingly without any recognition of its indefiniteness and elusiveness. Although the concept of generation has been acknowledged as problematic for a considerable time, and as the subject of extensive sociological discussion,[5] the term has been accepted as an adequate description of the entities between which justice over time has to be secured. In spite of their unwillingness to take up the subject, neither philosophers nor political theorists have been any more inhibited by the uncertainties and paradoxes that we have been considering than the contractarian and liberal theorists were inhibited by Filmer's skeptical commentary from using the concept of the people.

It will be the theme of our discussion of the history of the treatment of justice over time that thinkers failed to perceive these obliquities until the 1950s, when it became clear that the world's population was growing at breakneck speed and that its not unlimited resources were being increasingly damaged by human activity (see pp. 18–21, below). We shall insist on the significance of these events (for events they were in demographic, economic, and political as well as intellectual history) in showing up the inadequacy of established philosophical, ethical, and political analysis because it had no durational dimension. Up to the present, it will be insisted, there has been little progress in adapting traditional concepts to accommodate the newly recognized requirements.

It would nevertheless be both unconstructive and irresponsible to wait for a wholly new model of inquiry to be brought into being, with adequate and accurate terms for both the entities to be related and the nature of the relationships between them. Since answers are required of us now, we must do what we can with instruments whose inadequacies and capacity to mislead have been recognized and allowed for. This has, after all, been the character of the history of philosophy for as far back as it can be traced. The newer theories and the new developments have never waited on a solution to existing problems. Just such an attempt to improvise, using expressions as debatable as "the intergenerational tricontract" and "the intragenerational intercohort trust," is made by one of us in an essay in this volume.

The Metaphorical Model of Processional Justice

We should not wish, moreover, to leave the subject of the obstacles to understanding without some attempt to provide guidance, in this case of an almost entirely terminological kind—the elaboration of a particular metaphor for use when investigating justice over time. The image of the procession decidedly cannot cover the whole field we have looked over or dispose of all its contradictions and incoherences. It creates some puzzlements but clarifies many others, as the exposition that follows is intended to show.

When walking in a procession, an irregular moving assembly such as the Saint Patrick's Day Parade in New York City, rather than in a military formation in defined ranks, we can interact only with those walking in our immediate vicinity. We can have no knowledge of how long the procession is in temporal terms, that is, how long it would take for the whole of it to pass a particular point, but we can be confident that it is not of infinite length. We are conscious that our predecessors, those ahead of us in the procession, have acted in ways that control us to some degree, because we are liable to be slowed down or halted by a motion communicated along the line from them. But we are well aware that we can have no such impact on our predecessors. If we decelerate or stop, either of our own accord or because our predecessors make it unavoidable, there will be a similar impact on our successors, those who will come after us in the future, but they can have no such impact on us. "Us" here denotes the immediately surrounding part of the procession, an indefinite area, but one within which both action and reaction can take place, one part of the area in interaction with another, a forward, later part with a hinder, earlier part. We are conscious, moreover, of how irregular and indefinite is the boundary that separates our area from the remainder of the procession, fore and aft. We recognize a further crucial fact, that those to the front of us are in interaction with others in front of them, and so on indefinitely, and those at the back of us with those to the back of them.

In spite of its advantages as an aid toward grasping the reality with which we are concerned, the processional image has certain drawbacks, which we must now consider. The tense is wrong in both of the two later clauses in the previous paragraph. Those in front of us in the "real world," that is, those before us in time, are not *now* in interaction with those in front of them who are inaccessible to us, but *were* so; and those behind us, that is, after us in time, are not now but will be in interaction with those who will come later still. We do not move in time or through time, however; time moves over us: the sense that we have as a society of facing the oncoming future is lost in the processional metaphor, which seems to place the future behind us. The full effect on us of the actions of past persons is only sketchily conveyed by the slowing and stopping that has been described: likewise the multifarious and strenuous efforts we make, and quite spontaneously, with respect to future persons. Otherwise, we maintain that the image of a procession does convey the dynamic of the relationships that justice over time is required to respect, and suggests quite vividly how arbitrary and artificial all groups and boundaries inevitably are.

Philosophers, ethical and political, are required to transcend their own experiences as far as possible, and in this case to quit the time slice in which they find themselves in order to observe and to theorize from outside. Here the processional image is particularly useful because a visible segment of the procession apparent from a single point of observation does provide an intelligible sample of the whole, while preserving the condition that people should be perpetually entering from one side and leaving from the other. If the ideal observer strives to get up as high as possible above the procession to see as much as can be seen of it, however, he or she runs into the difficulty about length in relation to infinity. The observer would do best to stay metaphorically on the ground, but to seek a vantage point with the widest possible view of the procession as it passes. Stretching the imagination a bit, a well-placed observer might be able to descry individuals who come into view and disappear from view not by entering or leaving to the left or to the right, but by being created inside the procession, or disappearing within its body, that is, by being born and dying as it passes through the angular area visible from the chosen point.

The processional image might be prompted here by the spaceship image found in science fiction. The body of people in it are on their way to a destination so distant that they know that they themselves will not reach the planet to be explored, but rather their children and grandchildren, or even later descendants, engendered within the spaceship itself. The two pictures are incompatible, of course, but they help each other.

This is as far as we should be prepared to go in recommending the processional image of the conditions that have to be satisfied for an adequate solution to the problem of justice over time. It is hoped that the generations referred to by the contributors to this volume, mostly it would seem removed generations, along with the age groups, cohorts, and related individuals whose utility is debated, will be visible in the image. The generations that are in conflict according to David Thomson, for example, are portrayed as those in the later section of the observed present, to the right of the picture so to speak, opposing those in the middle and on the left, the relatively old in opposition to the relatively young. Those to the right of the picture are persons who have been companions of individuals now further on in the past, out of the picture but still in the procession; those to the left will become companions of those not yet in the picture, in the future. But the boundaries between the sections remain irremediably indefinite.

The working out of the processional metaphor, and the whole discussion of durational entities, might convince us that no bounded groups can be made concrete enough for the purposes of analysis. Justice over time would accordingly always have to be construed as justice between individuals—past, present, and future individuals—the titles "generations," "age groups," and "cohorts" serving only as indefinite indicators of those in similar temporal positions. The one collective institution with which such individuals could have relationships is the state, a concept and a corpus so far absent from the discussion.

Once the state or the collectivity enters into the analysis, however, an entirely different image of how justice over time might be secured makes its appearance. A deathless collectivity, identified with the political purposes of the state, and not itself subject to the limitations of duration imposed on political cooperation and exchange, might make dealing with the problems and the puzzlements much easier. But the image of an eternal, all-inclusive collectivity embracing everyone alive, and everyone who has been or will be alive, scarcely belongs in the arena of individual rights, government by consent of the governed, and the rule of law. Awkward as the processional image may be, awkward because the reality to be signified is itself so elusive, we are required to accept its logic in preference to the Hegelian march of the state through history.

Justice over Time in the History of Philosophy and Political Theory

The proposition that we shall defend in expounding the history of the manner in which philosophers and political theorists have dealt with justice over time has already been set down. In defiance of the adage that there is nothing new under the sun, we maintain that in the particular definition we use, justice over time did not exist as a subject of analysis or discussion, or even as a concept, before the 1970s, or before the 1960s at the earliest.

The definition of justice over time that we favor goes as follows. It consists in an obligation on all present persons to conduct themselves in recognition of the rights of all future persons, regardless of geographical location and temporal position. No generation is at liberty to ransack the environment, or to overload the earth with more people than can be supported, or even, though this is more debatable, to act in such a way as to ensure that the human race will disappear. This duty goes beyond beneficence, the idea that it would be better to act in this way and magnanimous to our successors. Rather, we are required so to conduct ourselves because of the rights of future persons. Many people believe in fact that we should do more; that is, ensure as far as we can that our successors in time will live better than we live.

It perhaps should not surprise us that the so-called grand theorists of ethics and politics should have failed to formulate a doctrine of the rights of time-separated persons in relation to and as distinct from the rights of time-contiguous persons and groups of persons. All those in the Classical and Christian European traditions incorporated some version of a metaphysical, providentialist doctrine into their writings, a doctrine that would look after the question of duration and succession. Making this assumption, Plato, Aristotle, Aquinas, even Hobbes, Locke, Rousseau, and Hegel, could be satisfied to write as if their principles, being just for their own times, could stand for all time. The famous provision for a civil religion inserted by Rousseau into his *Contrat social* appears to demonstrate the continuation of this circumstance into the age of critical rationalism.

The sense of posterity was lively enough in these thinkers, and frequently appealed to. The consciousness of the past and of its power to bind the present was equally clearly recognized. Richard Hooker, the great apologist for the Anglican Church and the English, later British, state, put it thus. "Wherefore, as any Man's Deed past is good as long as himself continueth: so the Act of a Publick Society of men done Five hundred Years sithence, standeth as theirs, who presently are of the same Societies, because Corporations as Immortal: we were then alive in our Predecessors and they in their Successors live still."[6]

The law and its institutional creations such as the corporation were regarded as having indefinite duration and the power to transfer obligations from past to present and to future. It was a requisite for contractual political thinking that this should be supposed to happen. The manner of such transfers was quite evidently metaphysical and providential, however, enabling people in Hooker's exposition to be present and responsible before and after their lifetimes. But the notion of transferring rights the other way, from future to present to past remained absent from his speculations, even though he provided the notional apparatus for such transfers.

It was not until 1790 that an eminent political theorist made an assertion that could be said to betoken an unequivocal obligation from future generations and persons to present and past generations and persons.

This was when Edmund Burke wrote as follows in his *Reflections on the Revolution in France*.

> Society is indeed a contract . . . a partnership in all art, a particular in every virtue, and in all perfection. As the ends of such a partnership cannot be obtained in many generations, it becomes a partnership not only between those who are living, but between those who are living, those who are dead, and those who are to be born. Each contract of each particular state is but a clause in the great primeval contract of eternal society, linking the lower with the higher natures, connecting the visible and invisible world.[7]

Here, however, seemingly specified two-way relationships over time tail off into transcendental speculation even more fanciful than Hooker's, typical of Burke at his cloudiest and aptly illustrative of the metaphysical assumption that continued to make unnecessary any critical examination of statements implying duration.

But it would be wrong to suppose that no theories, beliefs, or principles of action existed before the past twenty years that could be said to acknowledge in any sense the rights of future persons. In an agrarian society settled on the land, the village, the family group, and the population at large relied for their perpetuation on action taken to preserve resources from year to year, decade to decade, century to century. Anthropologists contemplating societies maintaining themselves thus in our day frequently report that their behavior implies awareness of a longer-term future, and the needs of those who will be present in that future. This is so even if the obligations are left vague and no clear distinction is made between present people as they will be later on and wholly future people. Indeterminacy on this point can be seen in the various versions of the text of the well-known Lockean proviso, now so frequently referred to in philosophical discussions of property rights, past, present, and future.

There it is laid down that everyone has exclusive rights to what is taken from nature and mixed with his labor or hers, "at least," Locke adds when the condition is first stated in his text, "where there is enough, and as good left in common for others."[8] Whether those others are existent persons, or persons still to come, is not indicated. It is reasonable to infer, however, that both classes are included, and that the rights of both do, indeed, limit the actions of those who do the removing, at whatever time, but Locke never expressly says so.

Considerably more important in the experience of our predecessors for whose condition Western political theory was originally worked out was their concern for generation, the word and the notion. We need not linger on this now familiar ground, except to note the restrictive tendency of generative thinking over time. The elderly English landowner of the eighteenth century, looking at the lines of little saplings he had planted, can probably be supposed to have had in mind a debt to his descendants, who would enjoy the avenues so created. He might have included all unborn Englishmen, even all Europeans, but hardly all unborn humans; his imputed generational sentiments do not include the final clause of our definition of justice over time, the rights of all possible future persons.

The last statement we can make about the indifference to this topic shown by thinkers before our own day has to do with their implicit reliance on religious revelation. This attitude is evident enough in the sentiments of Hooker and Burke, but it goes without saying that it completely informed the outlook of the population at large. In village churches up and down the country, in Britain as in the rest of Christendom, the most conspicuous decoration was a picture of the Last Judgment on the chancel arch facing the nave where the congregation assembled, portraying all humanity, past, present, and future, being consigned to Heaven or Hell. Christians knew that in the sight of God a person's date of birth on the human time scale was irrelevant, and that those not yet born also would be summoned to meet all other created humans and the Almighty. Such an assemblage, of course, would deny, or completely transcend, the processional limitations that we have insisted on here.

There are dangers in sketching the history of a concept, or in this case the lack of a concept, and we must guard against a simpleminded acceptance of the historical proposition under review. Perhaps a thorough full-length examination both of sophisticated doctrine and of popular presumption would reveal clear statements before our own day of a right residing in all future persons that obliged all current persons. Our predecessors as far back as ancient times could certainly have observed instances of losses imposed on one generation by its predecessors: the erosion of soil in the Mediterranean basin in Classical times; the destruction of forests in Elizabethan England; the extinction of wolves and bears in Britain; the pollution of streams such as the now buried river Fleet in London, or even the Cam in Cambridge, which was running with sewage when gazed upon by Queen Victoria and Prince Albert in the 1840s. The evidence was everywhere, and it is difficult to believe that no one ever saw it as a violation of the rights of posterity, as well as an outrage to themselves, which those in the nineteenth century were busy clearing up. All that can be confidently asserted, however, is that when it dawned on biologists, philosophers, moralists, and journalists in the 1960s that there really could come an epoch when the spring would be silent because there were no birds to sing, an overt tradition of speculation and assertion was simply lacking.[9]

Perhaps the most surprising manifestation of that lack is in the works of Thomas Robert Malthus, the formulator of the principle that population would always tend to grow faster than the means of subsistence. That "merciful and humane as well as eminently perceptive man" talks entirely in the present, however, reproaching his contemporaries for the improvident behavior that was the cause of the current misery and degradation of so many of them. This was sinful and God would punish them (Malthus was a clergyman); the rights of future persons were not cited.[10]

It would nevertheless be simpleminded to identify implicit belief in Christianity and the Christian revelation as the sole cause of persisting indifference to the rights of posterity. Revelation was being progressively rejected half a century before the time of Malthus, and the prophets of progress whom he attacked were often avowed secularists. But neither the skeptical Hume nor such enthusiastic idealists as Godwin or Condorcet got any closer to the intellectual position we are seeking. The challenge of progress that eighteenth- and nineteenth-century Europeans and Americans came to feel so powerfully may have implied duties for everyone, but those duties seldom or never seem to have been construed as owed to their posterity.

The extreme atomistic individualism of the classical economists, and of the utilitarian philosophers, especially Jeremy Bentham, which appeared during the lifetime of Malthus, did give rise to an attitude that at least brought into view the possibility of generations of the future having rights. This is not the place to go at length into the utilitarian texts of Bentham, James, Mill, and others to single out statements with this tendency. It is enough to assert that the insistence by utilitarian thinkers on taking account of the total sum of happiness of all distinguishable individuals, and reckoning increments and decrements, means and medians, was sooner or later bound to raise the question of the happiness of not yet existent persons, as well as that of those present at the time of writing. An exponent of the felicific calculus who wonders whether the satisfaction of animals, those who never will be human, should be taken into the reckoning is likely to think also of the satisfaction of those who will be human but who have yet to be born.

The first clear exposition of these questions with a deliberate statement of the interests, if not the rights, of persons still to come did not arrive until 1874, when Henry Sidgwick published *The Methods of Ethics*. After acknowledging the possible relevance of the pleasures and pains of all the "inferior animals" to the utilitarian system, Sidgwick proceeds thus.

> But even if we limit our attention to human beings, the extent of the subjects of happiness is not quite determinate. In the first place it may be asked, How far are we to consider the interests of posterity when they seem to conflict with those of existing human beings? Perhaps, however, it is clear that the time at which a man exists cannot affect the value of his happiness from a universal point of view; and that the interests of posterity must concern a utilitarian as much as those of his contemporaries, except in so far as the effects of his actions on posterity—and even the existence of human beings to be affected— must necessarily be more uncertain.[11]

These are pregnant sentences for the contents of the present volume, and a historian of thought might be permitted to remark on how effectively Sidgwick set the scene for the debates of the 1980s and 1990s, including the preoccupation with nonhumans a century before the event. But the definition of justice over time that we are pursuing here is still implicit, not overt. Rights and duties are not specified; posterity is undefined and is not necessarily all-inclusive; moreover, Sidgwick never elaborates or tries to solve the problems he has raised.[12] And as far as we can see, nothing new was added to Sidgwick's assertion before the late 1960s.

Even then, references to the threats of the growth of global population and damage to the environment were rather muted and treatments of the subject never became common. Among economists, "generational" relationships began to be discussed with respect to welfare as the result of an important study by Paul Samuelson, published in 1958. In 1967 Jan Narveson published a piece in *Mind* in which he seemed to take up where Sidgwick had left off, "Utilitarianism and New Generations."[13] Narveson's concern was with questions that were to remain characteristic of the discussion and that are discussed in the essays in this volume by Fishkin and Glover, for example, about duties to produce children and about numbers, implicitly (though not yet overtly) future numbers in the sum total of satisfactions. In 1968, M. P. Golding's essay "Ethical Issues in Biological Engineering" appeared.[14] He subsequently described the article as one "wherein I discuss obligations to future generations and some of the problems they provoke. I know of no other explicit discussion of this topic."[15] The frame of reference of this early work is noteworthy, for medical advances and dilemmas, whether or when to switch off life-support systems, intervention in conception and during pregnancy, genetic engineering, and even science fiction scenarios all have a future reference and have been part of the general field of inquiry, speculation, and ethical principle, as is evident in the essays here.

It was the appearance in 1971 of *A Theory of Justice* by John Rawls that marked the proper initiation of obligations to future generations as a topic of salient philosophical interest, just as it did for so many other topics of ethical and political philosophy.[16] Though Rawls had developed his theory of veil-of-ignorance contractarianism in a number of previous essays, concern with generations seems to have awaited his authoritative treatise, in which a whole section of his chapter "Distributive Shares" is titled "The Problem of Justice between Generations." It is not going too far to say that the majority of the work done on justice over time during the 1970s and 1980s, including much of the only previous collection of essays devoted to the subject before the present one, has been in the way of a commentary on Rawls's treatment.[17] The single exception came in 1984 with Derek Parfit's *Reasons and Persons,* itself already salient by the 1990s for the impact it has made in these areas, but also much engaged with Rawls.[18] Not simply a chapter, but the whole fourth and final part of that book is titled "Future Generations."

It took, then, more than twenty years, from the late 1960s to the late 1980s, following the recognition of the threat to the future from population and pollution, for the subject of justice over time to become a recognized branch of ethical and political theory. Even so it was not much written about, probably because of its forbidding intricacy, its unfamiliarity, and its difficulty, but by now it is an inquiry in progress. Important as we think it is to set the present collection in its historical, ethical, and political theoretical context, we shall not try to summarize here the declarations made about and the positions taken up on justice over time by Rawls, Parfit, or any other authors.

Positions like the following: that justice to future persons with whom we can have no contact is analogous to, perhaps logically identical with, justice to distant persons elsewhere in the world who are also inaccessible to us; that it is part of civilized behavior, of that which gives us satisfaction with ourselves, that we should take steps to shield posterity from harm; or Jan Narveson's belief "that when it comes to morality, only persons count. Possible persons are not persons. . . . What we owe to future persons is neither everything nor nothing, but merely something"; or Derek Parfit and Tyler Cowen's claim elaborated so persuasively here, that the social discount rate, by which it had been customary, especially among economists, to play down the rights of those in the future at a rate chosen arbitrarily, is a null argument, indeed a moral outrage.

It is for the readers of this volume to judge how effective, or perhaps how ineffective, the pieces we have published are as responses to the challenge of the times set forth in our Preface. It is for them to decide further whether the complications and paradoxes that have been laid out here and labeled those of processional justice have been properly taken into account, if indeed the readers of this Introduction are prepared to grant that this image, and the examples and provisions that we have set forth, are properly to the point. In fact the possibility must be reckoned with that this Introduction and many, perhaps all, of the essays may not address justice over time in appropriate terms. The present situation of ethical and political theory may still be defeated by the problems that it raises.

This recalls the lugubrious statement that had to be made a full "generation" ago (thirty-five years that is to say) in 1956, in the introduction to the first series of *Philosophy, Politics, and Society:* "For the moment, anyway, political philosophy is dead." We would not wish to go this far at the dawn of the 1990s, since rather than being an apologetic trickle in the faculties of philosophy, political science, history, and law, political philosophy is now in full spate, and it is usual to dwell on its revival over that "full generation." But we would both like to join in putting the following set of queries to our contributors and to their readers, as well as to others who might have written for us.

Is it not evident, as Fishkin makes clear in his essay, that considerations of justice over time show up the inadequacies of the time-slice theories of justice that have been preoccupying theorists? Might it not be significant that there is a recognizable tendency among the authors of these essays to dwell for as long as possible on the analysis they have in mind without referring to the time continuum except as a final comment, almost as if saying, I told you so? Is there any conceptual awareness of the difference between justice within a present, justice over lapses of time where only partial overlaps among persons is possible, and justice over lapses of time where no overlap takes place, that is, justice between removed generations? Is there any consistent consciousness of the elusiveness and ambiguity of a present? Of the distortions inherent in the language used for the concepts we have been struggling with? Of the possibility, or impossibility, of representation within what we have called the procession over time? Of the character of the collectivity, or the state, when viewed durationally? Is there not much evidence that the traditional language of philosophy of political theory, interfused as it always was with providence and metaphysics, is being made use of unaltered? Can we not perceive these highly problematic conceptual foundations in the attempt by John Rawls to assemble the "generations"—he uses the expression "generations" though he seems nearly always to be talking of individuals—in a manner that vividly recalls the doom on the chancel arch of a medieval church?

Once alerted to these considerations, the critic of the 1990s is disposed to dwell on a statement made earlier about the universalism of philosophical principle, in ethics and in politics, as well as epistemology and so on, and the particularism of political beliefs and political life. While Rawls is expanding his original position and bargaining behind a veil of ignorance (participants do not know in which generations they will find themselves) it becomes evident that the informing principle in the author's mind as he develops the constitutional life of the society in which generational justice is to be secured is none other than the constitutional life of the United States, of which he is a citizen. This is not the whole of humanity progressing as it does through time.

We ourselves have described a world of hypotheticals in crude Rawlsian terms. And one of us, Peter Laslett, makes use in his contribution of an ordered set of hypotheses, taking as far as possible the considerations we have put into our Introduction, in order to suggest a solution to the problematic issues of durational justice. Though this, we would claim, is only to do our duty, it may still be a question of whether it is enough. A theory taking proper account of justice over time is yet to emerge from the chrysalis of an established, irredeemably time-bound, traditionally legitimated political philosophy.

Notes

1. The difficulties already noted about discounting, difficulties amplified by Cowen and Parfit in this volume, constitute a critique of the one strategy commonly offered for dealing with this problem.
2. The phrase is from Laslett, "Conversation between the Generations."

3. Sir Robert Filmer, *Observations Upon Aristotle's Politiques Touching Forms of Government* (1652), in Laslett, ed., *Political Works of Sir Robert Filmer*, 226; Sommerville, ed., *Patriarcha*, 277.

4. *Two Treatises of Government*, preface, line 8. Other refuters of Filmer were more aware of his "needling effectiveness" as a critic of contractarianism, but no one seems to have addressed Filmer's durational critique of the people.

5. The locus classicus is Mannheim, "Problem of Generations." *Generation* has been given a historical-experiential dimension (the Depression generation, for example), as well as a procreative one. Theories have been advanced using cohorts as successive groups of entrants into the political and social worlds. But no generally accepted solution has been forthcoming, and the standard encyclopedic treatment of political generations (Marvin Rintala in *The International Encyclopaedia of the Social Sciences*, ed. David L. Sills [New York: Macmillan, 1968]) ends with a list of unanswered questions, the last of which is "What Is a Generation Unit?"

6. *Laws of the Ecclesiasticall Politie*, written in the 1580s and 1590s, in Hooker, *Works*, 88.

7. Burke, *Reflections*, 143–144.

8. *Second Treatise*, par. 27.

9. The reference is to Rachel Carson's book *The Silent Spring* (1962).

10. There are statements in the successive editions of his *Essay on Population*, especially in the second of 1802, which have a future reference and could be said to prophesy disaster (see Laslett, review of *The Works of Thomas Robert Malthus*, ed. Wrigley and Souden). But such an eventuality seems to be referred to divine providence rather than the responsibility of those he was addressing.

11. Sidgwick, *Methods of Ethics*, 385, reproduced unmodified in a book that was extensively revised up to the final printing of 1907. Sidgwick goes on to raise the question of whether the vast numbers of people to come may reduce average happiness by their very numbers, and whether, therefore, we should take action to limit the quantity. His decision is in favor of the largest number and the maximum total happiness, though the choices he opened up are still being debated, as our contributors testify.

12. Cf. the discussion in Barry, "Justice between Generations," in *Democracy, Power and Justice*, 500. Sidgwick shows no interest in issues of duration in his influential book *The Elements of Politics*.

13. Samuelson, "Exact Consumption-Loan Model of Interest"; Narveson, "Utilitarianism and New Generations."

14. Golding, "Ethical Issues in Biological Engineering," his own reference.

15. Golding, "Obligations to Future Generations."

16. Rawls, *Theory of Justice*.

17. Sikora and Barry, eds., *Obligations to Future Generations*. See also Daniels, *Am I My Father's Keeper?*

18. Parfit, *Reasons and Persons*.

I

Is There a
Generational Contract?

PETER LASLETT

In this chapter I wish to consider a very common concept in the discussion of justice over time, the concept of the generational contract. The closely related but conceptually distinct notion of generational trust will also be analyzed at some length, although it is much less frequently encountered. Running my fingers over the ways in which these expressions have been and are being used, I shall try to discover the hypothetical intergenerational interchanges that seem to be presumed by those who use such expressions. As this survey proceeds, I shall sketch out a general thesis about justice over time, using the two concepts as consistently as possible, and in as strict yet inclusive a theoretical sense as can be managed. For all the vagueness, looseness, and at times incoherence of references to generational contract, as well as the difficulties inherent in the notion itself, we shall find that such an exercise raises fundamental issues about social and political understanding, and challenging questions with respect to justice over time. There is a great deal here for political theorists and ethical philosophers to attend to, even though the exposition of generational contractualism soon gets complicated, and the phraseology tediously repetitive.

Appeals to generational contract and occasionally to trust are increasingly made both in protest against present injustices committed by contemporary age-groups one against another and in championship of future removed generations, especially in relation to the environment. Economists and policy makers intent on securing equitable treatment for those paying toward pensions and pension receivers sometimes refer to generational contracts and trusts, whilst the phrase "welfare contract," or "welfare compact," is quite often met with in connection with the Welfare State as a whole and the transfers it brings about, for health purposes as well as for those of income support. The succession to jobs by younger persons as they are vacated by older persons is also occasionally referred to as a contractual matter. All these are allusions to interchanges going on now or expected in the future, but allegations of breach of contract with past removed generations could also be advanced.

The notorious unrealism of contractarian thinking, pointed out originally by Sir Robert Filmer, repeated by David Hume, then reiterated by Jeremy Bentham and succeeding utilitarians, will be a given in this discussion. Generational contracts and trusts will be assumed to be entirely hypothetical, treated in fact just as John Rawls treated the social contract itself, when, in defiance or disregard of these criticisms, he made contract the point of departure of his *Theory of Justice.*[1]

The limitations imposed by the processional character of generational interrelationships and those of cohorts and age-groups will likewise be for the most part discounted. The reader is referred to the Introduction for an explication of how the perpetual intermingling of these entities as they follow one another in their unending procession through time makes the giving of boundaries to them for definitional purposes extremely difficult, if not impossible. It will be necessary to make entirely arbitrary assumptions as to who can speak and act for any generation or generational entity. We cannot, therefore, give the generational contract a local habitation and a name, any more than could be done for the social contract itself. Nevertheless, generational images, generational language, and the associations of generational relationships will be freely used in the argument that follows.[2]

The Intergenerational Tricontract

Attention will be directed toward a particular version of the generational contract, which, although it could cover only one of the types of transfers that go on between contemporary cohorts and age-groups, seems to be capable of yielding a fairly complete justification of obligations between noncontemporaneous, removed generations, provided of course that its implicit assumptions are granted. This generational relationship will be called the intergenerational tricontract.

By removed generations is meant those who do not overlap but stretch backward and forward from the present generation, itself thought of as a removed generation with respect to these others. The rights and duties within the present generation, subsisting between cohorts, age-groups, and other collections of people including the State, rights and duties that cannot be justified by reference to the implicit intergenerational tricontract, are referred to a trust or trust relationship between cohorts, in which age-groups are also involved in a somewhat indirect fashion. Though the terms of this trust remain constant, its distribution of social goods to beneficiaries is, or should be, in a state of continuous modification as time passes and removed generations in due course succeed each other.

The distinction between contracts, specifically the tricontract, between non-contemporaneous removed generations on the one hand, and the trust between contemporary cohorts on the other hand, is of cardinal importance to the exposition. At the risk of confusion arising from the many connotations of the word *generation*, I shall try to keep this distinction fixed in the mind of the reader by occasionally referring to the two concepts as the *inter*generational tricontract and the *intra*generational intercohort trust.

The argument set out here will repeat, develop, and modify some of the propositions originally put forward in 1970 and elaborated in 1979. These propositions maintained that the rights a generation has in preceding generations are matched by the duties that have to be performed toward generations yet to come.[3] There is, therefore, at all times a set of generational duties still to be met by rights. The image is that of a row of hooks linked into eyes, at the forward end of which is a hook without an eye, though an eye will be forthcoming from the next generation in the procession. In processional "reality," of course, the empty hook is always in process of forming and the complementary eye is likewise a perpetually emergent phenomenon.

In this construction of the intergenerational contract, three removed generations are in question rather than two, hence the name *tricontract*. If each successive generation is regarded as having both rights and duties, then the rights that any given generation (here generation 2) has in its predecessor (generation 1) are met by the duties it performs for its successor (generation 3). Although it is seldom clear quite what generational relationships are in the minds of politicians, or indeed of most analysts of transfers, when they refer to generational contracts, or even how many generations they suppose to be in question, it would seem that they usually presume the two-generational contract. This is understandable, because a two-generational, essentially procreative contract, appears at first sight to give a quite satisfactory account in ethical terms of the transfers between cohorts of persons who are at any one time in the productive phase of the life-course, those not yet in that phase (the children), and those who have left it (the elderly). Indeed, in much of the discussion, relationships between these contemporary cohorts or age-groups sharing the same time space are taken for the purposes of ethical analysis to cover relationships between removed generations not sharing the same time space. This view assumes, therefore, that if cohort and age-group interchanges can be justly arranged, those between removed generations will look after themselves, no such distinction as that between an *inter*generational tricontract and an *intra*generational intercohort trust being necessary.[4]

The two-generational contract, then, seems to be the standard version of implicit agreements between age-groups in the matter of the dependency of the younger and older members of society. Here the procreative character of that contract is easy to descry, since actual procreators (though not necessarily all of their lateral kin) are universally prior in time to those they procreate as well as being their generative originators. The assumption governing succession to jobs (the older generation getting out of the way to allow the younger one to take up employment in return for being supported by them in retirement) is also seen as a two-generational affair, however, though here procreation is only a distant reference. Let us look at the workings of the procreative contract between adjacent parental and filial generations as a metaphorical basis for justifying interchanges of this kind. We shall find it quite unsatisfactory in such contexts, let alone for the purpose of securing justice between removed generations.

The Two-Generational Procreational Contract

The procreational contract requires that children must support their parents when they can no longer support themselves in return for having been procreated and nurtured by those parents. The assumption evidently is that parents in conferring these benefits and children in accepting them are behaving in an implicitly contractual way. Hence the right of parents to appeal to a notional contract if they believe that they are inadequately maintained, and the right of children to do the same if they believe that too much is being demanded. This apparently explains how those no longer working can justify claiming pensions out of the taxes collected from their juniors still in the labor force; it also explains why those speaking for such pressure groups as "Americans for generational justice" may use contractual language when complaining that the retired are taking more than is justly due. The same reasoning applies when young persons not yet employed call for early retirement of those in jobs, or when that call is made for them and for others without work by politicians bent on reducing official unemployment figures.

But if the two-generational procreative contract can apparently provide in this way for issues between age-groups sharing the same time space, it has little to offer when it comes to more than one succeeding set of procreators and procreated and so to removed generations. Interchange between grandparents and grandchildren can be covered by the two-generational contract, though without a great deal of conviction. Grandparents occasionally look to grandchildren for support, and some legal codes have provided that grandchildren are obliged to supply it. In terms of the implicit two-generational contract grandchildren could be presumed to have this duty as a return for the procreation by their grandparents of their own parents, without whom they, the grandchildren, would not have existed. Perhaps procreators could be said to have fulfilled their side of a contractlike obligation to their potential grandchildren in this way and so to have the right to require those grandchildren to fulfill their contractual duties. Furthermore, this interchange over three generations could just conceivably be said to be repeated for succeeding triplicates and so to provide some ground for that justice over long periods of time, which those concerned with the environment, sense as such a strong imperative.

If their argument is no securer than this, however, environmentalists seem bound to lay themselves open to the retort often met with as a rebuttal of their claims. "Why should I do anything for future generations? They have done nothing for me." Insofar as environmentalists appeal to contractual arguments at all, we should perhaps do best to suppose that it is a tripartite arrangement they have in mind, rather than the two-generational procreative contract, which may appear to suffice for support flowing between contemporaneous age-groups. Tracing the implications of the two-generational procreative contract seems to me, however, to show up its inadequacy for all the purposes of securing justice over time, short term and long term.

It is an absurdity to construe the attitudes and behavior of children, the procreated, with respect to their parents, the procreators, in the mode if-you-do-something-for-me-now-I-will-in-due-course-do-the-equivalent-for-you. This is particularly so for procreation itself, which is surely the greatest of the goodies generators offer to the generated. How could a yet to be born individual make even a hypothetical contract with someone to bring him or her into existence? This is the potential person dilemma in an inverse form. The additional benefits a mother and father confer on their offspring—support, nurture, education, perhaps financial endowment, and so on—are likewise received as of right, as conferring no obligation, in the spirit of love in which they are offered, for as the Scripture reminds us, love seeketh not her own. Every observer of parental attitudes and most of all parents themselves recognize that what is done for children by those who bring them into the world is entirely spontaneous, proferred without expectation of return at the time or thereafter, and done as an end in itself. On reflection, of course, a mother or father would admit to a duty to act in this way, a duty which, if neglected, would give rise to self-reproach. But this does not explain why they behave as they do.

Nor does the willingness of children to be generous to parents in later life indicate that they do so by virtue of an implied agreement entered into when they were in receipt of parental largesse. It is inconceivable that a child would justify a claim to that generosity on the grounds that if parents denied the claim they would forfeit the right to support later on. To look upon the symmetrical interchange between parents and children as having anything to do with an agreement or contract between them seems to me to lack all power to convince. It does so even as a metaphorical construct, a simile, or an analogy.

The two-generational procreational contract, therefore, fails as an explication and justification of flows of support between cohorts or age-groups sharing the same present, contiguous to each other in the procession, as we might say. Obligations between removed generations cannot in consequence be addressed at all under the two-generational contract.

This is certainly not so with the intergenerational tricontract, whose terms have been spelled out and which seems particularly well suited to securing justice between removed generations. The tricontract, moreover, gives formal expression to a widespread conviction about the obligations of generations to those coming after them, not only removed generations but also those which overlap in the same time space and which under another aspect can be regarded as contemporaneous, successive cohorts or age-groups. This is the conviction that each generational entity must deliver the world to its successors in the condition in which it was received. Such a belief, as we shall see, leads to the suggestion that the world itself is held by each successive set of its human inhabitants in trust for those who will come after. No very precise notion of how such a trust could be constituted seems to be in the minds of those who recommend such a proposition. It must be held to be strictly distinct from that notional trust, or set of trust relationships (the intragenerational intercohort trust), subsisting between cohorts and age-groups that can be looked to for securing justice among them, rather than between removed generations.

Trusts between Cohorts, Extending to Age-Groups

To grasp the relation of the intergenerational tricontract to the trust between cohorts and age-groups, which together make up the pattern of relations over time with which we are concerned, it is necessary to examine each item more closely, at the risk perhaps of some verbal or even some conceptual confusion. We begin with the notion of all coevals; that is, the whole number of persons alive at the same moment, a cross section across the human procession taken at a point in time.

As a phenomenon, all coevals has two identities from the point of view of justice over time. It is on the one hand to be taken as representing a removed generation, the best we can do to grasp that entity for the purposes of discussion, while recognizing its shortcomings as an indicator. As such, all coevals has to be regarded as one of the components between which the intergenerational tricontract is presumed to be established. Considered on the other hand as a collection of its constituent parts, all coevals as an entity embraces the whole number of cohorts to which belong all members of an entire population alive at the same time. These cohorts—each comprising every person with the same birth date— are conventionally combined into age-groups for analytic purposes. Because of the processional character of cohorts and of the whole set of relationships and entities, and also because of the looseness of the language in general use for discussion of these topics, however, the additive process makes the connection between trust linkages associating cohorts and the relations of age-groups to one another rather intricate and difficult to follow.

The three age-groups into which cohorts are traditionally marshaled for the purposes of the discussion of rights, duties, and welfare flows are also, somewhat unfortunately, frequently called generations. Younger cohorts, children who normally have parents in older cohorts, are taken to be the "child generation," dependent in every way during their earliest years on their seniors and economically dependent until maturity. Cohorts in the middle age range, the independent, directive, wealth-creating producers, are represented as the "parental generation," and cohorts senior to them as the "grandparental generation," economically dependent if they have insufficient savings, because no longer earning, and frequently dependent in other ways as life nears its end.

Generations defined in this way as existing within a population of all coevals have to be held distinct from removed generations linked by the generational tricontract. It is between age-groups of the generational kind, assemblages of adjacent cohorts that is to say, that means of support are seen to flow, downward and upward from the parental generation, set in motion and regulated by the trust that subsists between the cohorts that constitute each of them. The fit, however, is not exact, like so much else in these generational constructions. This is because not all net wealth producers are parents, and by no means all parents are net wealth producers. It is quite wrong, moreover, to suppose all those in late life to be incapable of producing goods and services of use to others, and many youngsters can be producers as well.

The important point, however, is that the trust and trust relationships that we are discussing subsist between cohorts, rather than between age-groups of the generational kind, although these form the origin and destination of the welfare flows themselves. The picture is of cohorts, which together constitute each of the age-groups concerned, having trust relationships with each other, the provisions of which change as the cohorts age and so proceed from one age-group to another. It is in this rather elusive and indirect sense that age-groups themselves are caught up in the trusts and trust relationships that are presumed here to subsist between cohorts, and in which other bodies also participate, particularly collective institutions and above all the State.

It is important to remember that all coevals, considered as a generation involved in the intergenerational tricontract, communicate the rights and duties of the tricontract to every individual, regardless of his or her age or generative position. Everyone, therefore, has rights to what he or she receives from his precursors or hers, rights that are or will be met by the duties they perform to their successors. But they do not have, by the specifically contractual arrangement presumed here, any duties to those anterior to them, or any rights in those posterior to them. This being the case, the child generation receives transfers being made to it by the parental generation as of right under the tricontract. But that tricontract gives no title to the parental generation to transfers from the child generation, or to the grandparental generation from the parental generation.

The implied intergenerational tricontract cannot, therefore, serve to justify welfare flows upward in the generational order, backward in the generational procession, from juniors to seniors, from younger to older age-groups. Pensions, especially pay-as-you-go pensions from current taxation, and such transfers as care during the years of dependency that may come with old age are secured in other ways. The suggestion is that provision of these types of support is due under the trust, or set of trust relationships, that has just been described as subsisting between cohorts and in which in the indirect fashion set out above, generations of the age-group type are also involved. It is in this intragenerational intercohort trust that collective institutions and especially the State have to be regarded as a further party or parties. This trust, or these trusts—it is not possible to be even as roughly precise under this head as it is under the generational tricontract—are not confined to these parties, however, or to the purposes of justice between age-groups, cohorts, and generations. It or they form particular constituents of the generalized network of trust that characterizes the whole of society organized into the liberal State, and with the liberal State as its performative instrument.

Intercohort trust relationships in fact are specific instances of "that general fairness that cements mankind" insisted upon by John Locke.[5] The particularity of the trust or trusts that engage those in active life in any political society with one another, with their no longer active extant predecessors, and with collective institutions, political and otherwise, is conveyed by the terms used in the Introduction to define the mutual understanding on which the modern Welfare State is founded. There, however, the association is given the title *contract* rather than *trust*. "During its productive years, each generation pays to support those who are dependent on it, assuming that when its own dependent phases come, it will be supported, in turn, by successor generations. . . . Issues of distributive justice . . . come to be viewed as settled by a continuing implicit agreement."[6]

It is not without interest that the contractual arrangement sketched out in this passage has three parties to it, like the intergenerational tricontract, rather than the two parties of the procreational contract, and that the word *agreement* appears as the final term, for *agreement* is vaguer than *contract*. But that this implicit, perdurable agreement is better conceived of as a trust than as a contract is evident from the following circumstances. The interchange between the parties is not of the quid pro quo character intrinsic to contract, which requires that if I do this for you, you must do this for me; that is, exactly what is laid down in the contract, or its equivalent: any variation must be referred to me.

The interchange does, however, resemble trusts of the type familiar in everyday life, at least to those who deal in any way with property exchanges. In the trust, a trustor makes items of value over to trustees, not for the good of those trustees, but solely for the good of the beneficiaries. If a trust is what the lawyers class as discretionary, the trustees can and should vary the distribution of the assets, without necessarily referring to the trustor if available, provided always that the object of the trust, that is, the welfare of the beneficiaries, is enhanced. In selecting the trustees and specifying their duties the trustor must be presumed to know that they are sufficiently well informed of the relevant circumstances and of what would be best for the beneficiaries under changing conditions, and in view of how conditions might change in the future. If, for example, the accumulation of assets to be spent later on is indicated, that is what trustees should undertake. If the beneficiaries should need counseling in the extent and character of their justifiable expectations from the trust, it is for the trustees to supply it.

If we apply the trust notion to social goods originating in a parental generation as described above, being transferred to a grandparental generation, the trustee is the State, certainly when the social goods proceed from taxation. As time passes, individuals composing the cohorts that progress through the productive age-group make their contributions (that is, ordinarily pay their taxes) in the confident expectation—their just expectation under the trust—that those who come after will behave similarly. In due course those successors will expect their own successors to do the same. It is not a question in either instance of one party repaying another for benefits received earlier, which is why the transfer arrangement is more trustlike than contractlike. Nor is it a question of beneficiaries receiving a specified payment, never reducible, always increasable, at a particular time. This is because of the discretionary character of the trust, and because the trustees are obliged to provide for future demands due to anticipated demographic and economic developments by accumulating a balancing fund as necessary. A parallel process, though not of course requiring possible savings and such, would apply to understandings about succession to jobs.

Intercohort Trust Relationships and Variations in Birth Totals over Time

The outstanding practical difficulty at the present moment as to distrib
utive justice over time, a difficulty that particularly affects Western political societies but that will no doubt finally have to be faced by all
societies as their fertility falls and their life expectancy rises, comes from
variations in the relative size of birth totals. The issues are familiar
enough, but are worth reiterating here using the concepts of intergenerational contract and intragenerational intercohort trust that have been
elaborated. In the United States, where the problem is and will be particularly acute, it is identified as that of the Baby Boom, and its successor,
the Baby Bust, with their consequences for transfer flows and for the
age and period incidence of taxation, as well as for the material standing
of various age-groups.

In that country a very large child generation, consisting of babies born
to a relatively much smaller parental generation in the 1950s and 1960s,
is now on its way through the productive years, creating a correspondingly large "parental age-group of the generational kind." This parental
generation has no difficulty in providing transfers to its progenitors and
seniors, now comprising the grandparental generation, which last at
present enjoys standards never before attained in the history of the elderly,
to some extent as a consequence of transfers to them in the form of
health support, taxation privileges, and direct maintenance. There are
those who argue that the older cohorts have been enriched by these
transfers at the expense of both the child generation and the younger
cohorts of the parental generation. They add that this inequity has existed
for some decades in the administration of the Welfare State in Great
Britain, New Zealand, and other countries as well as in the United States.[7]

The current parental generation, that is, the cohorts of the Baby Boom,
however, are engendering a child generation of unprecedented relative
smallness, the Baby Bust. When in due course the Baby Boomers become
the grandparental generation, their demands for transfers from their
exiguous successors, who will then be the parental generation, will be
relatively enormous. It is already evident to expert opinion that the flow
of resources to them will have to be scaled down. Such a measure would
face of course the formidable political power of the American elderly,
organized to an extent unparalleled elsewhere, and defy the adage frequently repeated on Capitol Hill that the U.S. social security program
is the third rail of politics—touch it and you die.

Such a reduction in the per capita benefits of the retired would not only reduce their welfare but lower the amount that current earners can expect when they retire. Nonetheless, these earners undoubtedly believe that by making their payments they are ensuring that their retirement will be a comfortable one, at least as comfortable as that of the currently retired. The transfer arrangement between cohorts and age-groups in the United States apparently is and may well continue to be out of phase with demographic and economic development, to an extent that may be impossible to correct. Should this be so, using the terms of the present argument, this is a result of the mishandling of the intercohort, inter-age-group discretionary trust by its trustees—that is to say by the State—and by the collective institutions occupying trusteelike positions.

Distribution has not been sufficiently flexible to maintain justice over time in accordance with the principles of the intergenerational tricontract and the intragenerational intercohort trust. Payers into and recipients of benefits from assurance funds have been allowed to suppose that their rights and duties were indeed of the kind that the untenable two-generational procreative contract implies. Retired persons, therefore, tend to assume that having paid their taxes, out of which noncontributory pensions are financed, or having made a contribution or two to a sup-posedly funded pension scheme, or both, they have a right to an irre-ducible level of benefit in perpetuity. Other reproaches to the trustees might be that those trustees, here perhaps best understood as the political and administrative community at large, have been insufficiently informed to carry out their duties under the trust. Furthermore, the counseling functions that such trustees should presumably exercise have been ne-glected, misunderstood, or omitted, and succeeding cohorts have thus been left ignorant of the consequences for intercohort transfers of con-tinuing below-replacement fertility and of escalating life expectancy. Fi-nally, the trustees have failed to levy from the cohorts in possession of wealth and to put aside the resources necessary to even out the flow of transfers in the face of anticipated demographic vicissitudes.

These may seem to be extreme statements, though they go no further than those directed by David Thomson and others at the "Selfish Gen-erations" who have been allowed to develop vested interests in the extant transfer pattern rather than directed against its administrators. These last, and the politicians with them, might reply that the demographic and economic knowledge that would ensure a more equitable distribution between cohorts has not been available to them, and furthermore that much of that knowledge comes from uncertain and variable demographic and economic forecasts. They would perhaps add that the limitations on political action are perpetually underestimated by their critics; that the measures envisaged might lead to an unacceptable extension of the power of the State and its bureaucracy, especially the creation of a huge balancing fund at the disposal of the government of the day; indeed, that a transfer system properly adjusted to meet these requirements might be incompatible with an open, liberal society. In any case, to become part of legislative and administrative activity, a perpetually revisable pattern of transfers, revisable in relation to present and future probabilities and possibilities, would have to be accepted as an agreed assumption of the whole electorate, and this is not likely. When questioned on the point, United States citizens always maintain that social security benefits have to be made larger, but scarcely ever declare themselves willing to pay higher taxes to that end.

The suggestion that the liberal State could be defeated by the distributive requirements of justice over time, even permanently and finally defeated, is surely of great importance for the general subject of this volume. We are engaged, however, in the exploration of a particular model, the contractual model, and its efficacy with respect to justice over time, rather than in adjudicating a political polemic. And there is still more to be said. The issues facing the United States arising from a pronounced slump in numbers of births have been discussed here almost entirely in terms of taxation and money, but there are aspects of demographic vicissitude that go deeper than this. Continuously low and falling fertility will gradually reduce the numbers of available younger persons to support the elderly and will attenuate their kinship relationships, while narrowing lateral kin links and progressively elongating vertical kin links. The now quite familiar phenomenon of double dependency—that is, elderly persons and children being simultaneously supported by the parental generation—will increase. An adequately informed, properly regulated trust between cohorts involving the State might do something about such problems, but their causes seem scarcely open to political manipulation.[8]

It seems appropriate nevertheless to insist that at least some of the difficulties and misunderstandings have arisen from failure to take note of what can be done in the way of analyzing relationships between generational entities as they have been teased out here. I am myself disposed to go somewhat further and to propose a general principle of justice between generations, age-groups, and cohorts that officials, politicians, and the public at large could be persuaded to respect. In earlier versions of this essay it was suggested that rights and duties have a temporal tendency in themselves, an Aristotelian nisus it might be said. Duties point always forward in time and downward in the procreative succession, backward in the generational procession, and rights point always in the opposite direction.[9] I shall not press this claim further here, though I shall refer to it again when we come to the implications of the intergenerational tricontract with respect to communal reparations for past wrongs.

Further Characteristics of the Intercohort Trust Relationship

First comes the fact that transfers downward from the parent generation to the child generation are not, or need not be, referred to the intercohort trust and its collective trustees. This is because the cohorts in the parent generation transfer these social goods directly, as it were, to the child generation in accordance with the intergenerational tricontract and in repayment of what, in the past, the grandparental generation transferred to them. It can thus be seen that when the child generation comes to occupy the position of the parental generation and so to supply transfers to their temporal and generative predecessors, now the grandparental generation, they do not do so as repayment. In this way the absurdities of the two-generational procreative contract are avoided in the workings of the intercohort trust.

The second circumstance surrounding the intercohort trust relationship has already been hinted at. The trust fund, so to speak, that the State administers as trustee is the source of support for all citizens who happen to be in need, those who are suffering from economic as well as demographic reverses and physical disability as well as disability due to growing old. These circumstances go to the foundations of political society, one of the primary objects of which is to provide for just such vicissitudes, which are an unalterable element in the human condition. It could be claimed, then, that the failure to provide for a demographically induced dilemma such as the consequences of the Baby Boom and the Baby Bust was and is neglect of a basic purpose of political association.

The third feature of the trust between cohorts and so between age-groups of the generational kind follows directly from the second. It is evident from what has been asserted that cohorts in the productive parental generation can be said to be contributing to their own welfare, since as those cohorts grow older they will constitute the grandparental generation, which is the recipient of welfare flows under the trust. Here at last we can bring in transfers that do not necessarily go through the State as trustee, but can also go through private corporations that collect savings from individual members of cohorts in their earning years and pay them back to the same individuals later. The trust analogy is not quite satisfactory here because private corporations benefit from holding such savings, so their role is not one of profit-renouncing trusteeship.

A funded State pension scheme, however, would come close to the standard trust arrangement. Although the State, as trustee, can collect profits from holding and investing such savings and from accumulating reserves to provide for equitable redistribution over time, it is the society as a whole that benefits. Society here includes the trustors, members of the value-orginating cohorts, since all members of the political society gain from the insurance that such activities provide in the eventuality of sickness, unemployment, bankruptcy, and so on. The phrase "social insurance" appears in every explication of the Welfare State. Although there is a tendency to suppose that the insurance function of the collectivity, and especially of the State, is a peculiar attribute of contemporary Western industrial societies with their Welfare States, it has in fact characterized political societies everywhere and at all times.[10] Such considerations surely underline the value of the State as spreader of risks, again a basic feature of political collaboration.

A fourth and highly important feature of the trust between cohorts marshaled into "age-groups of the generational kind" is that it does not extend its distributional activity to cohorts and age-groups belonging to different removed generations. This follows from the fact that the production of later removed generations is not available to earlier ones. The production of earlier removed generations, such of that production as is still significant, is wholly available to later ones under the intergenerational tricontract, so that the intercohort trust is otiose. Since they are by the definition "removed generations" out of any possible contact with one another, cohorts comprised in the somewhat complex manner described earlier as included within and limited to removed generations cannot be regarded as involved in any trust with one another. Though this is to press the image of contract rather far and to stretch the representational capacity of a cross section to its very limits, it seems justifiable to suppose that the intercohort trust cannot serve to provide justice between removed generations. That function is reserved to the intergenerational tricontract.

I shall return to these questions in my final paragraphs. Meanwhile we must address a feature of the intergenerational tricontract that takes the argument on to different territory, territory scarcely less important, however, for the securing of justice over time.

Reparations for Past Wrongs and the Intergenerational Tricontract

If it is true, as our analysis of contract in relation to justice over time requires, that we have contractual duties only to future generations, duties that meet the rights we exercise and have exercised upon past generations, then it follows that we have no contractual duty to take responsibility for any misdoings our predecessors perpetrated as members of removed generations previous to our own. This principle has substantial implications, unwelcome to many theorists, such as George Sher, who contributes to this volume, and to many politicians, administrators, and citizens as well. According to its provisions, for example, reparations claimed by American blacks from American whites in our own day, or from the Pakeha by their Maori co-citizens, are not owed to them because of any ethical relationship between removed generations, certainly not under any version of the intercohort age-group trust. This does not mean, of course, that the history of such grievances, the extent and circumstances of the original wrong and its consequences for the victims, are not relevant to the claims for reparations. But it does mean that the claim has to be considered exclusively as a part of the contemporary political process, as an appeal to "that general fairness which cements mankind" made independently of contractual or trust relationships.

In what follows, the adjective *political* will be used to describe such pleas for reparations and their adjudication, so as to distinguish both from pleas arising from the intergenerational tricontract or the intragenerational intercohort trust. Passages from the earlier version of my "The Conversation between the Generations" (see note 3) are reproduced here, adapted to the present text. The relevant passage begins with Edmund Burke's notorious statement about the partnership between the generations (see the Introduction, p. 16), which concludes: "As the ends of such a partnership cannot be obtained in many generations, it becomes a partnership not only between those who are living, but between those who are living, those who are dead, and those who are to be born."

Although this does suggest a reason why I am obliged to earlier generations, in that we are interconnected through a project that must last longer than the number of years we are alive combined with those that elapse between our lives, this seems a tenuous link with which to justify rights and duties. It requires us to honor agreements with persons never able to be present to tell us what our promise means and how far it extends, quite apart from the crucial issue of whether an authority that might keep us to our word could exist. It is easily granted that the dead are entitled to respect, even if it might be difficult to define that respect for political and other purposes.[11] But it is quite another matter to suppose that we are bound to them in a contractlike way. It is worth noting that Burke speaks of the ends and advantages of this intergenerational partnership (conceived in a combined temporal and procreational way) but never refers to responsibilities. The transfer of guilt seems not to be in mind. Yet the transfer of guilt between generations is perhaps the commonest form of the conversation we are examining as it goes forward with those in past time, in the historic sense. It can raise disquieting issues, as may be evident from the following question.

Is an American WASP of our day morally responsible for the original enslavement of blacks, and for the perpetuation, the successive reimposition it might well be called, of white supremacy ever since? Can someone be born a white Anglo-Saxon Protestant in the United States without incurring this formidable moral liability?

To answer that a person who is born into a WASP family is born an American citizen, and is thus by citizenship legally answerable for this collective guilt, has two implications. First, that the political order of the United States is possessed of unbroken moral continuity over time: guilt is transferred from individual to individual, from generation to generation of Americans removed from one another by the passage of years. Second, that all American citizens, WASP and otherwise, are involved in the responsibility for the enslavement of black people and their subsequent exploitation: guilt is not confined to those who are descendants of slaveowners, or to inheritors of their possessions, or to that much larger company who themselves now profit from racial subjugation or have ancestors or relatives in that position. Indeed, unless some juggling with citizenship, its degrees and extent for different classes of persons, is undertaken, black American citizens would themselves seem to be guilty of their own moral degradation and that of their forebears.

The everlasting moral personality of the political order implied by this answer is of a wide-ranging character. Foreigners are nevertheless apparently excluded from the moral interchange that proceeds within the ongoing life of every collectivity over time, whatever the descent of these foreigners. It would seem to follow that the many British persons whose ancestors were slavers have no duties toward American blacks, whereas every American is deeply committed to them. This seems to hold notwithstanding the fact that most of the ancestry of most Americans was located in countries whose citizens were not involved in the subjugation of blacks.

The implication here is that my citizenship makes me liable for past misdemeanors committed by Britons within British territories but in some way absolves me from any of the responsibilities incurred by my ancestors with respect to persons who lived in the past within the moral entity we now call the United States of America. This is true, apparently, even though I could be living (as members of the Gladstone family still are?) on the invested proceeds of the great British slave trade to the North American continent.

All this strikes me as highly unpersuasive as well as unrealistic. Assuming an eternal moral person for the State, as Burke seems also to be doing, and investing it with moral claims that have no obvious boundaries is in my judgment totalitarian as well, however "legal" it may be. What is wanted is a relationship between generations that is individual as well as social, one that passes through mortal individuals rather than through deathless collectivities. Making an individual morally responsible for the acts of his or her procreative ancestors, especially when it is often impossible to identify those ancestors beyond a generation or so, quite unclear how far back the responsibility should go, and just as uncertain what its limits should be, is highly unrealistic. Obviously there is a great deal of work here for the conscientious analyst of ethical and political relationships.

Another example might be taken from contemporary Germany, whose present generation of citizens makes reparations to Israelis. This generation is apparently acknowledging moral responsibility for the actions of the pre–Second World War generation of German Nazis, although Germany was then a different geographical as well as political entity and not all its citizens were Nazis.

In view of the extraordinary arbitrariness of these circumstances, it seems to me that the action of the German taxpayer should not be taken as at all realistic. Insofar as he or she is performing an intergenerational duty, he or she must be presumed to be choosing to exercise feelings of guilt about the persecution of the Jews in an almost entirely symbolic fashion. Although this is not the place to analyze the case of Americans and slavery at the proper length, I suspect that acts of restitution by WASPs to blacks in the 1990s could be taken only as symbolic as well. To convert problems into symbolic issues in this way in no way solves them, because it does not take into consideration how such symbols are nominated, how and why they are effective, what part propaganda and ideology of all kinds play in the symbol system, and so on. But of one thing we can be certain. Obedience to symbols is scarcely a strict principle of moral entailment.

It might be an exaggeration to elevate the principles of the intergenerational tricontract set out here into those of moral entailment, though the suggestion that it is the nature of rights to go backward and that of duties to go forward in time could bring us closer. On these assumptions it is clear that no living American or British citizen, no contemporary of ours in the 1990s, can be said to have a moral responsibility for the enslavement of blacks, or for any act of discrimination against blacks that took place before the time of their own removed generation. No conscientious German of today is guilty on account of the persecution of Jews by Germans of the Nazi era. No Pakeha living in the 1990s should be required to answer for the progressive dispossession of the Maori or for breaches of the treaty of Waitangi of the year 1840.[12] But every American, every German, every New Zealander, Pakeha and Maori, everyone now alive is obliged to all contemporaries and, under the tricontract, to all future removed generations for actions taken during his or her lifetime. They must do all that is possible to ensure that enslavement, dispossession, racial discrimination, and persecution of the kind that has been analyzed shall never occur now or within the foreseeable future. What applies to acts of this description applies also to acts of environmental degradation, to anything in fact that prevents our handing down to our successors the world in the condition in which it was when passed on to us by our predecessors, if possible in an improved condition.

We cannot dwell here on the perplexities that these principles might give rise to if an attempt was made to apply them consistently to the whole unmanageable area of relations between generations. One issue, however, should be touched on if only in passing; that is, the transfer of property from the past to the present and to the future by inheritance or otherwise, which since the time of Locke has been held by political theorists to be a crucial characteristic of continuity over time, a view that is represented in several of the contributions to the present volume.

The right to succeed to property is the most tangible that a child has in his parents, and that right is ordinarily exercised only after the death of a parent. But what if the property bequeathed by a parent, doing his or her duty to the child, is itself based on injustice? What if it consists, to repeat the example, in slaves, or in the money made from selling and owning slaves?

Nothing that has been advanced here makes it a duty for a parent to confer on his or her children ill-gotten gains; such possessions, by the rules of reciprocity, belong to the persons from whom they were stolen. But if a child should by generational position inherit a disputed possession, the criteria as to whether the child should keep that inheritance are scarcely generational. He or she is guilty only if the courts of law, or the political process of which in the widest sense the courts are part, decide that the possession is now unjustifiable. It is true that children in such positions sometimes renounce their inheritances because they feel them to be the tainted products of capitalist exploitation or racial oppression. But it does not seem to me that the inheritor of such property could be justly condemned for failing to make such renunciation on the grounds that this puts him or her in the position of the predecessor who did the despoiling. The condemnation would surely be of the political and social system that permitted the original injustice, and if the inheritor was held guilty at all, it would be for failing to do all that was possible to alter that system, in the present and for the sake of the future. Once more the duty of the conscientious inheritor goes forward in time, though the means by which he or she fulfills this duty are outside the scope of intergenerational relationships. They belong again to politics, as do the duties of all citizens of all countries always to respect, but sometimes to seek to revise, the treaties made by their predecessors.

To construe politics in this situation, nothing could be better than to become familiar with the political argument now going forward in New Zealand between Maori and Pakeha. The conventional case for reparations is seen to be inefficacious once a conscientious attempt to address reparations is undertaken, with both parties present and with the whole historical record in front of them, insofar as that record can be reconstructed. The transfer of guilt from the original transgressors to their extant representatives soon appears almost irrelevant, and political negotiation on the basis of historical knowledge comes to dominate the interchange and the search for a typically political consensus.

Generational Contracts, Intercohort Trusts, and Their Argumentative Force

By exploring contemporary usage and attempting to give some theoretical consistency to its formulations and half-formulations, I have gone as far as possible in this context toward answering the question, Is there a generational contract? No doubt other analysts might work out more convincing interpretations. Still others might judge it best to abandon the set of concepts altogether, in spite of its currency among politicians, propagandists, and people at large.

It must be obvious that this is certainly not my own view, and the task of erasing such a widely accepted set of notions from the minds of ordinary citizens would be exceedingly difficult, certainly beyond the resources of ethical and political theorists. Perhaps the most formidable body of critics in what might be called the everyday world, however, would be the lawyers. Contract belongs to the language of the law, but if a lawyer's opinion were asked as to the efficacy of the definitions and principles that have been elaborated here, they would likely be judged barely defensible in court. It is a notable fact, however, that the doctrine of natural rights, condemned out of hand by Jeremy Bentham as "nonsense upon stilts," is nevertheless very much alive in contemporary Europe and America, indeed in the world as a whole. The lawyer's disposition to reject widely accepted and supported doctrines of this kind, and to look upon their use of legal expressions as being no more than emphatic language recommending dogmas that have only the vague principles of natural justice to underwrite them, is not calculated to advance the discussion of the genuine and difficult issues of justice over time.

The charge of incoherence leveled against the notions of generational contract and trust certainly has some justification nevertheless. Even the two cardinal concepts, closely allied as they are in legal language and practice, are not always to be held theoretically distinct, as can be illustrated by the idea of the world itself as a trust to successive humans. This notion was appealed to when the explication of the intergenerational tricontract was first introduced, and it undoubtedly has enthusiastic support among environmentalists, despite the difficulty of reconciling it with the interpretation of contract and trust that has so far been expounded. And the picture of the natural world being entrusted to humanity has several features that make it awkward in a theoretical framework, which is also true of other quasi-theoretical notions encountered in environmental discussions that are not touched on here.

For one thing, the entrustment of the world in perpetuity to successive humans would seem to oblige independently of the fact that the world supports them. Humans would be preserved, of course, since we are integral parts of the order of nature, or of "our planet" as it is frequently if somewhat arrogantly called. But animals are likewise part of the world of nature, and animals are even more likely to suffer when humans abuse their trust, as it is patent that they perpetually do. The preservation of all animal life, however, raises the question as to whether such organisms as the anthrax bacillus and the AIDS virus are entitled to protection under the trust. If so, humans seem to be obliged to preserve a world even if that world might fail to preserve the human race.[13]

It is by no means clear, moreover, how the entrustment of the world is to be conceived. Neither trustor nor trustee seems to be nominated, only beneficiaries, though the beneficiaries may perhaps be supposed to act in both of the other roles simultaneously. The want of a clearly distinguished trustee goes along with a feature of all arguments to do with "our planet," that the parties affected are not individual national societies, but a single entity, humanity as a whole. No existent State, therefore, and no alliance of States could act as trustee for the planet, only a world State. But a world State does not yet exist and seems never likely to exist, which confronts us with another fundamental issue in political theory; that is to say the issue of what constitutes the proper ethical boundaries within which that theory is to work.

The difficulties with the concept of the world itself as a trust to humanity serve to direct attention to the fact that ethical principles other than those informing contract and trust might be invoked for environmental purposes. This might be done in combination with versions of either of these two, or both of them, perhaps otherwise. Aesthetic and religious principles might be invoked and the issues construed in different ways than those expounded here. It is no part of my purpose to try to show that notional contracts and trusts provide the only approach to the ends in view, but to explore contractarian principles and practices for what they can yield to the point. A determined attempt to elaborate generational "justice" on sociobiological lines might be quite successful, for example, and perhaps quite close to contractarian analysis. It would leave for decision, however, whether such a construction was of any ethical significance.

There are some indications that the contractarian approach to justice over time, which focuses on separate temporal entities in negotiation with one another but leaves open the question of how these entities are bounded, may suffer from the fundamental limitation of failing to grasp the processional character of the phenomena that have to be understood and explained. This possibility was close to the surface when we found ourselves wondering how far it was possible to go in assuming a time space that a removed generation could be said to fill, and in what sense cohorts could be supposed for the purpose of argument to begin and end within that time space when it is clear that in processional reality they do not (see p. 8, above).

There are at any one time as many separable cohorts in existence as there are exact moments of time at which more than one living contemporary individual was born. These cohorts, nearly all of which are based in practice on a year of time rather than a moment, continuously intertwine with each other over the whole length of human history. They do so like the strands that wind round one another to create a piece of thread, each strand being shorter than the piece of thread itself, which unlike the strands is capable of indefinite extension.

Such a simile leaves no room for transitions between cross sections, which are assumed in the argument presented here to be at one and the same time static and yet representative of all the cohorts that are in progress through them. Strictly speaking, the notion of generations that can enter into contracts, or of intercohort trusts that are bounded in time by the temporal limits of generations, are unrealistic constructs, however that notion is formulated. This essay on the question of the generational contract therefore must close by repeating what was asserted at the end of the Introduction. Theorists, social theorists, political theorists, and ethical theorists have yet to get an effective hold on the realities that would have to enter into any truly adequate account of justice over time.

Notes

1. Rawls, *Theory of Justice*, 12. For a formal critique of contractarianism, see the devastating remarks made during the heyday of logical positivism by Margaret Macdonald in "The Language of Political Theory" (1941), published in 1951 as no. 9 of *Essays on Logic and Language*; cf. Laslett, "Social Contract," in *The Encyclopedia of Philosophy*.
2. To keep in touch with current usage, loose and confusing as that usage undoubtedly is, the word *generation* will be employed for all the entities that have been distinguished when the context makes the meaning fairly clear.
3. See Laslett, "Conversation between the Generations." The earlier version with the same title was given as a lecture in 1970 and published in 1972.
4. This seems to be the position of Norman Daniels in *Am I My Parents' Keeper?* I am in considerable debt to the account Daniels gives of generational and cohort relationships, however, as will be evident in what follows.
5. These words, however, come from a letter castigating publishers and their defalcations, rather than from any consideration of political theory as such. See the preface to Laslett and Harrison, eds., *Library of John Locke*.
6. See the Introduction, p. 8, above. *Generation* is there used in yet a further sense, as a bundle of cohorts proceeding all the way through the life course. But "its

productive years" corresponds exactly to the parental "age-group of the generational kind" used here. The cited passage goes on to pronounce the arrangement unreliable for the purposes of justice over time because it is defeated by variations in the size of succeeding cohorts, the Baby Boom and Baby Bust problem considered below.

7. See David Thomson's essay in this volume, with its references, and his book *Selfish Generations?*

8. See Hammel, Wachter, and McDaniel, "Chickens Come Home to Roost," and for further work on this highly technical field concerning other countries and periods, Laslett and Smith, "La parenté en chiffres." This issue of double, or multiple, dependency will cease to be confined to the grandparent, parent, and grandchild triad and will be extended to these three together with great-grandparent and great-grandchild relationships. See, e.g., Bengston et al., "Generations, Cohorts and Relations between Age-Groups."

9. See the references in note 1. During the conference on generational justice at the University of Texas at Austin in October 1988, these suggestions about the temporal directions of rights and duties proved almost entirely unacceptable to the participants, most of whom are contributors to the present volume. I hope to return to this theme in a later, fuller version of the present exercise.

10. It is the existence and persistence of transfers of all kinds through the collectivity in its varying forms that impresses the historical sociologist, who finds it difficult to accept that the twentieth-century Western Welfare State is all that much of a novelty, and who is prepared to believe that our much poorer ancestors made relatively more generous provision for economic and demographic casualties than we do, considering our inordinate wealth. See the writings of Mead Cain, e.g., his contribution to a volume in press edited by Margaret Pelling and Richard M. Smith, *Life, Death, and the Elderly*, with his references.

11. For the Kantian duty of respect to past persons, especially the treatment of them as ends and not instruments, instruments preparing for our arrival and activities, see Laslett, "Character of Family History."

12. The Pakeha are white English-speaking citizens of New Zealand. I owe all that I know of the interesting current situation in New Zealand, highly significant as it is for the problems under consideration and for justice over time in general, to Andrew Sharp's book *Justice and the Maori*.

13. Some environmentalists seem to go so far as to claim that notional contractual or trustlike relations can or should exist between all humankind and animate or inanimate nature. Such arguments are best excluded from discussion of justice over time in contractual terms. To be persuasive, implicit contracts or trusts have to subsist between humans, human individuals and collections of them, such as the State, as well as cohorts, age-groups, and generations.

II

Ancient Wrongs
and Modern Rights

GEORGE SHER

It is widely acknowledged that persons may deserve compensation for the effects of wrongful acts performed before they were born. Such acts are in question when we say that blacks deserve compensation because their forebears were originally brought to this country as slaves, or that native Americans deserve compensation for the unjust appropriation of their ancestors' land. But although some principle of compensation for the lasting effects of past wrongs seems appropriate, the proper temporal scope of that principle is not clear. We may award compensation for the effects of wrongs done as many as ten or twenty generations ago; but what of wrongs done a hundred generations ago? Or five hundred or a thousand? Are there any temporal limits at all to the wrongful acts whose enduring effects may call for compensation? In the first section of this chapter, I discuss several reasons for addressing these neglected questions. In subsequent sections, I discuss some possible ways of resolving them.

I

A natural initial reaction to questions about compensation for the effects of ancient wrongs is that these questions are, in the main, hopelessly unrealistic. In the case of blacks, native Americans, and a few analogous groups, we may indeed have enough information to suggest that most cur-

I am grateful to Patricia Kitcher, Philip Kitcher, and Alan Wertheimer for their helpful comments and suggestions.

rent group members are worse off than they would have been in the absence of some initial wrong. But if the wrongful act was performed even longer ago, or if the persons currently suffering its effects do not belong to a coherent and easily identified group, then such information will not be available. There are surely some persons alive today who would be better off if the Spanish Inquisition had not taken place, or if the Jews had not originally been expelled from the land of Canaan. To discover who these persons are and how much better off they would be, however, we would have to draw on far more genealogical, causal, and counterfactual knowledge than anyone can reasonably be expected to possess. Because this information is not and never will be completely available, the question of who, if anyone, deserves compensation for the current effects of these wrongs will never be answered. But if so, why bother asking it?

This relaxed approach to compensation has the virtue of realism. The suggestion that we might arrive at a complete understanding of the effects of ancient wrongs is a philosopher's fantasy and nothing more. Nevertheless, despite its appeal, I think we cannot rest content with a totally pragmatic dismissal of the issue of compensating for ancient wrongs. For one thing, even if compensatory justice is a partially unrealizable ideal, its theoretical limits retain an intrinsic interest. For another, even if we cannot now ascertain which persons deserve compensation for the effects of ancient wrongs, the insight that such persons exist might itself suggest new obligations to us. In particular, if the victims of even the most ancient of wrongs can qualify for compensation, and if our current compensatory efforts are therefore aimed at only a small subset of those who deserve it, then we will at least be obligated to enlarge the subset by extending our knowledge of the effects of ancient wrongs as far as possible. Alternatively, the discovery that desert of compensation is not invariant with respect to temporal distance might force us to reduce our compensatory efforts in certain areas.

These considerations suggest that clarifying the theoretical status of ancient wrongs may dictate certain (rather marginal) changes in our actual compensatory policies. But there is also another, far more significant implication that such clarification might have. Given the vastness of historical injustice, and given the ramifications of every event over time, it seems reasonable to assume that most or all current individuals have been both benefited and harmed by numerous ancient wrongs. For just about every current person P, there are likely to be some ancient wrongs that have benefited P but harmed others, and other ancient wrongs that have benefited others but harmed P. In light of this, neither the distribution of goods that actually prevails nor that which would prevail in the absence of all recent wrongs is likely to resemble the distribution that would prevail in the absence of all historical wrongs. But if so, and if the effects of ancient wrongs do call as strongly for compensation as the effects of recent ones, then it seems that neither compensating nor not compensating for the known effects of recent wrongs will be just. On the one hand, since the point of compensating for the effects of wrongful acts is to restore a just distribution of goods among the affected parties, the injustice of the distribution that would prevail in the absence of recent wrongs will undermine our rationale for restoring it. However, on the other hand, even if that distribution would be unjust, the distribution that actually prevails is no better; and so a failure to compensate for recent wrongs will be every bit as unpalatable. The only strategy that is just is to restore the distribution that would have prevailed in the absence of all historical wrongs. But we will never have the information to do this.

How to respond to this combination of pervasive injustice and indefeasible ignorance is a complicated and difficult question. One possible strategy is to argue that even if compensating for recent wrongs would not restore full justice, it would at least bring us substantially closer to a totally just distribution than we are now. A second alternative is to revise our account of the aim of compensating for recent wrongs—to say that the point is not to restore a fully just distribution among the affected parties, but rather only to nullify the effects of one particular set of injustices. A third is to accept Robert Nozick's suggestion that we "view some patterned principles of distributive justice [for example, egalitarianism or John Rawls's difference principle] as rough rules of thumb meant to approximate the general results of applying the principle of rectification of injustice."[1] A fourth is to abandon hope of achieving justice by either compensating or not compensating, and simply to start afresh by redistributing goods along egalitarian or Rawlsian lines. If their positions can be grounded in either of the latter ways, egalitarians and Rawlsians may hope to rebut the charge that they ignore such historical considerations as entitlement and desert.[2] But as interesting as these issues are, it would be premature to consider them further here. The choice among the suggested options arises only if ancient wrongs do call for compensation as strongly as recent ones; and so that claim must be investigated first. The discussion so far has been merely to establish the claim's importance. Having done that, I now turn to the question of its truth.

II

Intuitively, the effects of ancient wrongs do not seem to call as strongly for compensation as do the effects of recent ones. Indeed, the claim that persons deserve compensation even for the effects of wrongs done in biblical times appears to be a reductio of the ideal of compensatory justice. But we should be wary of intuitions of this sort. It is perfectly possible that they reflect only an awareness of the epistemological difficulty of establishing desert of compensation for ancient wrongs; if so, then all the problems limned above will remain untouched. To clarify the force of our intuitions, we must ask whether they can be traced to any deeper source in the notion of compensation itself Is there anything *about* compensation that reduces the likelihood that ancient wrongs may call for it? More precisely, are there any necessary conditions for desert of compensation that become progressively harder to satisfy over time?

Prima facie, the answer to this question is clearly yes. In its standard interpretation, compensation is the restoration of a good or level of well-being that someone would have enjoyed if he had not been adversely affected by another's wrong act. To enjoy almost any good, a person must exist. Hence, a necessary condition for X's deserving compensation for the effect of Y's doing A seems to be that X would have existed even in A's absence. Where A is an act performed during X's lifetime, this requirement presents few problems. As A recedes into the past, however, it becomes progressively more likely that the effects of Y not performing A would include X's nonexistence. If X's currently low level of well-being is due to his great-grandfather having been defrauded in Europe, the very same fraudulent act, which reduced X's great-grandfather to poverty, may have caused him to emigrate to America and so to meet X's great-grandmother. Because the prevalence of such stories increases as the relevant wrong act recedes into the past, the probability that the effects of the wrong act will call for compensation must decrease accordingly. And where the wrong act is an ancient one, that probability may approach zero.

This way of explaining our intuitions about ancient wrongs may at first seem quite compelling. But once we scrutinize it more closely, I think doubts must arise. If X cannot deserve compensation for the effects of A unless X would have existed in the absence of A, then not only ancient wrongs, but also the slave trade, the theft of native American land, and many other acts whose effects are often deemed worthy of compensation will turn out to be largely noncompensable. As Lawrence Davis notes, "were we to project the 200 years of our country's history in a rectified movie, the cast of characters would surely differ significantly from the existing cast."[3] Moreover, even if we were to accept this conclusion, as Michael Levin has urged that we do,[4] further problems would remain. Even in the case of some wrong acts performed shortly before their victims' existence (for example, acts of environmental pollution causing massive genetic damage), it seems reasonable to suppose that it is not the victim, but rather some other person, who would exist in the absence of the wrong act. And there are also cases in which wrong acts do not produce but rather preserve the lives of their victims, as when a kidnapping accidentally prevents a child from perishing in the fire that subsequently destroys the child's home. Since compensation may clearly be deserved in all such cases, it seems that the proposed necessary condition for deserving it will have to be rejected.

If we do wish to reject that necessary condition, there are at least two available alternatives. One is to alter our interpretation of the counterfactual presupposed by the standard account of compensation—to read that counterfactual as requiring not simply that X be better off in the closest possible world in which A is absent, but rather that X be better off in the closest possible world in which A is absent *and X exists.* A more drastic alternative, for which I have argued elsewhere, is to modify the standard view of compensation itself—to say that compensating X is not necessarily to restore X to the level of well-being that *X* would have occupied in the absence of A, but rather to restore X to the level of well-being that some *related* person or group of persons would have occupied in the absence of A.[5] Although both suggestions obviously require further work, it is clear that neither yields the unacceptable consequences of the simpler account.[6] However, it is also true that neither implies that the probability of desert of compensation will decrease over time. Hence, the shift to either of them will call for a different explanation of our intuitions about compensation for ancient wrongs.

III

A more promising way of explaining these intuitions can be extracted from a recent article by David Lyons. In an important discussion of native American claims to land, Lyons argues that property rights are unlikely to be so stable as to persist intact through all sorts of social changes.[7] Even on Nozick's extremely strong conception of property rights, the "Lockean Proviso" implies that such rights must give way when changing conditions result in some individuals being made worse off by originally legitimate past acts of acquisition. In particular, this may happen when new arrivals are disadvantaged by their lack of access to established holdings. Because property rights do thus change over time, Lyons argues that today's native Americans would probably not have a right to their ancestors' land even had it *not* been illegitimately taken. Restoring the land or its equivalent to them hence is unlikely to be warranted as compensation. But if this is true of native Americans, then it must be true to an even greater degree of the victims of ancient wrongs. If property rights are so unstable, then rights held thousands of years ago would surely not have survived the world's drastic population growth, the industrial revolution, or other massive social changes. Their violation in the distant past therefore may not appear to call for compensation now.

Because wrongful harm and deprivation of property are so closely connected, this approach initially seems to offer a comprehensive solution to our problem. Here again, however, a closer examination reveals difficulties. First, even if we grant Lyons's point that changing conditions can alter people's entitlements and that new arrivals may be entitled to fair shares of goods already held, it remains controversial to suppose that these fair shares must be equal ones. If the shares need not be equal, then the instability of property rights may well permit the preservation of substantial legitimate inequalities through both time and inheritance. Moreover, second, even if property rights do fade completely over time, there will still be many current persons whom ancient wrongs have in one way or another prevented from acquiring *new* property rights. Because these new rights would ex hypothesi not have been continuations of any earlier rights, they would not have been affected by the instability of those earlier rights. Hence, the persons who would have held them will apparently still deserve to be compensated. Finally, despite the close connection between property and well-being, there are surely many ways of being harmed that do not involve violations of property rights at all. As many writers on preferential treatment have suggested, a person can also be harmed by being deprived of self-respect, by being rendered less able to compete for opportunities when they arise, and in other related ways. Although these claims must be scrutinized with considerable care, at least some appear clearly legitimate. Furthermore, there is no reason to believe that the psychological effects of a wrong act are any less long-lived, or any less likely to be transmitted from generation to generation, than their economic counterparts. It is true that the psychological effects of wrong acts are often themselves the result of property violations; but the case for compensating for them does not appear to rest on this. Because it does not, that case seems compatible with any view of the stability of property rights.

IV

Given these difficulties, Lyons's insight about property does not itself resolve our problem. It does, however, suggest a further line of inquiry that may. We have seen that because property rights are not necessarily stable, we cannot assume that anyone who retains his property in a world without the initial wrong is entitled to all (or even any) of it in that world. A world in which that particular wrong is rectified may still be morally deficient in other respects. Because of this, the real question is not how much property the victim *does* have in the rectified world, but rather how much he *should* have in it. Moreover, to avoid arbitrariness, we must say something similar about persons whose losses do not involve property. If this is not generally recognized, it is probably because deleting the initial wrong act, which is properly only necessary for establishing what the victim should have had, is easily taken to be sufficient. But whatever the source of the oversight, that the operative judgments about rectified worlds are themselves normative is a major complication in the theory of compensation; for normative judgments do not always transfer smoothly to the actual world. By spelling out the conditions under which they do not, we may finally clarify the status of ancient wrongs.

Let us begin by considering a normative judgment that plainly does not carry over from a rectified world to our own. Suppose that X, a promising student, has been discriminatorily barred from entering law school; and suppose further that although X knows he will be able to gain entry in another year, X becomes discouraged and so does not reapply. In a rectified world (Wr), which lacks the initial discrimination, X studies diligently and eventually becomes a prominent lawyer who enjoys great prestige and a high salary. In that world, we may suppose, X is fully entitled to these goods. In the actual world (Wa), however, the compensation to which X is entitled appears to fall far short of the goods or their equivalent. Hence our normative judgment does not fully carry over from Wr to Wa.

Why does our normative judgment about Wr not fully carry over? In part, the answer to this question seems to lie in X's own contribution to the actual course of events. Given more perseverance, X could have avoided most of the effects of the initial wrong act, and this certainly seems relevant to what X should now have. Quite apart from what X does or does not do in *Wa,* however, there is another factor to consider here. Insofar as X's entitlements in *Wr* stem from what X does in law school and thereafter, they arise through a sequence of actions that X does not perform in *Wr* until well after the original wrong, and that X does not perform in *Wa* at all. These entitlements are not merely inherited by X in *Wr,* but rather are created anew by X's actions in that world. But if X's actions in *Wr* are themselves the source of some of X's entitlements in that world, then it will make little sense to suppose that those entitlements can exist in an alternative world (that is, the actual one) that lacks the generating actions. To say this would be to hold that what a person should have may be determined by certain actions that neither he nor anyone else has actually performed.[8] We are plainly unwilling to say things like this in other contexts (nobody would say that a person deserves to be punished simply because he would have committed a crime if given the opportunity),[9] and they seem to be no more supportable here.

In view of these considerations, it seems that the transferability of a person's entitlements from a rectified world to the actual one is limited by two distinct factors. It is limited first by the degree to which one's actual entitlements have been diminished by one's own omissions in this world, and second by the degree to which one's entitlements in a rectified world are generated anew by one's own actions there. In the case of X, this means that what transfers is not all of X's entitlements in *Wr,* but at best X's entitlement to the basic opportunity to *acquire* these entitlements—in this instance, the entitlement to the value of the lost opportunity to attend law school. Of course, the value of this opportunity is itself determined by the value of the further goods whose acquisition it makes possible. But the opportunity is clearly not worth as much as the goods themselves.

This reasoning, if sound, sheds considerable light on the general concept of compensation. But because the reasoning applies equally to compensation for both ancient and recent wrongs, its connection with our special problem about ancient wrongs is not yet clear. To bring out this connection, we must explore its implications over time. So let us now suppose that not just X, but also X's child Z, has benefited from X's admission to law school in *Wr.* As a result of X's wealth and status, Z enjoys certain advantages in Wr that Z does not enjoy in Wa. Assuming that X is fully entitled to his advantages in Wr, and assuming also that X confers advantages on Z only in morally legitimate ways (whatever these are), it follows that Z, too, is fully entitled to his advantages in Wr. Under these circumstances, Z may well deserve some compensation in Wa. Because Z's entitlement to his advantages in Wr stems directly from X's exercise of his own entitlements in that world, however, it would be anomalous to suppose that Z's entitlements could transfer in greater proportion than X's. Moreover, and crucial given the principles already adduced, it seems that Z's entitlements in Wr will have to transfer to Wa in even smaller proportion than X's.

The reason for this diminution in transferability is easy to see. Just as the transferability of X's entitlements is limited by certain facts about X's omissions in Wa and X's actions in Wr, so, too, is the transferability of Z's entitlements limited by similar facts about Z's omissions in Wa and Z's actions in Wr. More specifically, the transferability of Z's entitlements is also limited by Z's own failure to make the most of his opportunities in Wa, and by the degree to which Z's entitlements in Wr have arisen through his use of his own special opportunities there. Of course, the opportunities available to Z in Wr and Wa may be very different from the opportunity to attend law school; but this difference is hardly a relevant one. Whether Z's advantages in Wr and Wa take the form of wealth, political power, special skills or abilities, or simply self-confidence, the fact remains that they are, inter alia, potential opportunities for Z to acquire further entitlements. Because of this, the way they contribute to Z's total entitlements in these worlds must continue to affect the degree to which Z's entitlements in Wr can transfer to Wa.

Once all of this is made clear, the outline of a general solution to our problem about ancient wrongs should begin to emerge. Because the transferability of Z's entitlements is diminished twice over by the contribution of actions performed in Wr and omitted in Wa, whereas that of X's entitlements is diminished only once by this contribution, it follows that Z is likely to deserve proportionately less compensation for the effects of the original wrong than X; and Z's offspring, if any, will deserve proportionately less compensation still. Moreover, since few original entitlements are preserved intact over succeeding generations (quite apart from any instability of property rights, the consumption of goods and the natural noninheritability of many entitlements must each take a large toll), the progressive diminution in the transferability of entitlements from Wr to Wa must be absolute, not just proportional. But if the transferability of entitlements from rectified worlds does decrease with every generation, then over the course of very many generations, any such transferability can be expected to become vanishingly small. Where the initial wrong was done many hundreds of years ago, almost all of the difference between the victim's entitlements in the actual world and his entitlements in a rectified world can be expected to stem from the actions of various intervening agents in the two alternative worlds. Little or none will be the automatic effect of the initial wrong act itself. Since compensation is warranted only for disparities in entitlements that *are* the automatic effect of the initial wrong act, this means that there will be little or nothing left to compensate for.

V

This approach to the problem posed by ancient wrongs is not dissimilar to the one extracted from Lyons's discussion. Like Lyons, I have argued that a proper appreciation of the entitlements on which claims to compensation are based suggests that these claims must fade with time. Whereas Lyons argued that the entitlement to property itself fades with time, however, I have held instead that it is the transferability of that and other entitlements from rectified worlds to the actual one that becomes progressively weaker. By thus relocating the basic instability, we avoid the objections that the analysis of property rights is controversial, that some claims to compensation do not view the right to the lost property as continually held in a rectified world, and that other claims to compensation do not involve property at all. But although the proposed account is not open to these objections, it may seem to invite others just as serious. More specifically, the presupposition that entitlements are historically transmitted may itself seem controversial, the distinction between newly generated and continuing entitlements may seem problematical, and the status of wrongs that are neither recent nor ancient may not seem to be accounted for satisfactorily.

The first objection, that the historical transmission of entitlements is as controversial as any analysis of property, is easily answered. Put briefly, the answer is that this presupposition *is* controversial, but that unlike any special view of property rights, it is internal to the very notion of compensation that generates our problem. If entitlements were never historically transmitted—if a person's entitlements at a given time were never derived from the prior entitlements of others—then someone like Z would not be entitled to any special advantages in *Wr* and so would not deserve any compensation in Wa. Moreover, although it is less obvious, the same point holds even if Z is only minimally well-off in Wr, but is extremely disadvantaged in Wa. It may seem, in that case, that Z's entitlements in Wr are independent of X's—that Z, like everyone else in Wr, is entitled to a certain decent minimum no matter what X was entitled to or did in the past. But even if this is so, it cannot form the basis for compensating Z for the effects of the initial wrong act; for if Z is absolutely entitled to such a minimum in Wr, then he will also be absolutely entitled to it in Wa, and so the original wrong act will become irrelevant.

Given these considerations, some form of historical transmission of entitlements is plainly presupposed by any view permitting compensation for a variety of prenatal (and, a fortiori, ancient) wrongs.[10] But precisely because of this, there may seem to be a problem with our central distinction between continuing and newly produced entitlements. This distinction appeared plausible enough when we first considered X's entitlements in Wr. However, once we take seriously the fact that people can transmit, confer, and waive their entitlements, the distinction seems to blur. When a parent confers advantages on children by educating or bequeathing wealth to them, the entitlements acquired are related both to earlier ones *and* to the product of new generating actions. Moreover, something similar may be said to hold even when someone merely retains his own entitlement to property; for he too is acting at least in the sense that he is refraining from transferring or waiving that entitlement. Because human actions and omissions are thus crucial in perpetuating so many entitlements, the premise that this role cancels transferability from rectified worlds may well appear too strong. Given this premise, it seems to follow that not only ancient wrongs, but also recent ones, such as systematic racial discrimination and perhaps even fresh property crimes, are largely noncompensable.

These worries are serious ones, and would require careful consideration in any full account of compensation. Here, however, I shall only outline what I take to be the correct response to them. Put briefly, my response is that the transferability of entitlements from rectified worlds should be viewed as disrupted not by *all* intervening acts or omissions in those worlds, but rather only by those acts or omissions that alter previously established structures of entitlements. When an entitlement is already established in a rectified world and is naturally stable over a period of time, its retention during that period is totally explainable in terms of its initial acquisition. In this case, the entitlement need not be attributed to any further doings of the agent; and so those doings seem irrelevant to the entitlement's transferability to the actual world. Moreover, assuming the legitimacy of inheritance, something similar may well hold for advantages that are transmitted to one's offspring; for here again, the resulting entitlements can be viewed as natural continuations of initial ancestral acts of acquisition. The principle of the conservation of entitlements that underlies these remarks would of course require considerable elaboration to be fully convincing. But something like it does seem initially plausible; and anything along these lines will nicely preserve the conclusion that desert of compensation is not entirely momentary and evanescent.

A final difficulty remains. My argument has been that desert of compensation fades gradually over time, and that ancient wrongs therefore call for no significant amounts of compensation. But even if this is correct, it does not dispose of the vast intermediate class of wrongs that are not ancient, but still were committed one or more generations ago. Since the process I have described is gradual, my account suggests that such wrongs do call for some compensation, although not as much as comparable recent ones. But if this is so, then the account may seem at once too strong and too weak. It may seem too strong because it will classify as intermediate even the wrongs done to blacks and native Americans—wrongs that appear to be paradigms of full compensability. However, the account may also seem too weak, since it implies that many partially compensable wrongs remain undiscovered, and that the problem of how to act justly in the face of incurable ignorance is therefore unresolved. Because any response to one aspect of this objection will only aggravate the other, the difficulty seems intractable.

But this dilemma is surely overdrawn. As for the claims of blacks and native Americans, it may first be said that even if the initial wrongs to these persons do go back several centuries, the real source of their claims to compensation may lie elsewhere. As Lyons notes, the truly compensable wrong done to native Americans may have been not the initial appropriation of their land, but rather the more recent acts of discrimination and neglect that grew out of this; and the same may hold, mutatis mutandis, for the truly compensable wrongs done to blacks.[11] Moreover, even if the compensable wrongs to blacks and native Americans do go back a number of generations, they may be highly atypical of other wrongs of that period. We have seen that one reason that compensability fades over time is that victims neglect reasonable opportunities to acquire equivalent entitlements; and so if slavery or the appropriation of native American lands has made it especially difficult for their victims to recoup their lost entitlements, then these wrongs may call for far more compensation than others of similar vintage. Here the results of my earlier discussion provide a natural framework for further inquiry. Finally, even if these suggestions do not establish full compensability for blacks and native Americans, they do at least promise substantial compensation for them; and this is perhaps all that is needed to satisfy our intuitions on the matter.

The other horn of dilemma, that this account leaves untouched our incurable ignorance about compensable wrongs in the past, is also overstated. The account does leave us unable to identify more than a small fraction of the past wrongs requiring compensation; but by itself, this implies only that we cannot right all of history's wrongs. The deeper worry, that in rectifying one injustice we may only be reverting to another, is at least mitigated by the fact that the most significant period of history from the standpoint of compensation is also the best known. Given this fact, the likelihood that our compensatory efforts will make things better rather than worse is greatly increased. If this solution is less precise than we might wish, it is perhaps the best that we have a right to expect.

Notes

1. Nozick, *Anarchy, State, and Utopia*, 231.
2. For development of this charge as it pertains to entitlement, see ibid., chap. 7. For discussion involving desert, see Sher, "Effort, Ability, and Personal Desert."
3. Davis, "Comments on Nozick's Entitlement Theory," 842.
4. Levin, "Reverse Discrimination, Shackled Runners, and Personal Identity."
5. Sher, "Compensation and Transworld Personal Identity."
6. Although I have presented them as alternatives, the two suggestions need not be viewed as mutually exclusive. Indeed, the most promising approach appears to be to combine them. The first suggestion appears the more natural in cases where there are many close alternative worlds that lack the initial wrong act but contain the victim himself; the second appears indispensable in instances where the initial wrong is so intimately associated with the victim's existence that there is no such world.
7. Lyons, "New Indian Claims."
8. This point is discussed in a more limited context in Sher, "Justifying Reverse Discrimination in Employment," 166ff.
9. For discussion, see Nagel, "Moral Luck," in his *Mortal Questions*, 24–38.

10. Compensation thus is in one sense a strongly conservative notion. One can consistently advocate redistributive measures on compensatory grounds or on nonhistorical consequentialist grounds; but not, I think, on both grounds together.

11. Lyons, "New Indian Claims," esp. 268–271. See also Bittker, *Case for Black Reparations*, chap. 2.

III

The Limits of
Intergenerational Justice

JAMES S. FISHKIN

Recent efforts to reconstruct liberal theory have attempted to place liberty in a stable role within some broader distributional structure. These efforts aspire to be *systematic*. At least under favorable conditions, they presume to specify a unified and coherent ideal solution to substantive issues of public policy; that ideal solution is defined by the realization of a principle (or complex of principles in lexical order) that should be implemented without exceptions. Such an ideal solution is systematic in that it does not require any recourse to intuitionistic balancing or any trade-off of principles, one with another.

That relations among generations have *not* been a central focus of the debate has greatly enhanced the plausibility of this aspiration to systematic theory. There has been little attention given to the complex issues of liberty and of distribution that arise from the consideration that individuals must be created and nurtured if they are to be citizens of a continuing liberal state.[1] Liberal theory has seemed almost to assume that atomic individuals spring from nowhere into adulthood only to return, eventually, to the void. I argue here that once the moral relations among generations are explicitly confronted, the plausibility of any systematic solution is greatly undermined. I then propose a different way of thinking about the first principles of liberal theory—one that puts generational relations and other issues of justice on a new footing.

Initially, I focus on three areas: (1) procreational liberty and the interests of future possible people; (2) procreational liberty and intergenerational equity; and (3) the liberty of families to benefit their children and the relation of that liberty to equal opportunity. In each case, a crucial liberty, one that can be regarded as constitutive of intergenerational relations, is implicated. I argue in each case that instead of a systematic solution—where first principles hold without exception and with strict priority relations—the most plausible result is what I have termed "ideals without an ideal." Even under the best conditions that can realistically be applied, the fundamental commitments of liberalism do not add up to a single vision in clear focus to be gradually approached. Rather, they add up to conflicting principles, each of which, if implemented, would take public policy in a quite different direction.

The standard critique of this result is that it is a form of intuitionism, which appears to produce only indeterminate results and to license each of us to balance conflicting principles pretty much as we see fit. In the last section, I suggest how determinate results can, in fact, be obtained from an unsystematic version of liberalism.

The Liberty to Procreate

The liberty to procreate is problematical because our notions of individual human interests have not been refined to deal with problems involving future possible people. Our ordinary criteria either break down or yield bizarre results.

We would ordinarily assume that a person X can be harmed if and only if X is made worse off than X otherwise would have been. For ordinary cases, this assumption works well enough. If I punch you in the nose, you are worse off afterward than before (your nose is bleeding), and that is what we mean when we say you were harmed. If, somehow, it could be shown that your nose spontaneously would have begun to bleed at exactly that moment, regardless of whether you had been punched, most, if not all, of the case for your having been harmed (by my punch) would evaporate. Let us call this the identity-specific notion of harm: X must be made worse off than X otherwise would have been for X to have been harmed.

Although it is central to common sense as well as a central part of many legal notions (particularly in tort law), the identity-specific notion of harm is inadequate for the evaluation of the interests of future possible people (and hence inadequate also for defining the appropriate sphere of procreational liberty). In the examples that follow, I have been greatly influenced by the path-breaking work of Derek Parfit, although my conclusions are quite different from his.[2]

Let us begin with two simple cases, one at the level of individual choice, the other at the level of social choice. In the first, a woman has a disease or is under medication for a given period such that if she were to conceive a child during that period it would have serious disabilities (perhaps she has German measles and the child would be deaf). If she were to wait until after that period, she could reliably expect to conceive a normal child. Many of us would say that she should wait, and our reasons would have to do with the interests of the child. Notice, however, that we cannot do so within the confines of the identity-specific notion of harm. The child who is born with serious disabilities is not worse off than it otherwise would have been, because if the mother were to wait, that child would not exist at all. Another child would be conceived instead, as differentiable from the first as one sibling is from another. That child is not harmed by the decision to conceive a child during the risky period, rather than during the normal period.[3] Or if it is harmed, it is not a harm we can assess with the identity-specific notion.

Consider this social choice parallel. Let us imagine a Third World country facing massive population problems. Suppose that demographers and economists together establish that if nothing is done about the population problem, after several generations the country will face disaster—mass misery, malnutrition, starvation on a large scale. Let us call this the laissez-faire policy option. On the other hand, to simplify matters, imagine an alternative policy option—let us call it restriction—that would sharply curtail population growth over several generations. Without getting into the details of how this might be accomplished, imagine that the demographers and economists predict the attainment of great prosperity in the same country after several generations of restriction.

It is worth noting that the population that would exist after several generations of population restriction is not a proper subset of the population that would exist after several generations of laissez-faire. In fact, after several generations the overlap would quickly approach zero. Consider all the contingencies involved in determining the identity of a particular generation (who marries whom, the timing of children, who those children marry, and so on). My identity or yours would be different if any of these factors had been different (so that I could then no longer speak of "my" identity in the same sense). Based on some of Thomas Schwartz's calculations, I conclude that after several generations the overlap would be almost nil.[4] If that is the case, then condemning the laissez-faire policy is the same as condemning the decision of the woman to conceive during the risky period (leading to a child with serious disabilities). All those who would experience suffering and mass misery due to overpopulation cannot be said to be worse off than they otherwise would have been, because were it not for the laissez-faire population policy, they would not have been at all. Had the other policy been chosen, completely different people would have existed instead. The results of the two population policies—mass misery from laissez-faire versus prosperity from restriction—would be visited over several generations on people with entirely different identities. Hence whatever benefits or harms might be involved cannot be conceptualized within the confines of the identity-specific notion of harm.

This issue is not merely a philosopher's quirk. A flood of litigation has bedeviled the courts exactly because of this problem. Many "wrongful life" lawsuits have been brought on behalf of children whose prenatal defects should have been diagnosed by a doctor or a laboratory.[5] These lawsuits typically claim that the child should have been aborted—had the doctor or laboratory only been sufficiently competent to inform the prospective parents of the disability to which their prospective child would likely have been subject. The difficulty faced by the courts has been much the same as the one mentioned here. The ordinary way to conceptualize damages within tort law is to imagine returning the injured party to the position he or she would have been in had the injury not occurred. But in this case, that position is nonexistence. Nonexistence is, of course, not the same as death. Never to have existed is very different from having a life that is interrupted.

Given some of the bizarre implications of the identity-specific view of harm, one clear alternative takes on new attractiveness. Why not compare states of affairs by looking at benefits and harms disconnected from any considerations having to do with the identities of the individuals? One particularly noteworthy theory that does this is utilitarianism. Setting aside the notorious problems of interpersonal comparison, suppose that there was something called a utilitometer. Or suppose that at least rough interpersonal comparisons of the intensity of preference satisfaction could be used to compare the disutility experienced by the seriously disabled child with the utility that would be experienced by the normal one, or the disutility experienced by all those who suffer from mass misery due to overpopulation with the utility of those who experience prosperity resulting from population restriction. Utilitarianism has the property of allowing us to look at any two states of affairs and compare their benefits and harms without having to know anything about how the identities of the people in one state compare with the identities of the people in the other. Utilitarianism is the most notable theory that holds this property, but it is not the only possible one. Suppose we compared the two states of affairs in terms of an impartial distribution of Rawlsian primary goods or some other metric for benefits and harms that did not make essential reference to preference satisfaction. We can call such theories, utilitarianism included, identity-independent theories (for the assessment of interests). Derek Parfit is the most prominent example of a theorist who has argued for some variant of utilitarianism precisely on the grounds that it is identity independent; that is, it avoids the counterexamples inherent to the identity-specific view.[6]

The problem with identity independent theories is replaceability. The point can be made most dramatically with a science fiction scenario. Suppose that I could painlessly and instantaneously replace all the readers of this book with others who will appreciate it more. Furthermore, the new readers (let us call them replacements) will in general get more out of life. On whatever identity-independent dimension of value we are talking about, they will achieve higher scores. To simplify matters, if we assume that the dimension of value is utilitarianism, then the point is that they will add more utiles to life each day than their predecessors did.

Note that I have not specified anything about how this transition would take place. Perhaps, as in the movie *Invasion of the Body Snatchers,* creatures from outer space would take on your appearances and incorporate your roles and memories. Perhaps I have a machine that simply fabricates new copies. Or perhaps the paper you are reading contains a new miniature technology, a technology that will go into effect as soon as you reach a certain page. In any case, posing the issue in a science fiction scenario clarifies the vulnerability of identity-independent views to replaceability arguments without raising empirical complications about the fear and disutility experienced by those who are eventually replaced. (For this reason you must consider my example hypothetical or assume that you have already passed the crucial page.)

Of course, replaceability arguments are not limited to science fiction. Consider this speech about the collectivization of Soviet agriculture from Arthur Koestler's novel *Darkness at Noon* (the Commissar Ivanov is addressing the prisoner Rubashov):

"Yes, we liquidated the parasitic part of the peasantry and let it die of starvation. It was a surgical operation which had to be done once and for all; but in the good old days before the Revolution just as many died in any dry year—only senselessly and pointlessly. The victims of the Yellow River floods in China amount sometimes to hundreds of thousands. Nature is generous in her senseless experiments on mankind. Why should mankind not have the rights to experiment on itself."

He paused: Rubashov did not answer. He went on: "Have you ever read brochures of an anti-vivisectionist society? They are shattering and heartbreaking; when one reads how some poor cur which has had its liver cut out, whines and licks his tormentor's hands, one is just as nauseated as you were tonight. But if these people had their say, we would have no serums against cholera, typhoid, or diphtheria."[7]

The general problem is that for any identity-independent conception of interests, so long as the abstract structure of distribution, the payoffs to positions, is at least as good under the replacement scenario, there are no grounds for objecting within the confines of this kind of theory. In fact, if we are utilitarians and the replacement scenario would increase utility, we could be obligated to kill everyone and replace them with a new population of better utility maximizers. In the identity-independent view, people are simply vessels for holding so much utility (or whatever else is our metric of value). It is the utility that matters, not the vessels. If a vessel breaks, it is of no importance provided that another vessel can be found or created that will hold as much or more.

The very merit of the identity-independent principles in dealing with the earlier counterexamples to the identity-specific view—namely, that they disconnect the assessment of interests from the identities of the people affected—is what renders them vulnerable to this replaceability scenario. Because the interests are viewed anonymously, such theories permit us to object to the production of a deformed child or to the miseries of overpopulation without worrying about whether the better-off people envisioned by the alternative are the same people. But this anonymous consideration of interests leads these theories to neglect the question of whether the people under the replacement scenario are the same people as those in the original population. The general dilemma is that if we consistently tie interests to personal identity we face the identity-specific counterexamples, but if we consistently untie them from personal identity, we face the replaceability scenario.

It may be worth pausing to consider two creative efforts to avoid one horn or another of this dilemma. The first, formulated by Peter Singer, aspires to avoid replaceability. I will argue that it does not. The second, formulated by Jonathan Bennett, seems to avoid the identity-specific counterexamples. I will argue that it does not.

Singer distinguishes his "preference" utilitarianism from the sensate classical version: "This other version of utilitarianism judges actions, not by their tendency to maximize pleasure or avoid pain, but by the extent to which they accord with the preferences of any beings affected by the action or its consequences." From this property of preference utilitarianism Singer concludes: "Killing a person who prefers to continue living is therefore wrong, other things being equal. That the victims are not around to lament the fact that their preferences have been disregarded is irrelevant."[8]

Singer's notion is that some beings, for example, animals, fetuses, and infants, experience utility only in the primitive sensate sense. Singer therefore believes that replaceability arguments apply to them, and he explores the implications of this for the eating of meat and the permissibility of abortion and even infanticide. He believes, however, that the applicability of utility in this second higher sense of preference utilitarianism to more developed children and adults would block replaceability scenarios applied to such persons. It is in this sense that his distinction between preference and sensate utilitarianism might be viewed as a way out of our dilemma (at least when applied to older children and adults).

I believe that Singer's escape is illusory. Preference utilitarianism is, at bottom, identity independent and thus vulnerable to some versions of the replaceability scenario. This becomes apparent if one thinks carefully about what the "other things being equal" clause might mean in Singer's solution. Recall that in our various scenarios, the replacements also can be imagined to have preferences in a self-conscious and reflective sense. Satisfaction of those preferences might easily turn out to balance the frustration of the life plans of the previously existing population.

More specifically, if we imagine, as Singer seems to, a special disutility in an ongoing life being interrupted (whether or not the person is around to regret the interruption), we might, symmetrically, imagine a special utility experienced by each replacement, for example, utility from the miracle of his or her being brought into existence. The new person may well experience an "existence bonus" that counterbalances the disutility from the previous person's existence interruption. Any reader of Walt Whitman's *Song of Myself* will have a vivid sense of such an existence bonus. There is no reason, in principle, why one of these must be greater than the other. The theoretical vulnerability to replaceability arguments remains.

That vulnerability is built into the foundations of utilitarianism. It is unavoidably identity independent because it is what might be called a purely structural principle. It defines the sufficient conditions for approving a change based entirely on information available from a listing of payoffs to positions under one alternative as compared to another.[9] If the total (or average, in some versions) is higher under one alternative, then that must be chosen. There is no reason for utilitarianism (or any other purely structural principle) to be concerned with the issue of whether the identities of the replacements are different from the identities of the originals. Because utilitarianism completely unties human interests from personal identities, it avoids the counterexamples with which we started, but only by creating a vulnerability to replaceability arguments.

Consider a second strategy for avoiding our dilemma. It has sometimes been argued that we should count only the utilities of those who would exist were an action not taken. Bennett has developed one variant of this approach: "The question of whether action A is morally obligatory depends only upon the utilities of people who would exist if A were not performed."[10]

This proposal is useful for the particular examples directed against the identity-specific view. If the population planner compares the benefits of the restrictive policy with the misery experienced by persons who would exist were that alternative not taken, then a clear case is made for the restrictive policy. Similarly, if the prospective mother compares the benefits of having a normal child with the disutility of the child conceived during a risky period, then a clear case is made for her waiting.

This strategy does not, however, offer a genuine way out of the dilemma. Although it handles these two examples, it is still vulnerable to the basic difficulty we encountered with identity-specific positions. According to these views, it cannot be counted as a harm that someone is created to endure a miserable existence. This vulnerability arises whenever those who would exist anyway are benefited by the misery of a newly produced person. Imagine, for example, a population considering whether to breed a race of test-tube-produced slaves. The persons who would exist were this policy not adopted are the present population. They would benefit overwhelmingly from having a race of slaves. The only ones who would suffer are precisely those who cannot be considered in this strategy, that is, the ones who would not exist were the policy not adopted. They are the ones who would be harmed by the policy, yet their misery could not be taken into account by this proposal.

The two horns of our dilemma are constructed from partial pictures of the interests of future possible people. Each has something to be said for it. But relying on one consistently to the exclusion of the other would lead to disastrous or bizarre results.

Consider a more mundane area where no exotic examples are required to make the point: procreational liberty. Procreational liberty defines a sphere of choice of undeniable importance where single-minded reliance on either identity-specific or identity-independent notions of human interest would lead to disturbing results.

Identity-specific theories, if relied on consistently, give procreational liberty too broad a mandate, whereas identity-independent theories, if relied on consistently, give it an overly restrictive one. Identity-specific theories open up too broad an area of procreational liberty because they do not count as harms actions that, on other theories for the assessment of interests, might plausibly be counted as harms.

I am assuming the placement of procreational liberty within some variant of the harm principle; namely, that people acting individually or together, consensually, can do as they please so long as they do not harm (or invade the rights of) others.[11]

Suppose families produce seriously disabled or deformed children even when they know perfectly well that after a waiting period they could produce normal ones (or be reliably likely to do so). Is that not sufficiently irresponsible that it raises basic questions about the appropriate breadth of procreational liberty? I am raising this primarily as a moral question without getting into the admittedly complicated question of legal remedies or restrictions. I merely want to make the point that there is something objectionable about producing a child under such avoidable conditions and that what leads to viewing that action as objectionable is some consideration of the interests of the child—once those interests are considered in a manner different from that permitted by the identity-specific notion.

On the other hand, to consider the interests of possible children consistently in the identity-independent mode would lead to other bizarre results. Our procreational liberties, in the negative sense of permissibly free personal choice, would be encroached on by a host of new obligations and new restrictions. Suppose we were consistent classical utilitarians and applied that position to the question of whether to produce additional children. So long as the additional child would add (or was reasonably likely to add) more utility than disutility (including whatever utility and disutility were caused by the child but experienced by siblings, friends, and so on), then we would be obligated to produce that child. It would no longer be a matter of discretion, or a matter of permissibly free personal choice. We would be morally required to conceive and bring such a child into the world. Once such issues are put in the category of moral requirement, they no longer fall within the realm of procreational liberty. They no longer belong in the area of life where we are permissibly free to do as we please so long as we do not harm or violate the rights of others. They have moved into the category of duty or requirement where failing to do the action in question is morally blameworthy and fulfilling it is a duty or obligation.

Consistently relying on the identity-specific view overly demoralizes and broadens procreational liberty. Consistently relying on the identity-independent view of harm overly moralizes and narrows procreational liberty. Each of these familiar and coherent approaches, approaches that work well enough in ordinary life, yields unacceptable results for the interests of future possible people. These conflicting, incommensurable images do not fit together into a unified conception but serve, at best, to identify conflicting moral considerations that can be balanced out in particular cases. More about this general result later. For the moment, I would like to turn to another area of disequilibrium among first principles that arises in intergenerational relations.

Procreational Liberty and Intergenerational Equity

The basic difficulties with the identity-specific and identity-independent views of interests do not depend on variations in cohort size. Although I used overpopulation as one of the counterexamples to the identity-specific view, that position is vulnerable to crucial problems even if cohort size happens to remain constant. For example, even when population is held constant, there would be no basis, within the identity-specific view, for objecting to the woman who conceives the child who would be seriously deformed (rather than waiting until a normal child could be conceived). The same logic would apply to whole cohorts replacing themselves with similar numbers under conditions where, for one reason or another, there was a great risk of large numbers of seriously disabled children being born. As in the earlier case, the risk might be avoided by waiting, for example, until some condition, say, a toxic chemical, were removed. Within the confines of the identity-specific view, there would be no basis for objecting to the "harm" to those children. They would not be worse off than they otherwise would have been, because had the alternative been chosen they would not have existed at all.

In addition to the problems just discussed, procreational liberty raises the problem of the possible variation in size of generational cohorts. In the United States, for example, the Baby-Boom generation consists of approximately 75 million persons. When that generation reaches retirement, there will be only about two adults of working age in the population for each retiree, while now there are about 3.4.[12]

Suppose we assume a budget constraint such that benefits for dependent populations, whether the elderly or the very young, must be provided largely on a pay-as-you-go basis. This is much the case throughout the Western industrialized countries. To the extent that this assumption holds true, variations in cohort size will greatly affect the per capita sacrifices that each generation of working people is called on to make to support dependent populations.

It seems morally arbitrary, however, that the relative size of a generational cohort should determine the level of sacrifice people are required by the state to make for dependent portions of the population. At least within ideal theory, which assumes favorable social conditions for a just society, some principle of intergenerational equity seems plausible. I have in mind a requirement of equal per capita sacrifice (over the long term) for generational cohorts for the contributions they are required to make for dependent portions of the population (whether those portions are the elderly, the disabled, or the young). The intuitive idea is that justice should be neutral among generational cohorts. If justice requires that each make certain sacrifices, it seems unjust that the sacrifices should vary wildly with the size of the cohort into which one happens to be born.

Although the empirical issues are enormously complex, the basic point can be made in a somewhat schematic way. Suppose that two large cohorts, A and B, are followed by comparatively small ones, C and D. Perhaps a widespread change in way of life lowers the fertility rate. In any case, as A and B age, the number of working people corresponding to each retiree is sharply reduced. In a largely pay-as-you-go system, this means that the per capita sacrifice for C and D will have to be far greater than it was for A and B. Of course, the benefits for A and B could be reduced to lessen the sacrifices of C and D. But assuming that the cohorts that preceded A and B were comparable in size, they have already made contributions at a high level to support those cohorts. If their benefits were now reduced, then their long-term on-balance sacrifice would be greatly increased (in comparison with earlier cohorts). But if the benefits to A and B are not reduced, then the burdens on C and D will be far greater than those faced by A and B. In either case, the variations in cohort size, when combined with budgetary constraints, lead to large violations of intergenerational equity.

A similar point can be made in the other direction. Suppose that the small cohorts, C and D, are followed by two large ones, E and F. Then C and D will have further disproportionate sacrifices to make to raise E and F. But E and F will have a comparatively easy time supporting C and D in retirement. Cohorts E and F are large while C and D were very small. On a per capita basis the sacrifices required of E and F will be small.

Under realistic conditions, the kind of generational equity posited here cannot be achieved if cohort sizes vary substantially. Yet if procreational liberty is fully maintained, then there may well be great variation in cohort size. Even under ideal conditions, we face a basic conflict between pro-creational liberty (which permits such large variations in cohort size) and generational equity. Various strategies might be developed to mute the conflict a bit by softening the impact of our budget constraint,[13] but the basic theoretical vulnerability is unavoidable. Once justice is considered across rather than merely within generations, new patterns of moral conflict emerge. These patterns bring the relation of liberty to other aspects of distribution into disequilibrium, challenging once again the aspiration for a systematic solution with settled priority relations.

The Liberty to Confer Benefits (within the Family)

Once children are conceived, they need to be raised. The liberty of families to benefit their children is another area where intergenerational relations produce a fundamental conflict between liberty and substantive elements of justice.

The liberty of families to benefit their children falls within a broader sphere of negative liberty where people should be more or less free to do as they please—provided that they do not harm or invade the rights of others.[14] It is, however, an especially precious portion of that broader sphere because it protects the area of liberty that touches most of our lives most directly.

We can narrow this liberty down a bit more by focusing on what might be called the private sphere: the sphere of intimate consensual relations that do not harm or invade the rights of others. By intimate relations, I

mean those that are both private and affective. By private I mean interactions that require the option of privacy in that their character would
be changed if they were coercively subjected to public scrutiny or inter
ference or both. Family relations clearly exist within this private sphere.
My concern is the liberty to confer benefits within the private sphere—
and the way that liberty conflicts with other essential parts of any theory
of justice.

Elsewhere I have argued in some detail that liberty (within the family)
conflicts with two central principles of equal opportunity and that those
conflicts take the form of a "trilemma"—a kind of three-cornered dil-
lemma.[15] Even under the best conditions that could realistically be imagined, we cannot fully realize equal opportunity and at the same time
preserve a liberty I have called family autonomy. For our purposes here
I will call it the liberty of families to confer benefits within the private
sphere.

The trilemma is surprising for two reasons. First, this conflict of principles is in the context of what a Rawlsian would call "ideal theory"—
favorable conditions for the realization of principles. Imagine that resources are as abundant as might realistically be imagined for any prosperous country and that there is general compliance with the principles
proposed, both in the present and in the relevant recent past. As a result,
the conditions that would normally be expected to produce conflict
among our fundamental principles do not exist. When conditions are
not so favorable—when scarcity is extreme rather than moderate, when
there is a legacy of injustice rather than of general compliance—it is easy
to see how intractable dilemmas might arise. But *if* there is a solution
defining inviolable first principles, then it should define results for the
favorable conditions just described.

There is a second factor that makes the trilemma surprising. I am talking
about a pattern of conflict, not between liberty and equality of outcomes
but between liberty and equality of opportunities. Equality of opportunity has often been dismissed as a modest principle, weakly reformist
in its implications.[16] If even this weak principle conflicts intractably with
vital forms of liberty, then the conflict between liberty and equality must
be unavoidable. I believe that once the liberties connected to the family
are considered, that is indeed the case.

Let me turn, for a moment, to the aspects of equal opportunity at issue
in the trilemma. First, there is the principle of *merit;* that is, that there
should be widespread procedural fairness in the evaluation of qualifications for positions. By qualifications, I mean criteria that are job related

in that they can be fairly interpreted as indicators of competence or motivation for performance in the positions to be filled. Whether the measures of qualification are SAT tests, civil service exams, or the evaluation of publications for tenure decisions, we are all familiar with the culture of meritocracy. It is deeply embedded in the rationales and practices of most Western institutions.

But merit, by itself, is not enough. My reasons for this conclusion are dramatized by an example adapted from Bernard Williams. Imagine a warrior society, one dominated by a warrior class.[17] From generation to generation, the children of the present warriors become the new warrior class and rule in turn. At some point, critics achieve a major reform. From now on, there will be equal opportunity, they announce, because the best warriors will be selected through a suitable competition. An elaborate warrior Olympics is designed to select those warriors who are most competent. The competition is held, but it makes no difference. The competition is won, overwhelmingly or perhaps entirely, by the children of the present warriors.

At first, to make it simple, imagine that the causal mechanism is quite obvious. The children of the present warrior class are both well trained and well nourished. Imagine that the rest of the population is on the verge of starvation. This turns the equal opportunity competition into a series of wrestling and boxing matches between three-hundred-pound sumo wrestlers and ninety-pound weaklings. Clearly, such a competition would not offer an adequate realization of equal opportunity. Note, however, that its results would be supported by the principle of merit. The three-hundred-pound sumo wrestlers presumably really are better warriors than the ninety-pound weaklings. They are better warriors because they have had a lifetime of favorable conditions to develop the desired characteristics, whereas their competition has had a lifetime of grossly unfavorable conditions to prepare for the same competition.

Real equal opportunity, it might be argued, must get at those conditions, for those conditions determine the real terms of competition. The difficulty, of course, is that those conditions are protected by the liberty to confer benefits within the private sphere of family relations.

A more ambitious account of equal opportunity would add to merit a second requirement, that there should be equality of life chances. By this I mean that it should not be possible to predict the eventual places in society of newborn infants based on such arbitrary native characteristics as family background, race, sex, religion, ethnicity, and so on. This criterion captures what was objectionable about the warrior society.[18] It was possible (but should not have been) to predict the winners and losers in the competition merely by knowing the class into which they were born. Of course this principle is violated a good deal in our own society, as various sociological studies demonstrate. If we know father's income or education, we can make good statistical predictions of the life chances among any cohort of newborn infants.[19]

The causal mechanism that is operating here is, to a large extent, simply a more discreet version of what was blatant in the warrior society example. Advantaged families differentially influence the development of qualifications, talents, motivations, and so on in their children compared with less advantaged families. These favorable causal conditions prepare such children to do comparatively well in meritocratic competition. The principle of merit then becomes a mechanism for generating unequal life chances.

It is worth mentioning that in real life we do not fully realize any of these principles. But we attempt to approximate them, and to one degree or another we are relatively successful. My point is that, together, they do not add up to a coherent scenario for the relations between liberty and equality, even under the best conditions. Consider the options pictured below:

	Option I	Option II	Option III
Merit	+	+	−
Equal life chances	−	+	+
Liberty (in family)	+	−	+

Option I is exemplified clearly by the warrior society. Liberty within the family (the liberty to confer benefits) protects the process whereby advantaged families differentially benefit their children in the developmental competition so that, as a statistical matter, those children will achieve unequal life chances. Suppose we attempted to achieve both merit and equal life chances? Then, as pictured in Option II, we would somehow have to insulate children from the advantages their parents would wish to confer on them. Perhaps some system of collectivized child rearing would do the job. Or perhaps a school system could be designed that would even out advantages and disadvantages from class background and block the exit options of private schools, tutoring in the home, and so on.[20] Whatever the precise details, any such scenario would require a significant sacrifice of liberty within the family. A third possibility would be to preserve liberty within the family, but attempt to realize equal life chances in some way that was independent of the principle of merit. This third option might be termed the reverse discrimination scenario, because it would require that people be assigned to positions according to some pattern that departed systematically from merit. One strategy would be simply to hire less qualified people from comparatively disadvantaged backgrounds. An alternative version of this scenario would assign all positions randomly, perhaps through a job lottery. Regardless of the details, any version of Option III would require a significant sacrifice in merit (and in the values promoted by meritocracy—procedural fairness and efficiency).

Clearly, each of the three scenarios is a horror story. Achieving any two of the principles drastically precludes the third—under any realistic scenario of favorable conditions.[21] It is as if a three-cornered stool had only two legs available to hold it up. Even after any two sides are propped up, lack of the third is enough to undermine or destabilize the whole structure.

One reasonable response to this pattern of conflict would be to trade off these three principles in particular cases while avoiding any systematic attempt to fully realize any of them, given the cost in competing principles. Such a position would, of course, exemplify what has commonly come to be termed "intuitionism"—the trading off of competing principles in particular cases without any fully realizable systematic solution.[22]

The intuitionist position is unpopular and unsatisfactory, in part because it is widely seen as vague in its prescriptions. Such a charge is not entirely appropriate, however. When strong gains can be made without a corresponding loss in competing principles, or significant losses without a corresponding gain, then clearly a case can be made for choosing a policy option within the intuitionist framework. There will also be cases under other conditions as well. But the two possibilities just mentioned are the most obvious ones.[23]

Since we are far from fully realizing any of these three principles, there is clearly progress of the first sort to be made. The liberty to confer benefits within the family could certainly be increased by changing the incentives for the formation of two-parent (as opposed to single-parent) families. The welfare system, at present, provides an incentive for the formation of families that will confer few benefits. Policies that would lessen minority teenage unemployment would, indirectly, improve the incentives for the formation of two-parent families. In addition, more systematic and innovative proposals might be constructed that promote the liberty to confer benefits within the family by providing the conditions for maximizing choice in the institutions to which children are subjected.

Educational voucher systems might well be developed so that choice of schools would not be merely a privilege of the advantaged, but an opportunity throughout the society.[24]

It is also clear that we sometimes sacrifice one of these principles without any corresponding gain in the others (or in additional factors that might be identified). Preferential treatment based merely on race, when it is applied in competitive meritocratic contexts, will sacrifice meritocratic assignment but will not significantly serve equality of life chances. When preferential treatment is applied to members of a minority group per se, an institutional incentive is created to confer the benefit on the most qualified members of that group, that is, its most advantaged members. Hence the debate about mistargeting of preferential treatment, not to those who actually are disadvantaged, but to those who symbolically share racial, ethnic, or other characteristics with those who actually are extremely disadvantaged.[25] This objection, I wish to emphasize, applies to preferential treatment for minority groups per se, and not to preferential treatment that is carefully targeted through income and other criteria to those who are actually from disadvantaged backgrounds. In that case, my objection no longer applies, because it is possible that the sacrifice in merit, real though it may be, is made up by an improvement in equality of life chances. On the other hand, when preferential treatment is applied to mere membership in the minority group, no gain in equal life chances can realistically be expected to follow.

Toward Reconstruction

The thrust of my argument thus far has been that intergenerational relations define a series of issues that render implausible the aspiration to a systematic version of liberalism. At this point I would like to suggest a different way of thinking about the fundamentals of liberal theory— one that permits a robust and demanding form of unsystematic theory. Instead of presenting liberal theory as a unified and coherent ideal whose parts fit together in clear focus, intergenerational relations reveal that its basic constituents rest in disequilibrium. Political theory applied to intergenerational relations gives us "ideals without an ideal"—substantive principles destined to remain in conflict, even under the best conditions. In this section I suggest a basic strategy within which each generation can wrestle with these moral conflicts to its own satisfaction—producing answers more determinate than an intuitionistic framework would, at first glance, seem to permit.

Recent liberal theory has been distinctive for its thought experiments: transporting us to an imaginary situation or transforming our motivation so that we choose political principles under conditions in which only the morally relevant factors bear on the decision. Two kinds of imaginary devices have been employed—changes in the situation of choice and changes in the motivation (within which I include filtering requirements by which only certain motivations are selected, while the rest are prevented from bearing on the decision).[26] When the motivation for choosing principles has been altered or filtered in the interests of impartiality, I will classify it as refined; when people choose, or are imagined to choose, with unaltered motivation (as, realistically, we would expect to find them in actual life), I will classify those motivations as brute. When the situation for choosing principles is the one in which those who must abide by the principles live together as an ongoing enterprise, I will classify it as an actual choice situation. When the situation for choice is an imaginary one, held to be morally relevant but not the situation in which those who must abide by the principles live together as an ongoing enterprise, I will classify it as hypothetical (see chart 1).

Motivations	Situations	
	Actual	Hypothetical
Brute	I	II
Refined	IV	III

Chart 1

An example of category I is actual consent theory. According to this approach, if people consent in real life, they are obligated to uphold the state; if enough (whatever that means) do actually consent, then the state is held to be legitimate and everyone is somehow obligated.[27] Motivation and situation are as found. Neither is subjected to transformation in the name of impartiality or moral relevance.

Category II transforms the situation for choice but not the motivation. Nozick's state of nature is a good example, where the question of whether there should be a state at all is posed in the "best anarchic situation one reasonably could hope for."[28] The motivations of people in this state of nature are not altered; they must be given a realistic construction. We are to assume that some would join protection associations voluntarily; others would choose to be independent. A major problem facing Nozick's argument is whether his scenario for the minimal state is compatible with a realistic construction of individual preferences, in particular, whether independents would be fully "compensated" in being forced to join the state.

Category III transforms not only the situation, as in category II, but also the motivations for choice in that situation. In Rawls's original position, agents are to choose principles of justice so as to maximize their shares of primary goods without knowing who in particular they will turn out to be. They are endowed with an abstract preference for primary goods regardless of the details of their actual life plans; they will know the details only after the veil of ignorance is lifted. In Ackerman's space ship dialogues, entrants to a new world argue over the distribution of "manna" through a filtering device for relevant arguments (the "neutrality" assumption). The perfectly sympathetic spectator of the classical utilitarians has both an imaginary vantage point (omniscience) and a postulated motivation (this individual reproduces in himself or herself every pain and pleasure in the world and hence will prefer states of the world that maximize the net balance of pleasure over pain).

Of the possibilities in chart 1, the basic difficulty with the top row categories (I and II) is that they are subject to indoctrination problems, whereas the basic difficulty with the right column categories (II and III) is that they are subject to jurisdiction problems (rival hypothetical thought experiments, like rival courts from different areas, each claiming authority over the decision).[29] The only category offering a prospect for avoiding both is IV (the left bottom quadrant). I want to suggest a bare sketch of a position that would fit this category.

I propose that we consider four demanding conditions for political practices that together purport to be sufficient to claim obligations for support from their members, justifiably. If all members are obligated in this way, then there is a sense in which the system is legitimate and its practices accurately define the appropriate norms of political evaluation for that society.

These four conditions are:

1. The practices must be *consensual,* that is, they must have wide support throughout the society.
2. The practices must be (at least minimally) *voluntary,* in that exit should be unimpeded for anyone who might wish to leave.
3. The practices must supply *essential benefits.*
4. The practices must be *self-reflective.* By this I mean basically that they must be subjected to continuing critical examination through unmanipulated debate.

Suppose a society's political practices satisfied these four conditions. I am arguing that *the minimally voluntary provision of essential benefits through self-reflective practices produces obligations on the part of each member*. If those conditions are satisfied for all the members, then they all have some obligation to support the result (setting aside questions about the strength of that obligation compared with other moral claims). Such a system hence would achieve a full solution to the legitimacy problem in the sense that all its members would be obligated to support it.

The special merit of category IV as opposed to category III in our scheme is that the actual acceptance of certain practices (when they are accepted and evaluated in the required way) trumps the jurisdictional challenges that arise from the unending variety of claims from hypothetical thought experiments. When those practices survive the required rigorous conditions, they can presume to settle the basic questions about the political structure of that society—so long as the requisite conditions continue to be maintained. Rather than producing new and exceptionless first principles, this strategy aims at legitimizing institutions that can wrestle with moral conflicts, such as those posed by generational relations, in all their concrete particularity.

It is not my position that actual practices always override or trump the claims of philosophers attempting to prescribe from outside the consensus. But forms of consensus that are suspect can be distinguished from those that have a justified claim to reasonableness and acceptability. The conditions proposed here are meant to isolate those that are reasonable and acceptable. When a consensus is suspect there are good grounds for philosophical reform. But when it is both reasonable and acceptable, then it defines the appropriate grounds for evaluating the regime.

Of course within such a consensus there is always continuing room for philosophical, moral, legal, and political criticism of the most vigorous sort. In fact, a continuing openness to such criticism is a plausible condition for being confident that a consensus should not be placed in the suspect category.

A theory of legitimacy does not yield a systematic theory of justice. But in its place it yields a theory of the fully legitimate political system. And such a system, in all its many parts, can produce justice defined in all its concrete particularity. It is the justice that comes from people operating in roles whose norms have achieved self-reflective legitimacy. The result is the collective reasonableness of a political system that reexamines itself from generation to generation. If such a system can maintain a self-reflective consensus, then it maintains legitimacy and, in that sense, preserves a certain kind of social contract specifying moral relations across generations.

Notes

1. A notable exception to this general point is Ackerman's *Social Justice in the Liberal State,* where a great many important issues are developed about generational relations. Still, he does not discuss the particular points I raise in this chapter.
2. Derek Parfit presents a fertile and original attack on the identity-specific view in his *Reasons and Persons.* My discussion here has benefited greatly from his work. The critique of Parfit's position that I develop here extends one I made in "Justice between Generations."
3. A possible exception would be cases where the disability is so severe that one might claim that such a life is worse than nonexistence.
4. Schwartz, "Obligations to Posterity," esp. p. 6.
5. See, e.g., *Curlender v. Bio-science Laboratories,* 165 Cal. Rptr. 477, 489 (1980), where a limited claim for damages was granted on appeal.
6. See Parfit, *Reasons and Persons,* pt. 4. Although there is some ambiguity about the exact character of Theory X when applied to different number choices, it clearly avoids the person-regarding counterexamples by being a variant of utilitarianism in its basic identity-independent character.
7. Koestler, *Darkness at Noon,* 161–162. I was reminded of Koestler's treatment of this issue by Joel Feinberg's excellent essay "Rawls and Intuitionism."
8. Singer, *Practical Ethics,* 80–81.
9. For an extended discussion of the character and limitations of purely structural principles, see my *Tyranny and Legitimacy,* chaps. 10 and 11.
10. Bennett, "On Maximizing Happiness," 62.
11. I take the term *harm principle* to refer to any of the standard variations on John Stuart Mill's "one very simple principle" that "the sole end for which mankind are warranted, individually or collectively, in interfering with the liberty of action of any of their number is self-protection" (Mill, "On Liberty," 135). For a systematic account of variations on the harm principle, see Feinberg, *Moral Limits of the Criminal Law.*
12. Daniels, *Am I My Parents' Keeper?* 6.
13. If a cushion of resources were accumulated—and if it were somehow protected from pressures to spend it on current generations—then the pay-as-you-go assumption might be modified.
14. For this broader argument, see my *Justice, Equal Opportunity,* sec. 2.4.
15. Ibid., chap. 3.
16. See, e.g., Schaar, "Equality of Opportunity and Beyond."
17. Williams, "Idea of Equality."
18. This is essentially the move John Rawls makes. See his *Theory of Justice,* where he explains how "fair equality of opportunity" adds to merit ("careers open to talents") the additional requirement that "those with similar abilities and skills should have similar life chances" (p. 73).

19. See, e.g., Jencks, *Who Gets Ahead?* 82–83.
20. Ackerman's proposals for "liberal education" would go a long way toward fulfilling both of these functions. See his *Social Justice,* chap. 5.
21. I am assuming throughout this argument that there are background conditions of social and economic inequality in the adult generation. My discussion focuses on equality of opportunities, not equality of outcomes. Equality of opportunities is a rationing of chances to be unequal. If there were no inequalities of outcome, then equality of opportunities would follow in an empty, merely formal sense.
22. See, e.g., Rawls, *Theory of Justice,* 34–40.
23. See my *Justice, Equal Opportunity,* sec. 4.5.
24. See Coons and Sugarman, *Education by Choice,* for a detailed proposal.
25. See, e.g., Fiss, "Groups and the Equal Protection Clause." For a critique, see my *Justice, Equal Opportunity,* sec. 1.3.
26. Ackerman's theory employs neutrality as a filter. See the discussion below.
27. A good account of these ambiguities, along with specimen illustrations, can be found in Pitkin, "Obligation and Consent."
28. Nozick, *Anarchy, State, and Utopia,* 5.
29. For further discussion of such jurisdiction problems, see my *Beyond Subjective Morality,* sec. 4.2.

IV

Justice across
the Generations

RICHARD A. EPSTEIN

The recent revival of ethical theory has led philosophers, political theorists, and even lawyers to think hard about justice across the generations. The conceptual problems that lie in the path of this venture are difficult, for what is often at issue is what duties people alive today owe unborn future persons. The normal modes of inquiry are effectively barred in dealing with this question. Democratic processes with universal suffrage cannot register the preferences of the unborn, and dialogue between generations is frustrated when future generations, or at least some future generations, are of necessity silent. Because the usual sources of information are closed to us, the analysis often proceeds by examining hypothetical situations, most of which ask a question that is deceptively simple: what would we want the present generation to do if we were in the shoes of some future unborn generation?

For some, like John Rawls, the answer seems relatively straightforward: "Each generation must not only preserve the gains of culture and civilization, and maintain intact those just institutions that they have established, but it must also put aside in each period of time a suitable amount of real capital accumulation."[1] The emphasis is on a collective determination, undertaken behind a veil of ignorance, as to the optimal savings rate within each generation for the benefit of those that follow. As stated, the principle assumes a steady increase of the savings rate until some "steady state" is achieved, for "when just institutions are firmly established, the net accumulation required falls to zero."[2] In essence, the entire scheme is one that insists that the temporal priority of the present yields no moral priority for people alive in the present. The same sentiments are expressed by Bruce Ackerman, who has argued that "all citizens are at least as good as one another regardless of their date of birth."[3] Again, the clear implication is that some form of moral and, more important for these purposes, legal constraint is necessary to protect the legitimate claims of future generations.

I confess that my moral intuitions are not as well developed as those of either Rawls or Ackerman on this grand scale. Hard as I try I cannot determine precisely what it was that my parents owed me, or what their generation owed my generation or those yet to come. I am also somewhat overwhelmed by a similar inability to speak about what I owe my children, as distinguished from what I hope to provide for them. I shall therefore devote myself to a more modest task. I wish to worry less about moral duties and more about real prospects. My thesis is that the debate on equity between the generations focuses too much on duty, and too little on practice and incentive. There is little that coercion and duty can do specifically to ensure that the next generation receives its fair share of human and natural resources. In general, if we continue to create sound institutions for the present, then the problem of future generations will pretty much take care of itself, even if we do not develop overarching policies of taxation or investment that target future generations for special consideration. In saying this I do not wish to be understood as arguing that markets can solve all problems for the future any more than they can solve them for the present. I believe quite the opposite, that regulation is necessary to prevent aggression and overcome many coordination problems with common pools. My point is that no special forms of regulation are needed to take into account the problem of justice across generations.

Why should anyone want to adopt this leave-bad-enough-alone attitude? Because the alternatives are worse. The issue here is not that of intentions, or of obligations. It is that of the connection between means and ends. A classical liberal regime of limited government, focused regulation, low taxation, personal liberty, and private property does better by future generations than an alternative regime that consciously enlists large government to restrain liberty and limit the present use of property for the benefit of future generations. The use of collective coercion has to be carefully husbanded lest it do more harm than good.

To develop this thesis, I approach the problem of intergenerational equity in stages. First, I ask how intertemporal allocation works where there is no conflict between generations, so that the only problems are those of self-knowledge and coordination of present and future preferences. In this context I conclude that although problems of foresight and planning exist, there is nothing that any system of public regulation can do to counteract them. Whatever the philosophical conundrums associated with self-knowledge and personal identity, the correct and workable assumptions take the naive view that preferences are generally continuous, stable, and well ordered.

Second, I examine the conflict between the generations within the context of the family, where the utility of the parents depends in part on the welfare of their children. Here I argue that the natural parental investment in children creates a bias for the protection of the future that legal and social institutions should exploit, not undermine. Taxation and regulatory policies that are designed to secure equality of wealth in the next generation do so at the cost of reducing the levels of capital accumulation, so that intragenerational equity (if compelling at all) is at odds with intergenerational equity.

Third, I consider systems of public ownership that might be used to accumulate and invest present resources for future use. In this context, I believe that these efforts also tend to be self-defeating, if only because public institutions are less responsive to the future than private ones, given the short-term political pressures under which public institutions operate. What is true with respect to public assets is also true of public liabilities. The increase in public debt fuels public expenditures that constitute a covert transfer from future to present generations. A system of common law property rights would likely give greater protection to future generations than any regulatory or taxing substitute. The proper area for government regulations is with environmental pollution and other spillovers, where market solutions are weakest, both within and across generations.

The Self and the Future

The problem of equity between the generations presupposes that we can identify a conflict of interest between what people alive today want and what unborn people will want on some distant tomorrow. If one assumes a social pie of constant size, then the inference is that each of a finite number of generations is entitled to only one slice of that pie. Thus it would be greed (or worse, theft)[4] for members of the present generation to even nibble on a slice that in principle belongs to some future generation.[5] To understand how serious the risk of overconsumption might prove in practice, imagine a universe where temporal preferences remain, but any conflicts of interest between generations disappear. That world is captured by thinking of a single person with fixed endowments of capital and labor that must be spread over an entire lifetime.

The first question that this person has to confront is the duration of life. If that life is infinite because the individual is immortal, then the problem of sound asset use and conservation cannot be resolved. It is not possible to use equal fractions of a finite asset over an infinite period of time. If any minimum level of asset consumption is required for each period, then it cannot be satisfied for all periods simultaneously. The only distributions of finite assets that can last an infinite time must follow some exponential decay function, which rules out equal consumption over all relevant periods.[6]

The assumption of immortality also makes it impossible to plan actions or evaluate behavior, for no one ever has to bear the full consequences of an error in judgment or conduct. Immortal people do not face starvation, death in combat, or even old age. By hypothesis they have triumphed over scarcity, the basic fact on which all economic theories of allocation and all legal theories of entitlement depend. No one quite knows what he or she would do, or could not do, if granted immortality. What is true of single individuals is true of societies at large, for immortal groups cannot persist on finite resources. Any understanding of how choices are made over time must be based on people with finite lives.

With some fixed life, even of uncertain duration, the problem of resource allocation over time becomes tractable. The ordinary person will have to allocate between present and future consumption and present and future labor, depending on individual preferences (which may change) for both labor and consumption and subject to a fixed budget constraint. The resources that are used today will not be available in future periods. By the same token the consumption enjoyed today cannot be had tomorrow. Every individual has to face the problem of discounting future costs and benefits to their present value. Such discounting suggests that it is better to advance consumption and defer labor. But if there are diminishing returns to consumption in any given period, the countervailing tendency is to equalize net consumption over different periods. There is thus some pressure to defer net consumption. Exactly how these two pressures balance out is hard to predict in the abstract.

One implicit assumption in this model is that individuals retain constant preferences over time, or more generally will be the same people tomorrow that they are today. This proposition is not a necessary truth.

People's preferences may change substantially over time, and in principle these changes could be large enough to constitute a radical change in personal identity. But the denial of the continuity of persons has certain dramatic consequences for the ordinary business of life that are difficult to accept. Taken to its extreme, this argument holds that persons are reconstituted on a continuous basis. The person who orders a ham sandwich at lunch is not the same person to whom it is served ten minutes later.[7] People are constant only over the smallest slivers of time, so that every transaction necessarily involves a temporal externality: the person who buys the sandwich at noon is allowed to obligate the (same or different) person called upon to pay for it when served at ten past twelve.

Thinking of that sort is, however, both ruinous and wrong. It is ruinous because it undermines the possibility of any continuous and stable social order. No long-term arrangements, no contracts, no marriages, no friendships could exist if individual personality was as plastic as this model of personal identity suggests. Similarly, government regulation would be an impossibility, for no regulators could govern if their preference structures and personal identities were as unstable as those of the public at large. Out of sheer desperation we would have to assume what is in fact the case: that people should be regarded as constant (or predictably changing) in personality and character unless there is particular evidence of mental disorder (for example, the use of mind-bending drugs).

Fortunately we are not forced to choose between necessary social convention and philosophical truth. The entire system of biological inheritance depends on the ability of organisms to reproduce themselves over a life cycle. If organisms had preferences as transient and erratic as is sometimes suggested, then they could never raise their children to maturity, so the entire cycle of evolution would have ground to a halt long before any human being could write about it. There are enormous selection pressures toward stability in human personality because of the survival advantages that it confers. Organisms that know their payoff schedules when they act will receive higher returns than organisms that do not. Over time, the organisms that know those schedules will survive and those that do not will perish. Strong psychological continuity is the hallmark of human personality. From the standpoint of rank casual empiricism, I have always been impressed by how people change relatively little over time, and how easy it is to resume a conversation with someone I have not seen for a decade or more. There is no reason to fear that any radical instability defeats the individual's ability to plan for the future.

It is a truism nonetheless that individual preferences for work and consumption do evolve over time. Anyone who has seen other persons at different stages of their lives knows about the predictable cycle of life. Yet so long as ordinary people are aware of the problem, they will probably want to invest their assets in ways that permit some flexibility in future use, at least on matters where preferences are expected to change. There are good reasons why most people keep their pension funds in liquid and tradeable assets. It is enough today to know anticipated levels of future consumption, deferring decisions on the form of consumption until better information is obtained. The choice of a retirement home does not have to be made at age thirty-five, even if retirement income is set aside then. A mortality risk is involved, of course, but millions of people take advantage of simple lifetime annuities, which allow them to keep a constant (or other desired) level of income throughout their lives. There is a broad gulf between philosophical doubt about personal identity and imperfect information about future needs. Philosophical doubt (like assumptions of immortality) makes it impossible to think about routine transactions in a sensible way. Lack of information about future needs is an argument for private ordering. Individuals probably can anticipate their own futures better than others would, even if both predictions are mistaken. Insurance companies are always worried about adverse selection precisely because their customers know more about the true status of risk than they do. But all individuals have less incentive to conceal the truth from themselves. Where knowledge is imperfect, the costs of external regulation quickly outstrip the costs of self-regulation.

The Family and the Future

Thus far the discussion has been confined to cases of intertemporal decisions made over the lifetime of a single person. What happens when the future belongs to different people in a different generation? Here I begin with one assertion about human nature that I hope is not too controversial. Individuals do not seek to maximize individual utilities, but instead have heavily interdependent utility functions with their offspring.[8] The most powerful source of this interdependence is not disinterested benevolence, although surely that is an important force. It is genetic connection, which induces parents to take into account the utility of their children (and the reverse as well) in making decisions about present and future consumption.

The genetic code therefore creates a bias toward the future. The wise social system will exploit what nature has given us in an effort to span the generations. The trick is to forge connections across the generations that exploit this future bias. A simple example constructed from the practice of making trusts illustrates how this could be done.

Assume that there are two sets of parents, each with two children. Both sets of parents have accumulated a level of wealth sufficient to persuade them that the deferment of consumption from the present generation (where there is plenty) to the future generation (where there may not be) is worth doing. Yet because there is some risk that fortunes will reverse themselves in the present generation, the extra wealth has to serve double duty, both as insurance for the parents and as inheritance for the children.

Standard legal practices can cope with the problem. One such practice is to place the property in trust, under terms specifying that the income is to go to the parents for life and that after their deaths the remainder (the principal) is to go to the children. Given the possible fluctuations in the parents' position, they reserve the right to invade the corpus whenever necessary to maintain their existing standard of living. The parents (or their survivors) are given sole discretion as to whether the invasion should take place, and any such decision in their favor is not reviewable (so the trust instrument states) by any court.

Arrangements of this sort tend to be perfectly stable in practice. Parents who invade the corpus think long and hard about their decision. If anything, the common pattern is to reduce consumption, short of major medical emergencies and the like, in order to pass on their inheritance intact to the next generation, especially if the children face financial burdens that the parents have been lucky enough to escape. There are occasional deviations from the rule, but the infrequency of litigation, or indeed of disagreement, between different generations under a trust is powerful evidence of the strength of interdependent utility functions to bind families together over time. The bequest motive thus tends to defer consumption and promote investment.

This point can be made more vividly if we contrast the standard trust with an alternative arrangement, having identical formal properties but very different economic ones. Switch the trusts around a little bit: take one set of parents and make the remaindermen in their trust the children of the second set of parents. Then do the same thing with the second trust. To ensure that there is no sleight of hand, assume further that both trusts have identical assets and that both sets of parents are the same age, as are both sets of children. Under these two "cross" trusts, the parents are the tenants for life with the power to invade the corpus; the re-maindermen are the children of the other family.

There is no historical precedent for how the parents behave when the remaindermen behind the trust are someone else's children. The reason is perfectly clear. No sane person has ever created cross trusts in this fashion, because the business risks are too great. The interdependence of utilities between the present and the future generation is severed. Each set of parents has the incentive to strip its respective trust of all its assets. Those assets could then be placed in a second conventional trust, with their own children as the remaindermen. This is something akin to the prisoner's dilemma, given that the two sets of parents cannot bind themselves by contract to preserve corpus. Each set of parents will say: if we are honest, we will surely lose out because the other set of parents will not be; and even if they are honest, we can do far better by cheating on the trust in which we are tenants for life. It is a game that no one can win. Why then incur the transaction costs to make trusts that will be broken? Trusts rightly remain family institutions.

Suppose we change the rules of the game for these cross trusts. One possibility is to prevent the parents by law from reinvesting the trust assets in the conventional trust, with remainders to their children. Now their choices would be somewhat different, but even so the power to invade will not be exercised in a disinterested fashion. Each set of parents would measure the gain from personal consumption against the satisfaction that they derive from seeing a stranger take what they have left. Whatever altruistic impulses they might display would operate at far lower levels than those toward their own children. The invasion of the corpus will be well-nigh complete, with at most scraps remaining. The moral should be clear: where the freedom of the present generation to make unfettered dispositions is crimped, the alterations in its consumption patterns will reduce the total stock of wealth available in the future. The private law of inheritance and trust responds to just this concern. Where it provides that certain moneys must pass to particular persons, the recipients are the decedent's children, not strangers. In some cases conflicts will arise between parental desires and obligations, but only infrequently. The far greater conflict arises when property passes at death to strangers. Then there will be predictably more consumption within the first generation, with fewer assets to pass on to the next generation. The effort to redistribute wealth within the second generation reduces the amount of wealth passed on to that generation. We cannot have it both ways.

Bruce Ackerman has suggested one way around this problem, which is a tripartite bargain between the member of the present generation with wealth (whom Ackerman calls Manic Senior), his own offspring (Manic Junior), and some other offspring (Depressive Junior). In Ackerman's view the baseline position allows Manic Senior to consume all his excess wealth, that is, above and beyond his original allocation, but he can leave extra amounts to his own offspring only if he procures a waiver from other persons in that generation. In effect Ackerman sets up a bargaining game that contains an extensive set of outcomes that would be an improvement over the original position he postulates. Thus if Manic Senior has four units of surplus, he can consume it all and no one can object. But he cannot leave it to his offspring. Manic Senior and Manic Junior together, however, can buy off the outsider with any portion of the gain. If Manic Senior is aware of the problem in advance, he can arrange his affairs to increase the consumption value of his assets, and hence his own threat position. If Manic Senior raises his consumption to two units, then the payments to the outsider will fall between zero and two units. Part of that surplus will be dissipated by bargaining pressures, so that less wealth will pass to the next generation under a system that tolerates all forms of inequality across generations.[9]

Thus far this simple model has contrasted two extreme cases: those where the parents give all their wealth to their children and those where they give all to strangers. In practice it is possible for the law to adopt a mixed strategy, in which part goes to the children and part to strangers. An estate tax represents just such a practice. The higher the rate of tax, the greater the fraction of the wealth that goes, via the public treasury, for the benefit of (but not into the hands of) strangers. Given all this parents are likely to adopt a mixed strategy. They would compare the utilities of full consumption for themselves against the indirect benefits they would receive from having their children consume only part, taking into account any marginal benefits that those children would receive from their tiny interest in the common fund. In practice, some relatively substantial transfers probably will still be made, if only because as people grow older their consumption patterns become limited and they may wish to conserve wealth, given fears of major medical expenses, for example. The estate tax has not destroyed all transfer of wealth to the next generation, but it has surely inhibited it.

The effects of the tax are more substantial when taking into account conduct before death. Transmission between the generations does not begin at death. In practice it begins with prenatal care, continues with education and upbringing during youth, and most important, with educational expenditures lasts long past the point when children reach their majority. Indeed, as people today routinely live into their seventies and eighties, transmission at death often occurs only when their children are well into middle age and their grandchildren are adults. (One objectionable feature of the estate tax is that it ties taxation to mortality, and thus makes its incidence and severity capricious.) Many important intergenerational transfers therefore take place during life in forms that no system of transfer taxation can easily reach.

It is possible, of course, to seek to counteract the partiality that parents show toward their children during life, but the steps would be far more intrusive than any straightforward tax imposed on transfers at death. Inter vivos transfers are much harder to detect because the consumption of parents necessarily is closely entwined with the consumption of children. A simple gift tax on out-and-out transfers of money or property would not suffice; more radical intervention is needed. Children could be forced out of their parents' home, or a special tax could be imposed on families who educate their own children to provide scholarship funds in equal amounts for those who are in need. The coercive nature of the egalitarian enterprise would become more manifest, giving rise to powerful political resistance. Even as the ethic of redistribution continues to make major political inroads into the traditional institutions of private property, the 1980s tax reforms have effectively abolished the entire transfer tax system for all but the very rich, most of whom can evade huge portions of it through a combination of shrewd tax planning, which takes advantage of the $10,000 annual exclusion per each donor-donee pair, and solid longevity.[10]

The effort to secure a patrimony for the next generation also has powerful effects on production. The tax across generations works like any other redistributive tax. The tax reduces the private return on investment, which in turn leads to a reduction in investment level, to an increase in present consumption, and to an increase in disguised or tax-free transfers. Again the lesson seems clear. Transfer taxes may secure redistribution within the second generation, but they cannot secure any transfers of wealth to the second generation.

Public Investment and the Future

Another strategy to provide for the next generation is for the state to invest the proceeds of an income tax in projects that are expected to outlive the current generation. But there is little reason to believe that this approach will work either.

Let us start with the simplest model, which ignores all political complications associated with running collective investments. The critical question is how private individuals will respond to the changes in the level of collective investment made by the state. The best working assumption is that private individuals will consider their own total wealth to be the sum of their private wealth and the subjective valuation that they attach to the resources in government hands. My personal wealth is not solely the sum of my land, cash, personal effects, and the like. To that figure has to be added the subjective value that I attach to my interest in highway infrastructure, good (or bad) government, defense, and the like. Assets that are held in public solution are not owned by government as such. Rather, as with the corporation, an aggregate theory of ownership reflects the underlying economic realities. Each person takes into account on a pass-through basis his or her "fractional" public burdens and liabilities. This point is especially important with such public benefits as social security, which is an elaborate network of rights and liabilities among citizens and across generations.

The interdependence of public and private wealth, however, indicates the obvious shortfall to this strategy. Levels of private savings can be reduced to offset the increase in public savings and investment. As a first approximation, therefore, the total level of future investment is not likely to increase by adopting this strategy, given the individual ability to substitute private consumption for private saving. Such is the result of the so-called Ricardo Equivalence Theorem, proved anew by Robert Barro, under the usual restrictive assumptions that all individuals have identical tastes and wealth, that all have equally strong bequest motives, that population will remain constant over time, and that technology does not change.[11] Some reduction in private investment will offset the increased investment by the state.

What happens when these austere assumptions are relaxed? In any real-world setting, some individuals have bequest motives and others do not; population and technology can change; and most important, it becomes costly to monitor the people in charge of both public and private investments. Public and private investments are still substitutes for each other, but neither can be as efficient as it would be in a world without individual differences, political pressures, and institutional frameworks. When these complications are taken into account, the question concerns the relative rate of decline in the efficiency of both public and private investment. Unfortunately, the differences suggest that public expenditures will provide smaller net benefits to the next generation than private ones. The simplest illustration is the general disrepair of public bridges, highways, and buildings, especially in comparison with capital assets in private hands.

These differences are not random, but systematic. The root of the problem has to do with the connection between ownership (and liability) structures and the ability to create and preserve value over the long haul. Compare the ordinary business corporation, whose shares are publicly traded, with the ordinary government situation, where property, often of immense value, is held under public trust, such that individual citizen interests cannot be alienated in any organized market. Even citizens who leave the country do not sell their fractional interests of public assets to new immigrants, but are forced to abandon them.

The corporate form allows for large accumulations of capital. Limited liability centralizes the management of the firm and creates shares that are both fungible and freely transferable and hence marketable at a readily determined uniform price.[12] Once the shares are sold, the seller retains no contingent liability for the conduct of the firm. Prospective trading partners are protected by notice of the corporate status, and tort creditors can be protected either by minimum capitalization or by insurance requirements.

The corporation is organized to look to the future. The market in firm shares reflects the present discounted value of the future income stream from the corporate assets. A short-term accounting profit today, achieved by invading corpus, does not induce the market to capitalize an inflated figure to set share value. Instead the accounting entry is recognized for what it is—a return of capital—so that the market valuation takes into account both the lower level of real profit and the diminution in capital attributable to the invasion of corpus. External monitoring of corporate assets is not perfect, but financial experts usually can do wonders in piercing through the fog of balance sheet notes. Firm managers therefore have an insistent incentive to maximize the future income stream of corporate assets, for a sharp reduction in share price could expose them to derivative suits, displacement by shareholder vote, or hostile takeover bids in the market for corporate control.

Citizens qua citizens do not hold marketable shares in publicly owned assets. There is no way that I can take my fractional interest in U.S. military preparedness or in national parks and sell it to an outsider, whether I wish to abjure the benefits of a particular project or to leave the country. The absence of a ready market in shares reduces the ability and hence the incentive of citizens to value publicly held assets. It dulls their incentive to monitor the behavior of government managers. Where there is an invasion of corpus—say the sale of timber, water, or grazing rights at below market values—no private citizen can obtain a substantial gain by detecting the breach and calling present management to account. Publicly owned property has little in common with assets owned by public, that is, listed, corporations.

In some sense, the fitter comparison with the state is the private or closed corporation, where shares are typically inalienable, either because of charter restrictions or because of the understandable reluctance of outsiders to buy into family firms. Closed corporations nonetheless are usually characterized by a common interest of family members (interdependent utilities again) and an ease of monitoring that ordinary citizens cannot bring to government officials. Even so, matters often get sticky, and the changes between the generations are often best handled by some mandatory "buy-sell" arrangement funded by life insurance on key shareholders.

No such arrangements are possible with public assets. Public officials for their part have powerful incentives to use or dispose of public assets for private gain, and they are subject to pressure by interest groups who wish to get more than their fair share of the public asset for less than their fair share of the price. Public highways, for example, must be maintained, yet many user taxes do a poor job of matching the costs that different classes of users impose. If trucks weigh ten times as much as cars, their concentrated weight means that one truck mile causes far more damage to the roads than ten car miles. A formally neutral formula that makes user fees a linear function of vehicle weight necessarily contains an implicit subsidy of trucks by cars, from which the usual economic distortions result. There will be too great a use of trucks and not enough use of cars or other forms of transportation. What is true of taxes is true of regulation as well. The restriction of access to public roads and the creation of gratuitous monopolies in truck transportation is one of the sad tales of twentieth-century regulatory policy.[13]

These errors create more than distortions within a given generation. They also create distortions between generations. Public officials and private interest groups have a built-in preference for present consumption over future gains. In particular, officeholders run for reelection and have much to gain if the government current account appears to be high, even though its capital account is low. Their political incentives are to let deferred maintenance accumulate, for its costs come home to roost only after they leave office. Hence the problem with bridges and roads.[14]

The protection of future generations is hard, even when the political system, say through the pressure of environmental groups, works to preserve long-term assets in their original form. The difficulty is that one cannot determine the wealth of the next generation simply by counting the number of acres of virgin timber that have been purchased for national parks. The cutting of timber does not necessarily amount to a transfer from the future generation to the present generation. The use of the timber also has to be taken into account. If the timber in question is used to build long-term assets, such as housing, then long-term values may be diminished by nationalization as inefficient public uses are substituted for more efficient private ones. Again, standing timber can be a wasting asset, when the failure to harvest in a proper mode results in older trees with rotten wood crowding out the newer growths that might replace them.[15] Unfortunately, matters do not improve when a laudable public motive is absent. The timber company with a license to cut timber from public lands will care less about the damage to the land and the environment than one that owns the land on which the timber stands. In the first case the loss is externalized on the public at large; in the second it is not. Public officers generally are not as good at business as private ones, if only because they do not face the right incentives for either loss or gain. They are less able to monitor and control abuses by their lessees than private lessors are. Their errors can have adverse effects on the maintenance of assets held in public trust. Once institutional imperfections are taken into account, therefore, the public ownership of assets does not offer any presumptive protection to future generations.

Deficits

The problem on the asset side of the ledger can also arise on the liability side. It is quite striking that the size of the public deficit is ever increasing in an age when the fraction of GNP devoted to government spending, or subject to government regulation, is at an all-time high. Deficits are charges that must be paid off in the future, often by the next generation. The analysis here, however, again is quite tricky, because to determine the full social significance of the deficit simply by recording its amount is impossible. Other factors also have to be considered. Two bear special mention: the uses to which the borrowed capital is put and the soundness of the debt structure.[16]

First, it is necessary to have some sense of the expected life of the assets that are purchased with the borrowed funds. If these assets had an expected life equal to the length of the debt, and if the debt itself were paid off by revenues generated solely from the asset, then there would be no intergenerational transfer from the future to the present. Ideally, the value of the public asset in each period would exceed the amount of liabilities associated with its construction and maintenance for that period, so that everyone would emerge a net winner, regardless of when he or she lived or died. A system of revenue bonds, for example, in which the debts incurred to build a highway were funded only by the tolls the road generated would be a sound public project, even if the highway disappeared the moment the debt was discharged. Since the general credit of the state would not be on the line, the individual creditors to the project would have an incentive to monitor both its revenue and its costs: their own financial return would be jeopardized by any shortfall. For the project to go forward, therefore, it would have to have a positive expected value.

This regime of asset-based financing is not perfect, however, because the highway system could well generate external benefits beyond those captured by highway users. The road might be critical for defense in times of national emergency. Yet in this context the sound rule is to guess the size of that classical public good and to fund it out of the defense appropriation, and not from general highway funds. The defense establishment would then be forced to trade its use of the road system against other direct military purchases. The residue should be funded from user fees to avoid excessive construction. Building the wrong long-term assets does not promote the welfare of the next generation.

Unfortunately, many public projects are not funded in this fashion. If there is a long-term debt for an asset with a short expected life, then some portion of the cost is externalized on the next generation in ways that work against the goal of intergenerational justice. More to the point, public indebtedness today is not only incurred for long-term capital projects. Huge amounts of the deficit are incurred to generate short-term transfers to the present generation. It is no great news that the most powerful coalition in Washington today is the elderly; social security benefits, including medical services, have expanded far more rapidly than the cost of living and more than any other component of the welfare budget.

These transfers systematically thwart any claims of intergenerational justice. Barro's model of intergenerational transfers suggests that these shortfalls will be offset by private transfers from parents to their children.[17] But the frictional costs he excludes from his model are too great to be ignored. Some elderly people do not have children, and others will choose to consume a portion of their investment, given their own pressing needs. The parents of many working-age people have already died, eliminating the possibility of compensating private transfers. The level of future tax and benefit increases remains uncertain, and the political costs of deciding who gets how much further undermine the effectiveness of any private response to social security.

People can, of course, mitigate the costs of regulation, but mitigation never brings us back to where we would have been had the first misstep not been taken. An alternative system that granted a tax deduction for money put into private retirement plans could (like any other consumption tax) remove the additional taxation burdens imposed on private savings, without creating the uncertainty over both contribution and benefit levels. Even if participation in this program were mandatory, the implicit backward redistribution of the present social security system would be reduced. But as matters stand, the political pressures favor those who vote, especially in a regime that offers only negligible protection to private property.

My second concern with public debt is directed to the form in which this obligation is held. Consider two debt structures. In case one each of ten people owes a single creditor $10, for a total indebtedness of $100. In case two, ten people are jointly and severally liable for $100 to a stranger, without rights of contribution and indemnity among themselves. In a world in which all parties are perfectly solvent and thoroughly reputable, the two debt structures have the same economic effects: the austere assumptions of Barro's model are satisfied. The creditor's asset is worth $100 and each debtor is on the line for $10. The moment one recognizes the human tendency to avoid paying money, however, the two structures are no longer the same. Where the debt is joint, each party has incentives to make the others pay his share of the debt. In ordinary private markets, this problem is effectively (not perfectly, but effectively) counteracted by a general rule that allows any codebtor who pays more than his pro rata share to have indemnity and contribution against his fellow debtors. That debt structure gives the creditor the security of knowing that a single suit can satisfy the full claim, while providing the hapless debtor who has paid more than his proportionate share full recourse against those who have not.

That system of contribution and indemnity is not available in the public sphere, however. Instead, there is a built-in tendency to try to introduce methods for repayment that reduce each individual's fraction of the payment. One way to discharge the debt is with moneys raised by a progressive income tax. The shares of the indebtedness implicitly shift, as the poor pay less and the rich pay more. Alternatively, where the debt is refinanced by new borrowing the obligation remains constant across different classes of individuals. The total amount of indebtedness is not reduced by shifting between these payment methods, but the costs of trying to shift the incidence of debt, whether successful or not, result in some long-term social loss. An elimination of the progressive tax thus offers one important advantage: the choice between debt and tax financing will depend less on distributional consequences, thereby reducing the opportunities for strategic behavior and placing some gentle restraint against increasing the total amount of government expenditures. Indefinite property rights tend to reduce the value of the assets so owned. The analogue to the debt case just outlined is that ten owners with a one-tenth interest each in ten houses behave differently from ten owners each with his or her own house. In exactly the same fashion, indefinite obligations tend to increase the total economic cost of the underlying debt. The problem of rent seeking that arises with the acquisition of assets can be exacerbated by the avoidance of liabilities.[18]

Inflation presents yet another risk to long-term contracting. Since the government (at least the federal government) controls the printing presses, the temptation to discharge the public debt by increasing the money supply and inflating the currency is great. This stratagem reduces the real amount of fixed debt and hence works a short-term implicit transfer from creditors to debtors. Such a strategy might be viewed as self-defeating; because the public debt is internal (in that we owe the money to ourselves), what we gain in one capacity we lose in the other.

Yet the fallacy of composition works in this area as well.[19] The argument about internal debt is correct only if every person has the identical interest as creditor (such as that of a lender of private money to the state) as he or she does as debtor (such as that of a citizen). But debt instruments are never held by all citizens in precise proportion to wealth. Some people are not creditors at all; some have extensive amounts of government paper. Much credit is held by foreign creditors, who are especially vulnerable to domestic manipulations of the money supply. Political coalitions do have incentives to change the value of money in order to alter the size of the debt. The creditor's gains are offset by the debtor's losses, but as ever the transaction is *not* an economic wash; someone has to bear the costs of influencing the political process, and everyone has to bear the increased costs of uncertainty in the value of government bonds.[20]

To complete the picture, inflation also imposes risks on any long-term private indebtedness, for if private debtors can increase the rate of inflation, then they can secure an implicit wealth transfer from their creditors. (The converse is true of deflation.) Any reduction in the stability of long-term money markets necessarily increases the costs of borrowing in all markets and tends to invite huge amounts of regulation—for example, mortgage moratoria statutes and anti-deficiency legislation—which further impedes the operation of private credit markets.[21] There will be less long-term investment. Yet variation in inflation rates can be reduced most effectively if the discretion of public officials in setting monetary policy is controlled. Limited government again offers certain long-term advantages. A fixed rule, for example, which tied the expansion of the money supply to the prior year's increase in the GNP, would be a good thing. Whether public assets or public liabilities are involved, a small state with limited discretion is the best way to promote the welfare of the next generation. The real risk in politics is that collective ownership will work redistribution back toward the present, toward those who have the votes.

Property Rights and the Future

I have said enough to show that there is no obvious reason to think that any policy of redistributive taxes or social investment will aid the redistribution toward the next generation. Now I need only show that it is unlikely that any policy will be needed. The ordinary rules of property, contract and tort, enforced by a limited government subject to stringent eminent domain restrictions, are far more likely to achieve that end, if only because the protection of the future is the ordinary outgrowth of the consistent application of these rules.

Start with the ownership of labor. According to the libertarian model, each person owns his or her own labor and is not required to perform any special act to acquire it. It follows, therefore, that all newborns have a substantial set of endowments that they do not take in any way from the generation that precedes them. Some members of the new generation will have greater endowments than others, but if the concern is with intergenerational equities, then any inequalities within a given age cohort can be safely ignored, or handled by ordinary charitable contributions and welfare programs wholly without regard to the age of the payers or recipients.

Next are physical assets. Here land is necessarily permanent, and the improvements on it generally have an expected life beyond its present owner. These assets will be passed on, unless we think it likely that persons in the present will take great pleasure in destroying what they have created. This last risk seems quite small. Most people do make bequests to their children, and where wealth is sufficient, to such permanent institutions as universities, hospitals, and foundations. Regulatory intervention at common law has never been concerned with people who want to destroy what they own;[22] rather it has been to restrict the period of time during which assets could be tied up in trust.[23] Even if the present generation wants heavy consumption, it has to sell permanent assets in order to finance it. You can't take it with you; this powerful message indicates that much wealth stays behind—for the next generation.

The situation is more striking when we move to intangible assets. Some, like patents and copyrights, have value beyond the life of the current holder and can be sold. It is difficult to know how they could be destroyed, save by refusing to allow anyone to license the patent. Even that strategy would be self-defeating, because the government could then acquire the intangible property through eminent domain for use in the public domain at close to zero cost, its value in the hands of its present owner. In any event, the prospect is not worth considering seriously given the tiny fraction of assets for which destruction is plausible. The hard question with copyrights, trademarks, and patents concerns their ideal duration, which could vary from property form to property form. The trade off is that longer periods of protection induce greater invention, but at the cost of more limited use of the covered work, mark, or invention over time. The trick is to minimize the sum of the two costs. If this is done in present-value terms, future generations will be well served by the regime of property rights so created.

There is, moreover, a huge body of intangibles that are properly regarded as part of the public domain. Mathematicians who prove important theorems have their names immortalized. Pythagoras did not obtain exclusive rights to use his own theorem. The stock of human knowledge generally increases, and the next generation always gets a free ride on the present, just as the nondiscoverers in the present generation get a free ride on the discoverers. It all works out pretty well. Academic positions, government honors, influence, and income can all be obtained by persons who have contributed to knowledge even if they cannot copyright or patent their ideas as such.

The one major concern is the environment. But in this area it is critical to define systems of private rights for the present. The common pool problem with fisheries is not solved by allowing everyone to keep the fish that he or she catches. Some rule must be devised to preserve the long-term stock as well. The common pool problem is writ large when the issue is the preservation of diverse species or the prevention of the greenhouse effect. Some form of collective intervention is appropriate here, just as it is appropriate to prevent nuisances and the premature exhaustion of common pool assets. There are too many potential plaintiffs and defendants for ordinary litigation to work. But the same systems of regulation that help in the present—damages, injunctions, tradeable permits—work to our long-term advantage as well.

In his contribution to this volume David Braybrooke attacks me and other libertarians on the grounds that "gross inequalities in the distribution of private property pose enormous dangers of oppression." He then recommends other systems for the social control of assets to counter this problem.[24] But his concerns with the use of property to promote slavery or serfdom are misplaced on at least three counts. First, he ignores the political risk of the confiscation of the wealth of the rich by the poor through an artful series of taxes and regulations. Votes can offset wealth. Second, he does not recognize that the ability of the rich to confiscate the assets of the poor or to enslave them is so potent not because the rich have private wealth, but because nations too often develop expansive government structures that allow the rich to turn their economic power into political power. Third, a defense of the institution of private property does not require that the title of all present property holders be treated as paramount; nor is it an apology for any concentrations of wealth obtained by improper means, whether private force or state-sanctioned monopolies. Finally, it is not my purpose to give a mystical and intuitive endorsement either to the institution of private property or to the present holders of particular assets. Instead, it is to explain, in functional terms, why a strong system of property rights, tempered by a suitable recognition of collective action problems, offers the best prospect for protecting and enhancing the endowment of the next generation.

In this case the proof is in the pudding. Socialist countries such as the Soviet Union have been unable to provide a consistent pattern of economic growth or to protect their environment. Yet the democracies that have accorded even modest respect to private holdings have done a better job. In these countries, to be born later is to be born into a world that promises greater comfort and happiness in the future. In these societies, future generations have received benefits from past generations that exceed the level of transfers stipulated under any of the standard theories of justice between the generations. We can keep it that way be hewing to the same sound principles of private and public law that work to promote justice in the present generation. Indeed, there is probably nothing we could do today to neutralize the power of the next generation if it decided to act in selfish and shortsighted ways. If we govern ourselves well, we can and will leave the blessings of liberty for our posterity. At that point someone else will have to carry the ball.

Notes

1. Rawls, *Theory of Justice*, 287.
2. Ibid. His position seems to be remarkably static in that increased levels of productivity might well call for a positive savings and investment rate that will allow future generations to be better off than present ones.
3. Ackerman, *Social Justice in the Liberal State,* 203.
4. See, e.g., ibid.: "So far as ideal theory is concerned, the bad trustee stands no better than any other kind of thief."
5. Here I put aside the problem that in principle there are an infinite number of future generations, so that no one generation could have a finite part of any pie, no matter how large. In the short run, this difficulty could be overcome by assuming an expanding output via improved production. But if resources are finite, then in the long run extinction is the necessary fate of all living species, including humans, so that equality between the generations could never be maintained.
6. See Williams, "Running Out," 165, 169–173, which demonstrates that the resource owner will diminish the consumption in each period by the real interest rate, which in turn reflects the price of deferred gratifications. The formula he derives is $x = S(1 - a)$, where S equals the amount of the original stock, a equals the fractional use that each period represents of the prior period, and x equals that portion of the stock consumed in the period. Note that in order for the consumption to be equal in all periods, a has to be set equal to 1, which means that x, the amount consumed in the first period, is zero. If x is a market basket of all goods and services, then there will be no second period. If there is some threshold x^* below which an individual or group cannot sustain itself, then human survival and equal consumption over all periods are not mutually compatible.
7. John Donne (both lawyer and poet) made the same point far more elegantly in

"Woman's Constancy": "Now thou hast lov'd me one whole day, / Tomorrow when you leav'st, what wilt thou say / Wilt thou then antedate some new-made vow, *or say that now / We are not just those persons which we were* / Or that oathes made in reverential fear / of Love and his wrath, any may foreswear."

8. See generally Hamilton, "Genetical Theory of Social Behavior," 1.

9. Ackerman, *Social Justice in the Liberal State*, 204–207.

10. The changes are reflected in law schools, many of which no longer offer the course on estate and gift transaction, once a staple of the upper years and now taken by only a few students at the schools that still do teach it.

11. See, e.g., Barro, "Are Government Bonds Net Wealth?" 1095. The gist of Barro's argument is that where there is forced deferred consumption on the public side, self-interested individuals will increase their consumption of private assets to offset those losses. Under very restrictive assumptions—all persons are identical, the number of people is constant in each generation, no technological change—the offsets can be made well-nigh exact. See ibid., 1098.

12. See Easterbrook and Fischel, "Limited Liability and the Corporation," 89.

13. See, e.g., Hilton, "Consistency of the Interstate Commerce Act," 87.

14. See *New York Times*, Apr. 22, 1988, B3.

15. For a chronicle of difficulties with public management of forests, see Deacon and Johnson, eds., *Forestlands*.

16. Eisner, *How Real Is the Deficit?*

17. This notion is seconded by Becker, "Theory of Social Interactions," 1063, 1073.

18. See generally Buchanan, Tollison, and Tullock, eds., *Toward a Theory of the Rent-Seeking Society*. For an argument on the limitation of the anticipated level of rent dissipation, see Flowers, "Rent Seeking and Rent Dissipating," 431.

19. "We are committing the fallacy of composition when we argue from the premise that every man can decide how he will act to the conclusion that the human race can decide how it will act" (Hardin, *Collective Action*, 1). The term dates to Mackie, "Fallacies," 173. The fallacy applies to any movement from a single individual to any group, however small.

20. Uncertain levels of inflation convert any fixed income offering into a variable payment instrument whose maximum value is achieved when inflation remains at zero. Uncertain levels of inflation simultaneously reduce the return to creditors and increase the cost to borrowers. The sum of those two costs acts as a wedge that prevents gainful transactions from taking place when the difference between what the debtor demands and the creditor is willing to pay is smaller than the total levels of uncertainty.

21. A mortgage moratoria statute defers the creditor's right to foreclose on the underlying security and in exchange gives the creditor some additional rights of interest. This prolonged extension of the debt usually leaves the creditor with a bundle of rights worth less than what had been enjoyed before regulation, but the courts have been reluctant to disprove of all such statutes categorically. See, e.g., *Home Building & Loan Association v. Blaisdell*, 290 U.S. 398 (1934), which in sustaining one such statute gave a very broad definition of the inherent government rights under the police power—the ability to regulate for the health,

safety, morals, and general welfare for the benefit of the public at large. For discussion, see Epstein, "Toward a Revitalization of the Contract Clause," 703, 735.

An anti-deficiency statute denies the creditor the right to sue the debtor for more than the amount of the property given to secure the loan. To the extent that the value of property has dipped below the face level of a loan, the statute denies the creditor his remedy for the difference via a "deficiency judgment." Substantial deflation, such as that experienced in the 1930s, transfers enormous sums of wealth to creditors. These two types of statutes are highly imperfect and generally mischievous responses. A stable currency eliminates any need for either remedy.

22. One difficult case is whether executors should be required to obey instructions from testators to destroy their private papers after death. Note that if these instructions need not be followed, then testators may take to destroying the papers themselves before death, in some cases before a change of heart. Note also that the eminent domain option in the text may allow the state to condemn whatever papers are left, although the question is very vexed because there is no sensible way to determine just compensation. It is also possible for private parties to preserve their papers while limiting access to them. For a discussion of Franz Kafka's order to his executor, Max Brod, see Hayman, *Kafka*.

23. The two major rules are the rule against perpetuities and the rule against unreasonable accumulations. The point of both rules is said to be to prevent the "dead hand" from ruling the future. Stated otherwise, the risk seems to be the present generation's protection of grandchildren at the expense of children. There is no evidence that excessive short-term consumption is an important problem with private wealth, even though many philosophical examples treat deathbed consumption binges as one of the realistic choices of the dying. See, e.g., Ackerman, *Social Justice in the Liberal State*, 205. My view is that these rules are generally unnecessary, but largely harmless. See Epstein, "Past and Present," 667, 710.

24. See Braybrooke this volume.

V

The Social Contract and Property Rights across the Generations

DAVID BRAYBROOKE

Can an Earlier Generation Block the Revision of Rights?

Gross inequalities in the distribution of private property pose enormous dangers of oppression—oppression quite as intolerable as oppression by dictators or monarchs, let them be ever so absolute. The reduction time and again by the rich of the poor to slavery or to serfdom shows what this may come to, though the most intransigent champions in our time of private property give such oppression astonishingly little attention. The omission is astonishing, because the liberties that they hold dear, and the right of private property itself, are always liable to be overridden by private grandees—something which is happening at this very moment in the Brazilian interior, as overweening cattle ranchers squeeze out smallholders and rubber tappers.[1] At least one libertarian (Eric Mack) is willing to accept as within the right of private property one common mechanism of oppression—bargaining hard enough to lead to people's giving up all their worldly possessions as the only means on offer of meeting their vital needs.[2] But even Mack, I presume, would not accept a mechanism in which the oppression is brought about by using riches to hire thugs and assassins. Robert Nozick

I wish to thank Lars Osberg of the Department of Economics, Dalhousie University, also Thomas Cromwell and Leon Trakman of the Faculty of Law at Dalhousie, for timely and helpful advice.

never mentions the possibilities of such abuses as dangers inherent in unlimited accumulation of property in some private hands much more than in others. His "Lockean proviso," though designed to put limits on the disadvantages of appropriation, without being directly aimed at the dangers in question, serves even so as a precaution; but it comes into operation only in circumstances so extreme (for example, someone's engrossing all the available drinking water)[3] that it would not have done anything to forestall "the second serfdom" in sixteenth-century Poland or the spread of serfdom in seventeenth-century Russia.[4] Richard Epstein gives an arresting account of the difficulties of bringing redistribution about, but does not dart even a contemptuous glance at the dangers that an imperfect and inefficient redistribution might avert.[5] Loren Lomasky, the most reasonable of the libertarians that I have come across, considers at some length the topic "When Rights Are Wronged" without noting even in passing the dangers inherent in unlimited accumulation; they are simply invisible.[6]

Worse, such writers leave us with the implication that if the property that gives private grandees such power was justly acquired, we are morally bound to accept the unequal distribution, with all its dangers. In particular, on this view a moral prohibition stands in the way of taking against the dangers any precautions that invade the rights of property. Nozick acknowledges that we may lack the information to establish the pedigrees of present holdings of private property; he resorts to the Difference Principle as a rough-and-ready way of dealing with the past injustices that contaminate present claims.[7] Given spotless pedigrees, however, he leaves us with no limit to inequality short of the proviso. No doubt, he and the other writers in question are ready to deplore the abuse of rights that lead to oppression. Do they think that is in itself a safeguard? That such abuse will not happen because the grandees, all too glad to accept a sweeping justification for their own property, will agree that it would be wrong—a dastardly deed—to usurp the property of the poor? Given the manifold historical precedents to the contrary, the poor will not be wise to place much reliance on such inhibitions beforehand, or to rely on remorse after the event as an aid to bringing their complaints home to the oppressors. Nor will it be easy for the poor to find other means of making their just complaints effective. The oppressors, once at least they have consolidated their new power, will be in a position to make sure that the victims get no help from the government. Must we really believe that something—that anything—which happens in an earlier generation can impose on a later one such dangers, and leave it morally helpless to cope with them?

There are a number of ways in which earlier generations have been thought to have powers with respect to private property binding to this degree. People in those generations may simply have had powers under timeless rights of acquisition and transfer to build up—justly—unequal accumulations that cannot now (short of being able to invoke something like the Lockean proviso) be justly interfered with. Or though those generations perhaps need not have set up the institution of private property or elaborated it in such a way as to allow unlimited accumulations, they may have consented to the institution having just such a feature; and once consented to, the feature turns out somehow to be irrevocable. The consent might have been given in an explicit social contract, which set up the institution or brought in this feature; or it might have been given tacitly, by going along, not stipulating any limits to accumulation, with the benefits of an institution itself evolved without express design or express undertakings. In Locke's case, the consent comes—tacitly, maybe unwittingly—when people in the first generation to use money consent to its use.[8]

If the notion of a tacit, even an unwitting consent creates any uneasiness, one might try to dispel the uneasiness by invoking the notion of a social contract in this connection, specifically, a contract that has ratified the institution with the allowance for unlimited accumulations, along with the accumulations built up to date. (Such a function for a historical social contract is present in Locke's doctrine,[9] though he arrives without relying on it at rights to unlimited accumulations; the contract only ratifies the rights.)[10] If timeless rights extending to unlimited accumulation had operated, previous doubts would have been groundless; but the contract might be thought of as a way of resolving once and for all any doubts then and now, and bringing in people who might have disputed the timeless rights as well as rejected any gesture at tacit consent. With the contract, if there had been a contract, the rules would have been settled under which property was acquired (or transferred) along with the distribution of holdings at the time of the contract, all regardless of their consequences in disadvantages for later generations.

None of these conceptions of how rights of private property with unlimited accumulation were first recognized (or first set up) and applied in earlier generations gives a persuasive argument for binding later generations. The notion of a contract, whether to originate such rights or to ratify them, is, however, in some ways the most persuasive of the lot, at any rate if we accept for the sake of argument the assumption that enables the idea of the contract to operate at its strongest. We get to this assumption if we suspend belief and suppose that we are dealing with a contract actually agreed to at some moment in history. This gives the contract notion more weight, certainly in this connection, than any attempt to bring later generations into the contract by assuming that it is somehow continually renewed, generation by generation. If later generations are given full freedom to contract or not, will they not insist on modifying any terms that have become too onerous to bear?[11]

One project that libertarians have taken up in their campaign on behalf of private property is to reduce to a minimum the grounds for reconsidering contracts,[12] so it is a matter of some current interest to see how far a social contract can bind later generations with respect to property. It is a familiar fact that people making contracts in one generation bind people in later generations—their "heirs and assigns" and other people as well. Moreover, in doing something as explicit as making a contract, the people concerned may be assumed to have had a chance to proceed with care and use their best judgment. Finally, they would have taken into account each other's demands and (one might suppose) have voluntarily struck a mutually agreeable bargain. Hence one might say that full weight had been given to their moral agency. By contrast to the idea of a historical social contract, a timeless right carries an extra burden of metaphysical mystery—how could it have preceded human invention and consent? A right, not timeless but socially invented as a device contingently useful for certain purposes, invites being revised immediately it becomes less useful.

I shall begin, therefore, with the social contract and the support that it gives, whether by creation or by ratification, for legitimizing rights with unlimited accumulation, and legitimizing also the distribution of holdings at the time of the contract, with consequences extending in perpetuity to subsequent rightful transfers of the holdings. The arguments that tell against the contract will, with only a little recasting, tell against tacit consent and timeless rights for unlimited accumulation (indeed, against having—beyond any possibility of revision—private property at all). On the side of the disadvantages of unequal accumulations I shall concentrate on the dangers of oppression, though there are other disadvantages; on the side of precautions and remedies, I shall concentrate upon redistribution as a precaution against oppression, though there are other precautions and remedies (all of them revisions of property rights, if these are sweeping to begin with).[13] Redistribution itself may take various forms. It need not involve transfers of the sort most disturbing to Epstein by the government from the ever-deserving rich to the undeserving poor, clients of welfare programs.[14] I shall abstract from the differences in forms.

No Blocking by a Historical Social Contract

Even if the contract had been arrived at unobjectionably and had been unobjectionable in content at the time when it was agreed to should it hold forever? A friend of mine, who has spent more time in the real world than most philosophers, reports that in the real world contracts are continually being renegotiated. They are not insulated from changes in the circumstances, the capacities, even the conveniences of the parties in the ways that philosophers, taking an elevated view of promises, incline to think.[15] Professors of law corroborate his report. Patrick Atiyah asserts that the practice of promising diverges widely from the sanctity assumed by philosophers. He says, "Empirical studies of business attitudes to contracts and contract-breaking, both in England and in the United States, suggest that business men in fact expect and tolerate a considerable amount of contract-breaking, at all events on matters which they do not regard as of fundamental importance."[16] He quotes "a leading American contracts scholar," Ian Macneil, as going even further: " 'Beneath the covers we are firmly committed to the desirability of promises being broken, not just occasionally but quite regularly.' "[17] On matters that are regarded as of fundamental importance, moreover, scholars like Charles Fried, who, standing by a traditionally exacting view of promises, oppose Atiyah and Macneil, nevertheless agree with them that a reasonable view of practice in contracts will make liberal allowances for dissolving contracts, under such heads as unconscionability and mistakes as well as fraud and duress. For example, Fried holds that the mistakes need not be mistakes made by all the contracting parties; they may be one-sided mistakes (more familiar to lawyers, for some reason, as "unilateral" ones).[18]

It is clear that in some contracts people in one generation can bind not only themselves but also people in succeeding generations. Contracts for selling outright bundles of material property or for leasing them are important instances. However, a contract to respect the rules and the distribution of property at one time, along with the consequences of that system for all time, is not easily assimilated to such contracts. To dispose of given items of property under certain rules is one thing; to agree to the rules in the first place is another. The first is what in Macneil's view is a discrete "transaction"; the second establishes what he calls a "rela-tion." He says, "Relations, unlike promise transactions, have internal capacities for growth and change, capacities absolutely essential for the successful completion of any enterprise not capable of specific and com-plete planning ab initio."[19]

Even contracts for sale or lease may fail to bind subsequent genera-tions—for a variety of reasons, of which I wish to seize just on the imperfect information that one or another party may have had at the time of contracting. When those Indians contracted to sell Manhattan Island for twenty-four dollars, they had no notion of how valuable it would become and no way of investing the proceeds safely and profitably for 350 years. That in itself does something to impair the contract, morally if not legally. (The law evidently speaks with two voices here.)[20] Their imperfect information on this point was connected, moreover, with imperfect information on another, if the contract reflected the sort of misunderstanding typical, I believe, of early contracts between the Indians and the Europeans. The Indians thought they were giving the Dutch something like the right to use the island as Indians would use it, as a place for transitory residence, gathering, and hunting. They did not understand themselves to be giving the Dutch the right to exclude the Indians from Manhattan forever afterward, while there rose upon it farms, dwelling places, wharves, sheds, and countinghouses.

The problem with imperfect information multiplies enormously if we shift from contracts for sale or lease to contracts to respect the rules and the distribution of property as they stand at a given time, with all the consequences therein implied as legitimate. Locke and other seventeenth-century contractarians could not predict how private property would work out, with new dimensions of oppression in industrial society, which makes them inexpert guides to present-day applications. Do we even now know enough about the institution of private property to know that all the present features of the institution will remain useful, or even tolerable, in future circumstances that we can predict no better than they? How much worse off with respect to information about the institution must people have been at earlier stages of social development![21]

Contracts are not in principle—as a class—irrevocable; the most solemn can be revoked when the parties are mistaken about the consequences. If anything is a "relation" in Macneil's sense, essentially requiring "in-ternal capacities for growth and change," it is the enterprise of civil society, the success of which depends so much on the exercise of those capacities that "successful completion" does not come into the picture. Success, it may reasonably be held, is survival in terms on reflection mutually satisfactory to all the parties. Would not the only legitimate form of social contract be one understood to have ample provisions for renegotiation, binding at most only so long as the institutions that it set up, or ratified, went on working as earlier contracting parties expected them to? On a reasonable view, it would be a form no more binding than this, even on the original contracting parties.

Insisting that any mistake must be a mistake made by all parties if the contract is to be revised will not help those who want from the social contract an impregnable defense of property rights with unlimited accumulation. The most plausible supposition is that neither the larger property holders nor the smaller ones would have foreseen the grandiose proportions of future inequalities or the dangers that they entailed; then the mistake would be one made by all. However, if it was a mistake made only by the smaller holders, whom the larger ones failed to inform fully, the narrow rule excluding merely one-sided mistakes gives way to the rule against fraud. (It was just such a fraud that at one point Rousseau ascribed to the first social contract.)[22] Either way, ratification of the distribution of property and of the rules of acquisition by the social contract could not bind future generations.

Historically, it is reasonable to assume, the farther we go back toward the origins of the institution of private property, the more imperfect we shall find information about the future operations of the institution. (To assume the contrary would be tantamount to assuming that at some time in the past the rate of social change had begun declining significantly and for good.) This point is crucial for any claim that a generation originating the institution in a social contract can bind future generations who discover the institution to be operating in unexpectedly disastrous ways. Nor does the problem of imperfect information go away with the succession of generations. A contract made as recently as a generation ago—a contract made in this generation—will be made with imperfect information. Modern contract theorists sometimes choose to deal with difficulties about information by assuming both perfect information about possible social institutions and the perpetuity of certain values very general yet capable of determining what the best institutions will be for all time.[23] (The perfection of information may be qualified by waiving foreknowledge by the contracting agents of their personal advantages under the institutions; and the very general values give only a "thin theory" of the good.)[24] It is not often noticed that the combination of assumptions, besides being heroic, has preposterous consequences for the application of the theories. Since we do not have perfect information, we cannot identify the terms of a social contract specifically enough to commit ourselves or our successors to any fully determinate institutions in perpetuity. We cannot commit ourselves and our successors for or against inheritance, for example; or for or against a nearer approach to equality than the Difference Principle might bring about. We certainly cannot commit ourselves to the Difference Principle—in perpetuity! In a society of universal affluence, where would be the motivation to observe it with strict lexical priority![25]

I have been arguing that if the parties to the contract had imperfect information, the contract would be liable to reflect mistakes that would need to be corrected in succeeding generations. But suppose their information, though imperfect, included grounds for fearing that unlimited accumulation of private property would lead to oppression. Is there any way of conceiving how they might have deliberately agreed notwithstanding to accept unlimited accumulation as a feature of the right of private property? Would the contract be any firmer if they entered into it with eyes fully open to this point? I do not think so.

The nearest thing that they could have had for a rationale is perhaps to have argued that respect for the right of private property ranks first among the very purposes to be served by having a civil society in the first place and a specific form of government in the second. Locke ranks it first, making the ranking more convincing by including life and liberty in property (in his official large sense);[26] their claim to ultimacy is thus in a position to color the claim of property in the narrow (material) sense. How could we get behind property, especially in this large sense, to reach more fundamental purposes, which we would need to cite to criticize the workings of the institution? Locke's modern disciples take a similar view: private property is in the first place private property in one's body, and life and liberty surely are at stake with what one does with one's body or suffers being done to it.[27]

None of this, however, goes any distance toward showing, even if private property is so fundamental, that unlimited accumulation must be accepted along with private property. It is difficult to maintain that there cannot be a society at all without private property, since there are examples of self-sufficient societies that have essentially done without it (monasteries; the Oneida Community; the Hutterites). It is palpably more difficult to maintain that there cannot be a society without unlimited accumulation. Even among modern industrial societies limits of varying stringency exist, and the more egalitarian societies persist from decade to decade in health at least as good as that of the others.[28]

Moreover, reflection on the complications that come to view when life and liberty are joined with material property works out against holding the distribution of material property and the rules of acquisition to have been created and ratified in perpetuity by the social contract. The complication cannot hide the danger of unequal accumulation; all that it does is bring the danger inside the category of private property. One of the unsettling discoveries to be made about the institution of property is that gross inequalities in material possessions lead time and again to infringements on the life and liberty of people at the short end of the inequalities. They therefore can claim that the contract has been violated to their disadvantage when the government does not prevent these infringements as much as possible and rectify them when they occur. Thus a conflict emerges internal to the institution of property in the large sense; and how is this to be resolved? More important, how are guarantees that it will be resolved with justice to those whose lives and liberties are at stake to be put in place without modifying, contract or no contract, the distribution of material property and the rules affecting this distribution?

If present-day Lockeans were to ignore effects on life and liberty apart from effects on material property, they would still have the uncomfortable difficulty to deal with that the rich, with their large accumulations of material property, are in a position to invade the property rights and holdings of the poor. In this way, too, unequal accumulation creates a danger internal to the right of private property itself. Are we to suppose that there is no morally acceptable means of taking effective precautions against the danger? And will not effective precautions almost surely require modifications of the allowance for unequal accumulation? Every other form of precaution is liable to be undermined by machinations that the rich alone can finance.

The trouble with a rationale—certainly the trouble with this rationale—is that if it falls before objections, it may seem to take down with it the principle that it was to defend. Could the original contractors have done more to convince and bind us if they had kept silent about any rationale and simply declared their willingness to put up with unlimited accumulation in spite of the dangers? But if they expected serious dangers of oppression to arise within their own lifetimes, questions would arise about their sanity, and hence about their competence, if they ignored the dangers—unless they had no choice and were coerced into omitting to take precautions against the dangers. In either case, the contract would be invalid even in the first generation. On the other hand, If they thought that the dangers would in all probability arise only for a later generation, would not a contract that benefited them regardless of the dangers in which they placed their successors be unconscionable? The dangers of oppression take many forms, and there are dangers in unlimited accumulation besides oppression. Yet how can it fail to be enough to make the contract unconscionable in the eyes of champions of rights to private property if keeping to the contract in the later generation disregards serious and growing dangers of large property holders setting at nought the property rights of smallholders? It is not, I am assuming, a contract that any pretense can make the later generations parties to; if they were, they could, aware of the dangers, refuse to agree to terms that led in that direction; or, misled, agreeing unaware, repudiate their mistakes and denounce the contract as invalid.

No Blocking by Timeless Rights

Here, if the defense of private property with unlimited accumulation is to continue, it must move beyond any notion that a right of this kind originates in a contract or gets some support by being ratified by one. The contractors, if there were contractors, may have had no choice in another sense; they were, it might be claimed, faced with a right that did not in any way depend on them yet demanded strict obedience nevertheless. Some champions of the right to private property might wish to claim that the right (extending to very unequal accumulations) is intuitively sacrosanct and has been known, and known to be such, from time immemorial. As a sacrosanct timeless right, it is in an impregnable position and has no need of support from anything like the consent of those affected, much less from anything like an explicit contract. Indeed, if contracts are subject, as has just been argued, to revision, that shows (it might be said) that it would be a mistake to give any coloring to the notion that rights depend on a contract.

Implausible as this position may be, it is one way of interpreting the intransigent confidence of Nozick and his school in the right to private property and their failure to relate the implications of the right to changing historical circumstances.[29] It entrenches the right to private property deeper than the most solemn contract—and deeper than the rights (effects of the practice or institution of promising) created by any contract.[30]

But it is a position at odds with the history of the concept of rights, both in origin and in conception. Rights as we know them came into being in the Middle Ages; natural rights, under natural law, were first asserted later still, by several centuries.[31] Aquinas's exposition of natural law has nothing to say about natural rights. Again, natural rights, and most preeminently the natural right to private property, have changed so radically in conception as to be ascribed to women as well as men, on points that formerly were held to be prerogatives of men, and to exclude slavery. Both changes, in the perspective of human history, are very recent: women were in a subordinate position respecting property for millennia; for an equally long time human beings held others of their kind as property.

Nozick says little or nothing to forestall inferring that his timeless right of private property is so naively conceived as to be vulnerable to these objections.[32] Giving him and his school the benefit of the doubt, we might take them more plausibly as holding that though the rights hold timelessly as features of the basic furniture of the cosmos, we do from time to time make discoveries about them in history. For example, we discover after several millennia that women have just the same rights to property as men and after time immemorial, that neither men nor women have the right to hold other men and women as slaves. This might be treated as no more than an empty extravagance of metaphysical idealism, which did not stand in the way of allowing for the same historical phenomena that other thinkers would consider revisions, to adapt to changing circumstances, of rights that were from the beginning social devices constructed by fallible human beings.[33] If it allows us to make discoveries like those that the nineteenth century made about property for women and property in slaves, it allows for changes in our beliefs about rights more radical than any modifications that I am contemplating in the right to material property; for I do not suppose that these modifications would, like those, be called for in all circumstances.

It is all the same more than a little odd to claim that the right to property is intuitively sacrosanct in the conceptual vicinity of natural law, where, as in Locke's case, the notion of natural rights starts up, given that natural law was the object of intensive attention for centuries before rights got attached to it. Locke himself makes little of them in his essays on natural law.[34] Never mind. The champions of intuition could say that rights were sacrosanct all along; it just took all those centuries to get beyond earlier formulations of natural law to discover their existence, and centuries more to get a correct view of certain particular features of them. The champions of intuition might be so reasonable as to concede that even now not everything might be known about these or other features.

With only some reservations about not identifying rights with economic individualism,[35] I am quite ready not only to accept the concept of rights as an instrument of natural law, but also to accept it as having been a suitable instrument (had it been known) from time immemorial. Natural law itself may be conceded to have been not merely a matter for possible discovery but a matter of actual practice for as long. Consider those principles some combination of which are necessary and sufficient conditions for human beings to flourish together; very likely a core of these principles will appear in every such combination, but here I need not assume this. Some such combination of principles must have been heeded whenever a human society did manage to flourish, were it only for a time. But there would have been more—even now there is more—to discover about these principles of natural law, and more to discover about the rights.[36]

I say discover; "discover" does not by itself discriminate between the two positions, idealist and nonidealist, respectively, distinguished above. What according to one position is discovered about a right that has been in reality the same all along is according to the other position discovered about the relation of a changeable right to different circumstances. In either case, however, the basic consideration is the one that underlay the previous discussion of the contract. Imperfect information in an earlier generation will lead to a new view of the right in a later generation, when circumstances require a new view.

If we were to stand by intuitions in these matters, it would seem to respect history, social development, and human powers of invention best to join the theory of natural law in seizing as the object of intuition in the foundation of ethics the necessity of providing somehow for needs and whatever else fosters human flourishing.[37] But this implies very little about a right to material property. Does private property come into the first principles of natural law by way of provisions that must be made to meet human needs? That there must be such provisions in all times and places is indeed a matter of first principles (at least until the Second Coming becomes imminent); moreover, the requirements in question can be specified: food of a certain nutritive value, adequate clothing and shelter, safeguards against terror and harassment. However, the implications respecting the institution of private property do not go very far. To make use of food, one must ingest it, and at that point it must be appropriated to the exclusion of other people's being able to use it. Yet all other provisions (as Locke quite failed to notice) can be shared.[38] Other ranks in the army do not own their clothing and may be asked to turn it in upon demobilization (whereupon a thoughtful government may make them a gift of blue serge suits). Members of the Oneida Community, like affectionate brothers and sisters, shared their clothes; they did not own them.

The mutability of any right of private property associated with natural law follows from there being alternative social arrangements (however limited practically in duration or in the number of people that they can embrace). Natural law, as Aquinas expounds it, applies in detail in different ways in different circumstances. Some exponents of natural law (including Locke, perhaps even Aquinas) may have thought that an extensive right to acquire and hold (material) property was something that could be deduced to hold in all social circumstances (waiving perhaps the Garden of Eden or a community of saints), or at least predicted to be the best option among suitable constructions.[39] This, however, is a simple failure of imagination, if it is not simple ignorance.[40]

We may discover the content of natural law by observing what arrangements promote human flourishing in flourishing communities. In some circumstances, perhaps in a great variety of circumstances, an extensive right to material property does promote this. But the conclusion that it does is an empirical judgment, relative to the circumstances observed. In other circumstances, human beings and communities have flourished and realized their common good to a very impressive degree without such a right: the Oneida Community and the Hutterite communities on the prairies in Canada and the United States are cases in point. Moreover, where an extensive right to material property is present, the communities in question will be found to limit it in a variety of ways, without apparently impairing their chances of flourishing. At any rate, it begs the question (a priori) to deny that this is so. It would take a good deal of intricate argument to show that the Hutterites or the members of the Oneida Community or the monastic orders in the Middle Ages have been less successful in the pursuit of the common good than (say) competitive capitalistic societies, in spite of the prodigious diversification of commodities in the last.

One provision that Aquinas makes for alternative social arrangements equally satisfactory to natural law, given a difference in circumstances or even without a difference, is his distinction between two ways in which an arrangement may fall under natural law. It may be a deduction from the principles of natural law and in that case holds for every human group in all circumstances (like some principle limiting assault and murder within the group); or it may be a construction (like the choice of a particular form of punishment as a means of enforcing the prohibition of assault or murder).[41]

In the perspective of natural law, rights of any kind are best viewed, I think, as constructions rather than deductions; and that is how, I contend, we should look upon any right, even a natural right, to private property. That it is a construction rather than a universally applicable deduction follows from the existence of alternatives, such as I have described, which in some circumstances would serve to promote human flourishing as well or better. If in most circumstances—and even everywhere after a time—a right to private property will turn out to be a feature of the arrangements most conducive to flourishing, it is a matter for contingent observation to settle whether this is so in any given circumstance. Moreover, that rights, including the right to private property, are constructions is in keeping with the history of natural law, in particular the centuries given to its formulation and study before the modern notion of rights became attached to it. It is in keeping with the history of practice as well as the history of theory: evidently, either deductions alone had sufficed hitherto for whatever success in flourishing (sometimes very considerable) that societies had attained or those societies had arrived at alternative constructions reasonably adequate for purposes much like those served by rights.

Respect for Rights in the Later Generation

Grant this to the libertarians. Even if rights are not so sacrosanct as to be precluded from any change, a problem remains about justice in the treatment of people who have relied upon them before any change is put through. Are they not justly entitled to the property that they have justly acquired by the exercise of the unchanged rights and under the motivating expectations thereto appertaining? Of course they are, but that cannot be sensibly taken to mean that their entitlements must be respected in perpetuity and without qualification. It means that, like a solemn contract about matters important to the parties, the entitlements call for grave respect and honor in all circumstances short of disaster.

I could pursue the analogy with contracts further; something like a contract occurs when someone acquires something and is recognized by the rest of the community to have done so rightfully. But then, as with a contract, the entitlements may be withdrawn, if people have been mistaken in recognizing them, and overridden in the face of disaster—not to speak of duress and unconscionability, though these things of course have been all too common in the history of acquisition. I shall not, however, pursue this analogy here, since it might produce some confusion between arguments on the present point (which do not touch upon the social contract) and arguments like those above in which the social contract is in view.

Instead, let us consider how given a respectable occasion for doing so the entitlements might be overridden as painlessly as possible. To take a disadvantage of private property other than the dangers of oppression with unequal accumulation, consider Locke's strictures on the failure of English grandees to make the best use of their land.[42] This failure might lead in the course of generations to a steadily increasing shortfall in the food available to the community, and hence to famines (which were common in Western Europe through the first half of the eighteenth century and even later something not too remote to be a matter of fear).[43] Suppose that it is proposed to remedy a present instance of this difficulty by turning unproductively used land over to people who have convincing plans for using it better.

A minimally painless procedure, consistent with encouraging thrifty husbandry in the first generation, might be to let anyone who had acquired land legitimately, by appropriation or transactions, to retain it for a lifetime; to respect the proprietor's gifts and legacies until the succession of a generation not present during the proprietor's lifetime; then to give notice during the lifetime of that generation of expropriation to take place at the end of the lifetime. There would then be vanishingly little difference, one might expect, between the original proprietor's actual expectations and the expectations that she or he would have had given this modification of the right to material property. Should not a community—should not a later generation in the same community—have at least this much room to modify the right? Or should it go down in famine, wrapping received expectations in the colors of a sacrosanct right?

It will perhaps be said that the right will not lead to this disaster; all that the right requires is that present owners be compensated if expropriation is undertaken. I doubt whether all champions of rights are so reasonable, and in any case the combination of expropriation and compensation will not win the hearts of all proprietors; they may prefer to keep their family seats regardless. What would normally be their right is still overridden and their expectations have been defeated. Moreover, it is easy to confuse compensation as a wise strategy for a government wishing to put through a reform of the institution of property with compensation as a matter of right.[44]

To be sure, if the modification that we have in view is to be really as painless as possible, some compensation should be paid. We must recognize, however, that the community may be in such straits as to find it difficult or impossible to pay the compensation now or in the foreseeable future. Even if it were not, should it hand over with the compensation a claim in perpetuity to a substantial share of national income? The claim, like the original entitlement, might diminish in force over time.

The community will not always have the time to move painlessly if a disaster is to be avoided. Suppose one of those grandees (let us take a Scottish grandee this time) takes it into her head to convert all her enormous holdings to deer parks and sheepwalks, turning out thousands of crofters to shift for themselves. At best, they may find passage to America in an emigrant ship that will lose half its passengers to disease before the voyage is over. Is the community to stand by, mindful of the duchess's right, and let this disaster happen? The very fact that the right to material property can be carried to such lengths—not oppression, perhaps, because not continual, but the abuse of an oppressor's power—as to give proprietors the opportunity of creating social disasters on this scale should show those willing to consider it modifiable at all (or open to new discoveries) that it is subject to modification (or new discoveries) even when this means overturning expectations that the proprietors have relied upon, and overturning them in some cases with little notice and no commensurate compensation.

Notes

1. *Times* (London), Dec. 28, 1988, 9. Arguably, the rubber tappers are being driven off what has hitherto been a common, so the case may be regarded as one of doubtful initial appropriation by the rich to the exclusion of the poor. When a rubber tapper is assassinated, however, his rights to life and liberty—aspects of the Lockean right to private property, broadly conceived—are violated. Violations by the cattle ranchers of the rights of smallholder farmers to their land have been reported in later stories.

2. Mack, "In Defense of 'Unbridled' Freedom of Contract," 433–435. Mack says, "If a bargain is struck, then those purportedly most vital needs will be satisfied." (Why "purportedly"? Is the naked bargain too uncomfortable to comtemplate?) He continues, "So the powerfully positioned bargainer is just the one who, if an exchange is allowed, renders what appears to be the more vital service."

3. Nozick's official formula for the proviso is "A process normally giving rise to a permanent bequeathable property right in a previously unowned thing will not do so if the position of others no longer at liberty to use the thing is thereby worsened" (*Anarchy, State, and Utopia*, 178). This might lend itself to broader operation, especially considering that whole trains of transfers beginning with original appropriations and coming down to the present have to meet the test (180). Nozick's gloss (178–182) on the proviso is very restrictive, however, based as it is on a "baseline for comparison" as to worsening that is "so low as compared to the productiveness of a society with private appropriation that the question of [it] being violated arises only in the case of catastrophe (or a desert-island situation)" (181). Nozick says, "This proviso (almost?) never will come into effect" (179); further, "I believe that the free operation of a market system will not actually run afoul of the Lockean proviso" (182)

4. For Poland, see Braudel, *Wheels of Commerce*, 265–272; for the reference to serfdom in Russia, I depend on C. Vann Woodward's review of Peter Kolchin's *Unfree Labor: American Slavery and Russian Serfdom*.

5. See Epstein in this volume. Cf. chap. 19 of his *Takings*, which considers and attempts to refute a variety of arguments for the redistribution of wealth and income and entirely overlooks the possibility that redistribution might be a precaution against the rich using property rights to oppress the poor. Epstein, allying himself with the eminent domain clause of the U.S. Constitution, says, "With the possible exception of charitable deductions, the eminent domain clause in principle forecloses virtually all public transfer and welfare programs, however devised and executed" (324).

6. Lomasky, *Persons, Rights, and the Moral Community*, 141–146. I rate him "most reasonable" because he sees the need to find a rationale for basic rights and offers quite a persuasive one in game-theoretical terms based generally on people's having projects to pursue (60–79). Moreover, he allows that even so the rights are given determinate forms in a social structure subject to the decisions of the people affected (101–105, 107). Nothing in his rationale, so far as I can see, gives the least ground for accepting unlimited accumulation, a topic he never takes up.

7. Nozick, *Anarchy, State, and Utopia*, 231. Cf. the informational demands of "the principle of rectification" that would redress departures from valid pedigrees (152–153).

8. *Second Treatise*, par. 46.

9. *Second Treatise*, pars. 45 (not by itself entirely conclusive on ratifying unlimited accumulations, but in context inviting such a reading), 95, 124, 131.

10. See again the paragraphs just cited. It is a puzzle worth pondering that Locke should have maintained so strongly that a later generation could revise the form of government, discarding absolute monarchy when the disadvantages of this form were discovered. And yet—humane as his conception of the due exercise of property rights may have been, if one accepts the views of recent scholarship, for example, John Dunn's in *Locke*—he made no provision at all for revising the

David Braybrooke

right of property, unlimited accumulation and all, tacitly and even unwittingly set up with consent to the use of money.

11. Nevertheless, I believe that a plausible notion of a continually renewed social contract, not too nakedly dependent on a question-begging invocation of "tacit consent," can be constructed out of Locke's *Second Treatise* by playing the notions of oath taking (which alone makes one a full member of the commonwealth, a civil society with a specific form of government), emigration, and the dissolution of the commonwealth against one another. But in Locke the continually renewed social contract suffers from the fatal omission (just noted) to allow for reconsideration of property rights.

12. Cf. Mack, "In Defense of 'Unbridled' Freedom of Contract," 127, and Epstein's article "Unconscionability," to which Mack refers.

13. Other disadvantages include wasteful use of resources by frivolous grandeur and mistreatment, not continual enough to be oppression, of tenants or employees. Other precautions and remedies include injunctions or restraining orders against uses of property contrary to the general welfare and the formation of labor unions.

14. Cf. Epstein, *Takings*. Rather than have the government make the transfers, redistribution might proceed along the plan suggested by Rowley and Peacock, *Welfare Economics,* chap. 7: the government might require people to break up their own estates, by spreading their legacies more widely and uniformly among their heirs and by leaving bequests to charities once the aggregate going to all the heirs together reached a certain limit.

15. J. T. Stevenson is the friend who imparted this information to me.

16. Atiyah, *Promises, Morals, and Law,* 140.

17. Ibid.

18. Fried, *Contract as Promise.*

19. Macneil, "Many Futures of Contract," 765–766.

20. Cf. Fried, *Contract as Promise,* for an example where the contract is not set aside in spite of an unexpectedly grievous burden on one party (64) and for an example in which the failure of the seller to foresee how valuable the property would become was held to invalidate the terms of the original contract (59).

21. I am treating the mistakes that I am considering as mistakes of not foreseeing kinds of developments that would compel reconsidering the contracts. Leon Trakman has pointed out to me that people may be given relief from contracts when developments occur of kinds recognized as making fulfillment impossible, e.g., one's stock of goods is seized by an invading force. At the time of contracting, it was reasonable to deem such a development so improbable that it could be disregarded.

22. *Second Discourse, On the Origin of Inequality,* pt. II, pars. 31–35. Rousseau goes on to insist that such a contract must be revocable (par. 46).

23. Rawls, in *Theory of Justice,* is, of course, the leading instance.

24. Ibid., 395–399.

25. Or to observe the Difference Principle itself cast in lexical form, which still precludes even the least sacrifice by someone less affluent to bring about however great a gain to the person who stands just above. Rawls, *Theory of Justice,* 83.

26. *Second Treatise*, par. 123.
27. Cf. Mack, "In Defense of 'Unbridled' Freedom of Contract," 428–429. The boldest and most thoroughgoing account of rights based on one's right to one's own body—some would say the most bizarre account (Lomasky, *Persons, Rights, and the Moral Community*, 263, calls it "splendidly entertaining")—can be found in Wheeler, "Natural Property Rights as Body Rights." This article, too, has had the honor of being reprinted in Machan, ed., *Main Debate*, 272–289.
28. See the diagram plotting the Gini Index of Inequality for various developed countries against their rate of growth in Gross Domestic Product in Osberg, *Economic Equality in Canada*, 180. Osberg points out, commenting on the diagram, "The country with greatest equality (Holland) has the third highest growth rate," though it is "not that much higher than the most unequal nation (France)" (179).
29. Libertarians vary in their awareness of changing historical circumstances: Nozick and Wheeler are much less alert to them than Lomasky is.
30. A paper by Susan Tatton has impressed upon me the importance of looking to contracts for the creation of rights.
31. Cf. Tuck, *Natural Rights Theories*, 7–31.
32. The rights present in the state of nature are spelled out for material property in the entitlement theory (Nozick, *Anarchy, State, and Utopia*, 10–12, 150–153). Agents in the state of nature at least understand as with Locke the basic natural law principles of their rights (11); in any case the rights hold timelessly (151) and have to be discovered themselves rather than constructed.
33. Lomasky's idea that rights become fully determinate only in ways that reflect variations in cultures might function as a compromise between these two positions; but I expect that under pressure it would turn into a softened expression of one or the other. Lomasky, *Persons, Rights, and the Moral Community*, 101–105, 107.
34. The assertion cited above of a conceptual connection between justice and the right to property may not make so much of rights as it seemed to. Perhaps it is an assertion that comes up only after the device of rights has been invented. Locke's *Essays on the Laws of Nature* run almost to the end without mentioning rights at all; they come up only in the last essay (VIII).
35. See Teichgraeber, *"Free Trade" and Moral Philosophy*, 23–25, 58–59, on the turn toward economic individualism that natural law took with rights as Grotius conceived of them.
36. For there always being more to discover about natural laws, see Aquinas, *Summa Theologiae*, 1a2ae, Q. 94, arts. 4 and 5, Q. 96, art. 6, Q. 97, art. 2; 2a2ae, Q. 120, art. 2.
37. James Griffin, though he is not so much a partisan of the concept of needs as I am, lends support to this point by maintaining in his book *Well-being* (307–308) that the right to material property is not basic enough to figure anywhere near the foundations of ethics.
38. As Lomasky claims, they all must be in hand for a time if a person is to use them; but they do not, contrary to Lomasky's headlong inference, have to be private property. *Persons, Rights, and the Moral Community*, 120–121.

39. Aquinas says (*Summa Theologiae*, 1a2ae, Q. 94, art. 61) that private property—like slavery—exists, not by inference from natural law, but as a contrivance of reason for the convenience (*utilitatem*) of human life. He would not have denied that there can be communities flourishing without slavery—for example, monasteries.

40. It is quite different from holding (as Locke did) that it is demonstratively true that without property there is no justice (*Essays on the Laws of Nature*, 212–213). Even this proposition does not imply that material property accompanies justice, and if it necessarily did, it might consort with infinitely many particular restrictions on the right. Yet the proposition might get in the way of understanding that the common good can in some circumstances be achieved without an extensive right to material property, especially if this right is confused with a right to property in the extended sense that includes life and liberty.

41. I shall neglect here the possibility that deductions, too, may vary with circumstances. Accepting it would come to much the same thing as regards being able to revise rights. I shall also neglect the possibility of all but eliminating the distinction between deductions and constructions by introducing a prescription of optimization. Accepting that would not make rights less revisable; on the contrary, rights and other institutions would in principle be liable to change whenever circumstances implied that human flourishing could be optimized otherwise. But optimization is not a notion that belongs in natural law; and natural law is the better for it, considering that to be practical morality must content itself with something like Herbert Simon's "satisficing." See Simon, *Models of Man, Social and Rational*, 61, 70–71.

42. See Richard Ashcraft's reading of *Second Treatise*, chap. 5, together with Locke's remarks on productive and unproductive people in his discussions of the rate of interest (Ashcraft, *Revolutionary Politics and Locke's Two Treatises of Government*, 244, 267–270). Ashcraft ends up by saying, "Locke's chapter on property is one of the most radical critiques of the land-owning aristocracy produced during the last half of the seventeenth century," at least as applied to "the useless members of that class" (273).

43. Jean Fourastié has pointed out (*Causes of Wealth*, 272–289) that a demand for "Bread!" was one of the slogans of French revolutionaries as late as 1833 (or 1848?). It would be quite incongruous in Western Europe nowadays—though not in some other parts of the world.

44. In addition, the view of compensation as a matter of right is liable to be confused by the unfortunate habit (which Locke shares with many of his successors) of taking something like the land that a pioneer clears for subsistence farming as prototypical of material property. The urgency of compensation, as a matter of right, palpably diminishes when those to be compensated own a hundred or a thousand times as much land as their families need to subsist.

VI

Future People, Disability, and Screening

JONATHAN GLOVER

Our interests may conflict with those of future generations. For instance, if we use fuel resources in ways that most benefit ourselves, future people may go short. This raises the question of justice between generations. How should our actions be constrained by fairness to people not yet born? There are two crude but popular views about social decision making. According to one, all that matters is that issues be decided democratically. The other is that economic decisions should be left to the market. Both majorities and market forces can generate notoriously unjust outcomes. Future generations provide a dramatic illustration of this, since those yet unborn have no vote and no purchasing power.

But the principles of justice that should guide our relations to future generations are not obvious. We have limited knowledge of what their circumstances and needs will be. We do not know how many of the generations stretching into the future should be considered, and to what extent, if at all, those farther off should be given less weight. Other problems are created by the effects of our actions on both the size and the composition of future generations. Different economic and social policies will affect such variables as where people live, which will affect which people meet one another, and so in turn will determine which people are born. Justice is made more complicated when different people, and different numbers of people, will exist to feel the impact of the policies under consideration.

Both political and everyday decisions unintentionally affect who is born. For instance, the man my grandmother first loved was killed in the First World War. If he had lived, my maternal grandparents would almost certainly not have married, and so my mother would not have been born, nor would I, nor my children, nor their descendants. Our existence is one minute consequence of the First World War. More trivial factors affected our existence, too: for instance, my grandfather's decision to learn marine engineering in Newcastle rather than in Belfast. Had he made the other choice, he would not have met and married my grandmother and our fate would have been nonexistence.

We also affect who is born by deliberate choice. For those not wanting to have children, contraception has enlarged the options beyond the rather bleak alternatives of chastity and abortion. With the development of more advanced reproductive technologies, the present generation has new powers of prediction and intervention. One issue raised by those powers is the topic of this chapter: should we aim for the birth of "normal" babies rather than those with disabilities?

Many people will think that this question need not detain us for more than a moment: the answer is yes. Surely everyone agrees that it is better if a baby is born without a disability? Although I have a lot of sympathy with this brisk response, the question is not so easily disposed of. It raises some of the most abstract issues in ethics. To a surprising extent, those abstract issues make a difference to social policy.

Our own decisions affect the likelihood of a disabled child being born. A simple case is the decision to smoke in pregnancy. Another is the decision to abort a fetus after exposure to rubella in pregnancy or when prenatal tests have detected some disorder. Others arise as a result of in vitro fertilization (IVF): the egg, having been fertilized in the laboratory, has to be transferred to the womb. If several eggs have been fertilized, tests may show that some are normal and some have a disorder. Deciding which egg to transfer will determine the kind of person to be born. Also relevant are decisions about the genetic screening of potential donors of semen or eggs.

"Gene therapy" can also lead to such decisions. When disorders are caused by the absence of a gene or the presence of a "wrong" gene, it is attractive to think of inserting or deleting genes in embryos as required. In our present state of medical development, this procedure carries a serious risk of unwanted side effects. It is much safer to conduct genetic testing before implanting a fertilized egg than to try to delete or insert genes. But the day may come when this sort of gene therapy can be performed without harmful side effects. Choosing between a normal baby and one with a disability will become a genuine possibility.

One kind of intervention against disability is uncontroversially right. This is any treatment that does not prevent the existence of the person with the disability but aims to alleviate or cure the disability. (The mirror image is that it is uncontroversially wrong to give a disability to someone who otherwise would be normal, for instance, by smoking during pregnancy.) What is controversial is to eliminate or prevent the disability by eliminating or preventing the existence of the person who has the disability. This controversial policy is the basis of screening programs.

Two Cases of Disability
A Girl

In 1987, there was a debate in Britain about lowering the time limit for abortion. The proposed lower limit would have excluded some cases where prenatal tests reveal severe disability. As part of the debate, two parents wrote to the *Guardian:*

In December 1986 our newly-born daughter was diagnosed to be suffering from a genetically caused disease called Dystrophic epidermolysis Bullosa (EB). This is a disease in which the skin of the sufferer is lacking in certain essential fibres. As a result, any contact with her skin caused large blisters to form, which subsequently burst leaving raw open skin that only healed slowly and left terrible scarring. As EB is a genetically caused disease it is incurable and the form that our daughter suffered from usually causes death within the first six months of life. In our daughter's case the condition extended to her digestive and respiratory tracts and as a result of such internal blistering and scarring she died after a painful and short life at the age of only 12 weeks.

Following our daughter's death we were told that if we wanted any more children there was a one-in-four probability that any child we conceived would be affected by the disease but that it was possible to detect the disease ante-natally. In May 1987 we decided to restart our family only because we knew that such a test was available and that should we conceive an affected child the pregnancy could be terminated, such a decision is not taken lightly or easily. . . .

If the time limit for abortions was to be reduced below about 22– 24 weeks such testing would be of no value as the results would not be available in time for the pregnancy to be terminated.

We have had to watch our first child die slowly and painfully and we could not contemplate having another child if there was a risk that it too would have to die in the same way.

Anyone will feel sympathy with the determination of these parents that any future child of theirs should be spared the life their daughter had. Given that determination, their only hope of having their own biological children depends on abortion being available after the test results. This is part of the case for such abortion being legal. But to those who believe that abortion is murder, or something close to it, the case may seem insufficient. To avoid going into this familiar debate, it is worth thinking about the position if the birth of a child with such a disability could be avoided by means other than abortion.

Suppose there is a large-scale IVF program, using donated semen or eggs, to help infertile couples have children. Should donors be screened to exclude carriers of EB? Some of us believe that it is better not to bring into the world babies who will have only a few painful months of life. Those of us who think this have a reason to screen the donors. We have a reason, in the case of EB and similar disorders, for choosing to bring into the world a normal child rather than one with a severe disability.

A Woman

The same issue of the *Guardian* included another contribution to the debate:

Thank God this "abnormal" fetus was conceived in 1947. I was born with spina bifida. My parents were told I would die within three days (wrong!) wouldn't walk (wrong!) and would be ineducable (wrong!). Yes, they were devastated but they picked themselves up and got on with the job of being responsible parents who wanted their children to achieve their potential. I attended normal schools from the age of seven, have a degree and two post graduate professional qualifications. I worked for many years as a Probation Officer and now as an Independent Guardian ad Litom (court social worker). I have a husband and two small children.

Yes, life can be difficult sometimes (isn't it for everyone?). Yes it cost money to get me where I am now (but a nuclear weapon would cost a damned sight more and probably cause more damage.) . . .

Years ago we kept "the handicapped" in institutions, out of sight, out of mind. Now, we can destroy them before we need to look at them or think of them. But we the handicapped are still here, still playing a part in society. Funnily enough, not only do many of us contribute to society, we even enjoy being alive.

Many of us who face daily the problems of being disabled, are amongst those pressing for stricter abortion laws because we know life is good and believe in protecting the weak from the strong.

Let us together build a caring society which has room for all its members no matter what race or disability.

Spina bifida can be screened for prenatally and is widely accepted as one of the conditions that justify abortion. But this letter raises an extremely difficult question for those who support such a policy. As the writer says, she is playing her part in society and enjoying being alive. Is anyone in a position to make the Godlike judgment: "It would have been better if you had been aborted"?

Again, to avoid the complications of the abortion debate, suppose that donors of eggs and sperm can be screened in an effort to prevent conception of children with spina bifida. (For most forms of spina bifida this would not be possible, but one rare form is genetic and such screening might one day be effective.) The objection to abortion as murder falls away. But the other difficult question remains. The writer says, "Thank God this 'abnormal fetus' was conceived." Is anyone in a position to make the Godlike judgment: "It would have been better if you had not been conceived"? If we doubt our ability to make such a judgment, we have a reason for opposing policies that deliberately avoid the conception of children with severe disabilities such as spina bifida.

Degrees of Disability and the Compromise Policy

The case of the girl gives a reason in favor of intervening against disability, whereas the case of the woman gives a reason against intervening. What should we do when such strong reasons point in opposite directions?

One response is to take the view that each reason applies in its own case. The two cases are very different. The woman is glad to be alive. The girl never reached the stage where she could have understood such questions, but those closest to her thought she had little reason to be glad to be alive. One could support intervention against conditions as severe as EB, but oppose intervention against those less severe, such as the degree of spina bifida experienced by the woman.

It is worth distinguishing disastrous disability (where life is so bad that death would be a release and it would be cruel to bring someone into the world to face such a life) from moderately severe disability. The boundary between the two degrees of disability obviously is blurred, and reasonable people will often disagree about a particular case. And character and circumstances can make a difference. Some people with terrible disabilities reveal extraordinary qualities, which enrich their own lives and those of people around them. Sometimes a terrible medical condition can be transformed by a loving and supporting family. But a blurred boundary does not mean there is no difference between the cases that fall on either side. It is reasonable, therefore, to see one of the cases considered here as disastrous and the other as moderately severe. (There is also a boundary problem between moderately severe disability and less severe conditions. I am relying on an intuitive understanding that color blindness, for instance, is not even moderately severe.)

The compromise policy would recommend screening against disastrous disability, but not against moderately severe disability. It is attractive because it acknowledges each line of thought that arises out of the two cases we have looked at. But both parts of the compromise policy must be examined. Before that, however, the policy of screening against disastrous disability needs to be considered in the context of some general objections to screening.

Objections to Screening

Disabled people who oppose selective abortion or screening programs make a point that is hard to answer: supporting a screening program is in effect saying that it would have been better if every disabled person had never been born. This forceful point is critical of the arrogant assumption that anyone is qualified to play God and decide who is or is not fit to be born. Implicit in such a criticism is the negative effect that such a view has on the rights of disabled people.

Playing God

Is it objectionably Godlike to decide that it is better for one person to live than another? We want to say that all people are of equal value and that no one is in the position of being able to estimate the worth of another person's life. Who are we to make these huge decisions about who shall live?

This line of thought evokes a strong response, but it is not decisive as an objection to all screening policies. The suggestion that it is arrogant to presume to make such decisions is false in at least some cases, including those where the disability is disastrous. The parents of the girl with EB need not be the slightest degree arrogant to want no other child of theirs to have such a life.

And when couples in quite ordinary circumstances choose to have or not to have a child, they indeed are making a Godlike decision. Perhaps we are not sufficiently awed by this familiar choice. It is possible to look at one's children and be retrospectively unnerved by how their very existence depends on decisions that one participated in and that could so easily have been different. But even if those familiar choices should be more impressive than they are, they provide a context in which it is hard to argue against reproductive decisions on the grounds that by making such decisions we are presuming a Godlike power over the existence of other people.

Disabled People and Equality of Respect

Having a severe disability is not a reason for being treated in any way as a second-class citizen. Opting for the existence of normal rather than disabled people is sometimes presented as a civil rights issue. Do such decisions violate the rights of people with disabilities? This criticism arises particularly in the context of prenatal screening leading to abortion. There its main force depends on one's view about whether fetuses have rights.

Some people would argue that such screening is effectively a form of discrimination against disabled people in general. Among the worst problems that disabled people must confront are the attitudes of many other people. And screening programs aimed at preventing the birth of disabled people could reinforce those attitudes. It may be difficult to feel self-esteem when people are doing all they can to avoid having a child like you.

That it is a threat to equality of respect clearly is a possible objection to screening. But equality of respect is a complex concept. Showing respect for people has two aspects. The first requires that we respect their rights: for instance, that we do not assault them, steal their property, tap their telephones, or prevent them from expressing religious or political beliefs. (Deciding exactly what people's rights are is a problem, but that does not undermine the claim that showing people respect requires not violating their rights, whatever they are.)

The other aspect of showing respect is more difficult to pin down, but hardly less important. It is a matter of attitude. It is a matter of not treating people with contempt or condescension. It is absent, to different degrees, in a caste system, or in a snob, or in someone who never listens but always interrupts. It is what makes our attempts to teach children to be courteous and considerate more than indoctrination in a set of arbitrary rules.

Much of what is involved in equality of respect is compatible with screening. Aiming for the conception and birth of normal people, for instance, is perfectly compatible with insisting that the rights of disabled people be fully respected and with seeing them as equals. Medical treatment presupposes that health is better than sickness, but those who believe in it treat sick people as their equals.

It may be said that the case is not parallel: the screening programs aim not to cure disabled people but to replace them with normal people. But even so, treatment as equals is possible. Something similar could be said about people who are not disabled. At the time I was conceived, if there had been a choice between my conception and that of someone just like me but more athletic or more imaginative, it might have been better if the other person had been conceived instead of me. I incline to this view, and if you do as well, this need not affect your attitude toward me for the worse. (Of course, a major disability may be more central to someone's life than not being athletic is to mine, so the chances of a screening program leading to loss of esteem are greater. But it is true of all of us that someone better in some ways could have been conceived instead. Accepting this about a particular person does not mean that one feels contempt or condescension toward him or her.)

The Slide to Positive Eugenics

Many people believe that gene therapy and genetic screening of embryos is dangerous. They believe that these policies may lead to eugenic policies that are positive rather than negative; that is, designed to "improve" people who suffer from no medical disorder.

Positive eugenic programs raise large and controversial questions. Which characteristics are to be encouraged and which discouraged? Who is to decide on a matter so fundamental to other people's futures? Is there not a risk of appalling and perhaps irreversible mistakes? Most people shudder at the thought of positive eugenics. Perhaps this reaction is too hasty. Before banning positive eugenics in principle forever, it may be a good idea to ask whether in the distant future such a ban would counteract some huge gain, and whether it is certain that the problems of positive eugenics could never be surmounted. But even if such programs should not be absolutely excluded, a strong case can be made for a ban on them at least for now. The problems they raise are so deep, and so far from being solved, that it would be wise to consider carefully their dangers and problems.

There are good reasons for resisting any current proposal that is likely to result in positive eugenics. But there is no obvious reason why gene therapy or embryo screening must slide into positive eugenics. No doubt the boundary between medical and nonmedical intervention is sometimes blurred. But conventional boundaries often exist (as in the speed limit) where there is no sharp boundary in reality. To avoid positive eugenics, it seems more rational to draw the boundary where we really want it.

Evaluating the Objections

The playing God objection is not a clear one. For it to be taken seriously would require some explanation of why deciding which kind of child to have is so much more presumptuous than deciding whether to have a child at all.

The apparently Godlike policy of "replacing" one potential child with another is not necessarily sharply distinct from the familiar decision about having a child at all. The boundaries of replacement are blurred. Go back to a "natural" version of replacement. Suppose the man my grandmother first loved had not been killed in the First World War. Suppose they had married and had three children: first two boys, Michael and Henry, and then their younger sister, Susan. Which of those children, if any, did my mother (who was my grandmother's only child) replace? As my grandmother's "first" child, was she replacing Michael, or as my grandmother's daughter, was she replacing Susan? Or was she replacing Henry, who would have been born on the same day she was? And would there have been one particular grandchild whom I am replacing, and a particular great-grandchild whom each of my children counts as replacing? And must my mother have replaced one of the children my grandmother would have had in her alternative marriage, or one of the children my grandfather might have had in an alternative marriage?

In this case, the idea of one child replacing another becomes too vague to be worth discussing. It seems better just to talk of the children and grandchildren of the alternative marriages who were not conceived, and of the offspring of the actual marriage who were conceived, without attempting these comparisons.

Something close to this may be true of the couple who decide not to have a child who would be disabled. Suppose that after deciding against implanting an embryo that would develop into a child with a disability, they wait a few months before conceiving again. Who is their next child replacing? Is she replacing the child who would have developed from that embryo, or is she replacing the child they might have conceived immediately after deciding against implantation?

Or suppose several attempts to conceive a normal child result in fertilized eggs found to have a disorder and thus not implanted. When a normal child is finally conceived, is that child a replacement for the first nonimplanted embryo, or for the most recent? Again, it seems less misleading to give up claims about replacement and to talk instead about deciding not to have one child and deciding to have another child, without bringing in the comparison. If this is correct, in such cases the supposedly Godlike decision about replacement collapses into two decisions of a kind made all the time.[1]

Although this weakens the playing God objection by blurring the boundary between replacement and everyday decisions, it does not make talk of replacement wrong in all cases. When a couple have decided to have only one child and they abort a fetus with a severe disorder, the child they later do have can be seen as replacing the one who would have been born. And the same holds when there is a choice between implanting one of only two embryos. These few special cases can be described as "clear replacement," and the larger number of other cases as "blurred replacement." Cases of blurred replacement seem no more vulnerable to the charge of Godlike arrogance than everyday decisions about whether to have a child. But it is hard to see why clear replacement should be either more arrogant or more morally objectionable than blurred replacement. That would require us to accept that it might be objectionable to transfer one embryo out of two, but perfectly acceptable to transfer one out of three. How the presence of a third embryo could make such a difference is difficult to explain.

To be convincing, the objection to screening that foresees a positive eugenics would need more evidence. The most serious objection is based on the interests of already disabled people.

Because attitudes to disability are among its greatest disadvantages we are reluctant to say anything that might seem to belittle disabled people. And in light of how some people triumph over disability, it is difficult to assert that a particular disability totally excludes a fulfilled life.

These responses seem appropriate. But they may distort our thinking about the problem. Our reluctance to believe that a disabled person necessarily has a less fulfilled life may lead to denying the need for screening programs that assume that the birth of a normal child is preferable to that of a disabled one. Such a preference may seem like a form of prejudice against the disabled.

But these thoughts in fact do not follow from the responses mentioned. Although a particular disability may not make a fulfilled life impossible, it is likely to make such a life more difficult. Consider the theoretical possibility of screening to ensure that only a disabled child would be conceived. This would surely be monstrous. And we think it would be monstrous because we do not believe it is just as good to be born with a disability.

If this is true, then it is not intrinsically wrong to prefer the birth of a person without disability and to base screening policies on that preference. It is desirable, however, to resist any tendency for such policies to spill over into discriminatory attitudes toward those who are disabled. If such a spillover cannot be avoided, this argument must be weighed against the case for favoring the birth of a normal person.

Disastrous Disability
Wrongful Life

In some legal cases it has been argued, on behalf of people with severe disabilities, that they were harmed by being brought into the world. The idea of "wrongful life" first appeared in American lawsuits in which illegitimate children claimed damages. In general, such claims were rejected. Later, wrongful life suits centered on children born with severe disabilities or diseases. Both parents and children acted as plaintiffs. The defendants were usually laboratories. Sometimes an action was brought against the parents themselves on the grounds of "negligence," for not having aborted the fetus.

The legal aspects of these cases are not important here. The central moral issue raised is whether parents and doctors ought to take what steps they can to prevent the birth of a child at risk of extreme disability. To put it more strongly, does a child have a right to life without severe disability, or failing that, a right to be prevented from being born?

One question about any such right is exactly on whom it imposes an obligation. Is it the duty of doctors and genetic counselors to prevent the conception or birth of such babies? This seems implausible. In general, their obligation is to provide information to enable the potential parents to make that decision. Perhaps things are different when the intervention of doctors, through IVF and so on, is required to bring the child into existence. But if there is a right not to be born with severe disability, it imposes duties mainly on the parents. This right may clash with the rights of the potential parents.

We must be cautious about assuming that there is a right not to be born with a severe handicap. Nonetheless, there are cases where it might have been better for the child not to have been born. This is related to the questions of suicide and voluntary euthanasia. Whatever the best approach to these questions, they arise because some kinds of life are perhaps worse than not to be alive at all. In one way, these questions are different, because the person is alive to make his or her own judgment about them. But if people can see death as being in their own interests, it seems equally possible that parents or doctors could think that not being born might be in the interests of a potential child. But a potential child is not like a potential immigrant, someone waiting to be admitted. Here the problem is whose interests are at issue.

Harm and the Comparison with Nonexistence

The claim under consideration is that to be brought into existence with an extremely severe disability may not be in the best interest of a child. This entails a general problem of comparing existence with nonexistence.

When medical techniques determine that some people rather than others come into existence, can those people be said to be better or worse off for the intervention? There are obvious difficulties in making comparisons between being alive and any state of being unconceived. This is a problem if we ask whether anyone is worse off when a child with a disability is born rather than a normal one. (And the idea of replacing someone else is not always clear-cut.) Yet despite these slippery conceptual problems, it does matter whether a normal or a disabled child is conceived. We need to think about these problems in a way that does not undermine this thought, but that avoids sliding into paradox or absurdity.

One approach is to find some notional way of making the comparison with nonexistence, perhaps by treating it on a par with being unconscious. Just as it is better to be unconscious than to experience the pain of a major operation, so it could be better not to be conscious at all than to experience certain kinds of life. Being dead or being unconceived could be treated as equivalent to permanent unconsciousness. This provides the necessary comparison, but at the cost of a certain artificiality: a particular person is unconscious during the operation, but no particular person exists in the state of being unconceived. The claim has to be that if a child is brought into the world with a disastrous disability, that child will have a life that is worse than no life. And this is a good reason for preventing the conception of such a child.

Moderately Severe Disability
The Family

Many people would take as axiomatic that it is better, when possible, to bring into the world a child without even a moderate disability. There is a problem with this view. Moderate disabilities are a substantial disadvantage, but not such that it would be better for the person not to have been born.

One approach would be to base screening policies on the interest of the parents in having a fully normal child. This is a difficult issue, because the effect on a family of having a child with a disability varies enormously. Sometimes the disabled child has qualities that enrich the family. Sometimes the other members of the family are enriched by the qualities brought out in them by the care they need to give. In other families, however, the unavoidable demands create exhaustion and strain, making the parents feel that, in Philip Larkin's words, "something is pushing them to the side of their own lives" and contributing to depression and divorce. And sometimes the demands of care for the disabled children consume attention that otherwise would go to the other children in the family.

This is a matter where everything depends on the individual case. But there is evidence that a substantial number of parents would support screening for some conditions. A 1983 survey of parents of children with Down's syndrome in the *Journal of Medical Ethics* asked what they would do if they knew that an expected child would have a severe mental disability. A total of 78 percent said they would want the pregnancy terminated. If it is reasonable to suppose that abortion arouses greater opposition than screening, it seems likely that at least this percentage would support a screening program.

It has been suggested that parental interests do not justify preventing the conception or birth of a disabled child, and that the child should be adopted. In some cases where parents do not want to bring up a child with a disability, people may be willing to adopt. But to the extent that the interests of the parents are being considered, it is worth remembering that giving away a child is not easy. From the parents' point of view, a screening program may be the best alternative.

While acknowledging that parental interests are important, supporters of screening policies may think that more is at stake.

Who Is Harmed?

Let us put to one side the interests of other people, such as family members, and consider only the handicapped person. Take a case where the rest of the family is not worse off because of the birth of a disabled child. Suppose this child has a moderate disability. Has the failure to prevent the child's existence done any harm? It would be hard to argue that the disabled person has been harmed, for he or she is leading a worthwhile life. There is no reason to think that the alternative (no life at all) would have been better for that person. Can the wrong decision have been made if no one is worse off as a result?

According to one moral principle, something is wrong only when it makes someone worse off than he or she would have been. This person-affecting principle, apart from its general plausibility, is thought to have played a useful role in reproductive ethics. One version of utilitarianism holds that a good way of increasing total happiness is to bring into the world more happy people. This conjures up two nightmares. One is a world where people are obligated to have many children in order to increase total happiness. The other, what Derek Parfit called the "repugnant conclusion," is a world with a huge total of happiness resulting from enormous numbers of people whose average level of happiness is low.[2] Jan Narveson once argued that the utilitarian principle should be interpreted in person-affecting terms; that is, to make people happy, not to make happy people.[3] This seems to offer a way around those unattractive alternatives.

The person-affecting view also has the virtue of backing up one part of the compromise policy on screening. The child with a moderate disability has not been harmed by the absence of a screening program. Where the family and others are not harmed, the person-affecting principle gives no support to such a program.

Two Surrogate Mothers

The person-affecting principle has a platitudinous air, but reproductive ethics can make paradoxes out of apparent platitudes. The difficulty can be brought out by considering a surrogate mother variant of a case discussed by Parfit.[4]

There are two kinds of surrogate mothers. One provides the egg, and so is fully the biological mother. The other, the "womb-leasing" surrogate mother, does not supply the egg. Agencies often screen potential womb-leasing surrogate mothers in the interest of the future child, for instance to exclude those who are likely to smoke during pregnancy. It is surely right to protect the future child in this way from risk of disability.

Should a similar screening take place for the egg-donor surrogate, for instance, to exclude carriers of genetic disorders? In this case, a different surrogate mother will result in a different child. So where the disability is a moderate one, the person-affecting principle would not require screening. The disabled child is not worse off than he or she would otherwise have been.

Some people believe that the need for screening should not depend on the type of surrogate. For those who take this view, the person-affecting principle is inadequate.

Gene therapy and other genetic engineering, if safe versions are developed, will also raise problems for the person-affecting principle. It is not clear that there is any way of drawing a boundary between genetic changes that occur in the same person and those that cause a change of person. So the boundaries of acting on the person-affecting principle may become blurred.

Impersonal Harms

There may be certain biological mechanisms that favor the conception of normal babies over those that would be abnormal. Imagine that a factory emits a chemical that reverses one such mechanism. This mechanism now favors the conception of children who are blind. The pollution seems to have done some harm. But to whom is the harm done? It has not made those children worse off than they would have been, since otherwise they would not have existed. The case that any particular person has been harmed is hard to sustain. Yet we are surely justified in seeing the pollution as harmful and in trying to stop it.

If this is correct, reproductive ethics as a field is characterized by impersonal harms and benefits. Harm can be done even though identifiable people are no worse off than they otherwise would have been. In explaining why it is better to avert the conception of someone with a severe medical condition, we can use the idea of impersonal harms, without having to resort to metaphysical claims about benefits to a particular nonexistent person.

Many find the idea of impersonal harms counterintuitive. One reason for this is a general one underlying the appeal of person-affecting approaches to ethics. For some of us, anything put forward as a moral rule whose justification does not lead back to people (or—not to exclude other animals—at least to conscious beings) has no force. It is a natural progression to think that for an action to be right or wrong someone must be better or worse because of it. The idea of an impersonal harm then seems an evasion of this requirement. Yet the idea is necessary for a plausible account of reproductive ethics.

There is a way of retaining the intuitive spirit of the person-affecting approach while bringing in the substance of the idea of impersonal harm. This is to expand the person-affecting principle through comparisons with alternatives. The pollution that damaged the filter mechanism did not make the blind children worse off than they would have been. But their state is worse than that of the children who would have been born in the absence of the pollution.[5] This comparative version of the person-affecting principle is perhaps a more palatable version of the impersonal approach. By eliminating the impersonal flavor, this approach clearly remains rooted in people and their lives, rather than derived from mere abstract rules.

Disability and Population Size

One reason Narveson introduced the person-affecting approach was to avoid a commitment to creating as many happy people as possible. Does the move toward including impersonal harms lead back to this unattractive commitment?

The creation of many happy people may be in itself a good thing. The idea of it being a duty, however, is outweighed by other considerations, such as loss in the quality of the lives people would lead. But the move to impersonal harms need not involve valuing larger numbers. When picking the best apples, there is no commitment to picking as many as possible.

This discussion has tended to undermine the part of the compromise policy that excludes screening for moderately severe disabilites. It has done so by criticizing one main argument against screening, which appeals to the claim that no one is harmed by the absence of screening. The counterclaim is that the children born because of screening will on the whole benefit more than the children born because of the absence of screening, and that this is relevant. Also relevant are the interests of other members of the family, such as the parents of children with Down's syndrome.

People are faced with different choices. (They normally must choose between different probabilities rather than between the certainty of one outcome or another, but this can be ignored here.) One choice is that between having a normal child and having a moderately disabled child. The appeal to impersonal harms gives a reason for choosing the normal child.

In another kind of choice, the condition may be so severe that the parents (like those of the girl with EB) are not prepared to risk conceiving a child who would have to endure it. Their only option may be to have no child. But the existence of a screening program, by removing the risk, could make a child possible for them. This is a strong point in favor of such a program.

Another choice is that between the risk, or even certainty, of having a child with a moderately severe disability and having no child at all. Here a widely held feeling conflicts with the results of looking in a more detached way at the two outcomes. The widely held feeling is that it surely cannot be right deliberately to produce a child who will suffer from a fairly severe disability. But the couple want the child, and the child, while regretting the disability, will not regret having been born. So no one is made worse off by the decision to have the child. And as no possibility exists of having another child without the disability, there is no impersonal harm. In such a case, the arguments support having the child.

The main arguments of this chapter support screening programs. But there is one argument that tends in the other direction: the danger of undermining respect for people with disabilities. It is important that screening programs be accompanied by social policies that protect and enlarge the civil rights of the disabled. It is even more important that equality of respect be extended to all. Individual differences of ability are quite irrelevant.

Notes

1. This line of thought was suggested to me by Christopher Shields.
2. Parfit, *Reasons and Persons,* chap. 17.
3. Narveson, "Utilitarianism and New Generations."
4. Parfit, *Reasons and Persons,* chap. 16.
5. Hare, "Abortion and the Golden Rule."

VII

Against the
Social Discount Rate

TYLER COWEN AND

DEREK PARFIT

When deciding how to use resources, or to protect the environment, or when selecting other policies with long-term consequences, governments and their advisers often use a social discount rate. With such a rate, possible costs and benefits are assumed to be less important if they would come further in the future. Such a discount rate applies not only to the costs and benefits that will later come to existing people, but also across the lives of all future generations. In this chapter we consider the arguments for such a discount rate and conclude that they are not sound.[1]

The Effect of Discount Rates

There are two primary methods of choosing a social discount rate. The first method uses the marginal real rate of return on private capital as a proxy for the opportunity cost of postponed consumption. One well-known study estimated such rates of returns at 12.41 percent.[2] After adjusting these returns for risk premiums, discount rates of between 5 and 10 percent are typically generated. The second method estimates the social rate of time preference by examining the real rate of return on the almost riskless obligations of the U.S. Treasury. This procedure usually generates discount rates between 1 and 2 percent.

If we are considering the further future, the choice of a

We wish to thank Amihai Glazer, Gregory Kavka, Daniel Klein, Randall Kroszner, Alan Nelson, and Kenneth Small for useful comments and discussions.

Table 7.1
Estimated Number of Future Benefits Equal to One
Present Benefit Based on Different Discount Rates

Years in the Future	1%	3%	5%	10%
30	1.3	2.4	4.3	17.4
50	1.6	4.3	11.4	117.3
100	2.7	19.2	131.5	13,780.6
500	144.7	2,621,877.2	39,323,261,827	4.96×10^{20}

discount rate has a significant effect on our evaluation of costs and benefits. Table 7.1 shows how many future benefits are, at various discount rates, worth as much as one present benefit.

Suppose the benefits in question are lives saved. According to a social discount rate, a single present life may be worth more than one million lives in the future. With a rate of 1 percent, these million lives must be far in the future: nearly 1,400 years. With a rate of 10 percent, the distance need only be 145 years.

Why should costs and benefits receive less weight, simply because they are further in the future? When the future comes, these benefits and costs will be no less real. Imagine finding out that you, having just reached your twenty-first birthday, must soon die of cancer because one evening Cleopatra wanted an extra helping of dessert. How could this be justified?

Many arguments have been proposed.

Non-economic Arguments
The Argument from Democracy

Many people care less about the further future. Some writers claim that, if this is true of most of the adult citizens of some democratic country, this country's government ought to employ a social discount rate. If its electorate does care less about the further future, a democratic government ought to do so as well. Failure to do so would be paternalistic, or authoritarian.

To assess this argument, we must distinguish two questions: (1) As a community, may we use a social discount rate? Are we morally justified in being less concerned about the more remote effects of our social policies, at some rate of *n* percent per year? (2) If most of our community answer yes to question (1), ought our government to override this majority view? The Argument from Democracy applies only to question (2).[3] To question (1), which is our concern, the argument is irrelevant.

The point might be put like this. A democrat believes in certain constitutional arrangements. These provide his or her answer to question (2). How could a commitment to democracy give the democrat an answer to question (1)? Only if he or she assumes that what the majority want, or believe to be right, must *be* right. But no sensible democrat assumes this. Suppose that some majority want to wage an aggressive war, or care nothing about the slaughter of innocent aliens. This would not show that they are right not to care. In the same way, even if most of us do care less about the more remote effects of our social policies, and believe such lesser concern to be morally justified, this cannot show that it is justified. Whatever most of us want or believe, this moral question remains open.

It may be objected: "In some cases, this is not a moral question. Suppose that, in some referendum, we vote for a social policy that will affect only ourselves. And suppose that, because we care less about what will happen to us later, we vote for a policy that will bring us benefits now at the cost of greater burdens later. This policy is against our interests. But since this policy will affect only ourselves, we cannot be acting wrongly in voting for it. We can at most be acting irrationally."

On the assumptions that most of us accept, such claims would provide some defense of the social discount rate. But the defense seldom applies. Most social policies will affect our children, as well as ourselves. If some policy would be against the interests of our children, this could be enough to make it wrong. Similar remarks apply to the interests of those people who are not yet born. It *is* a moral question how much weight we ought to give to the interests of these people. When those affected have no vote, the appeal to democracy provides no answer.

The Argument from Probability

It is often claimed that we should discount more remote effects because they are less likely to occur.[4] This argument also confuses two questions:

1. When a prediction applies to the further future, is it less likely to be correct?
2. If some prediction is correct, may we give it less weight because it applies to the further future?

The answer to (1) is often yes. But this provides no argument for answering yes to (2). Suppose we are deciding whether to cease or increase our use of nuclear energy. We are considering possible accidents from the disposal of nuclear wastes, with estimates of predicted deaths from escaped radiation. In a small accident, such deaths might all remain statistical, in the sense that we would never know which particular deaths this accident had caused. When considering possible accidents, we must think far into the future, since some nuclear wastes remain radioactive for thousands of years. According to a social discount rate of 5 percent, one statistical death next year counts for more than a billion deaths in four hundred years. Compared with causing the single death, it is morally less important if our chosen policy causes the billion deaths. This conclusion is outrageous. The billion people would be killed further in the future. But this cannot justify the claim that, compared with killing the single person, we would be acting less badly if instead we killed a billion people.

The Argument from Probability does not lead to this conclusion. It could at most lead to a different conclusion. We know that if radiation escapes next year, we will have no adequate defense. We may believe that, over the next four centuries, some kind of countermeasure will be invented, or some cure. We may thus believe that if radiation escapes in four hundred years, it will then be much less likely to cause deaths. If we are *very* optimistic, we may think this a billion times less likely. This would be a different reason for discounting, by a factor of a billion, deaths in four hundred years. We would not be making the outrageous claim that if we do cause such deaths, each of these deaths matters a billion times less than a death next year. We would instead be claiming that these more remote deaths are a billion times less likely to occur. This would be why in our view we need hardly be concerned about the escape of radiation in four hundred years. If we were right to claim that such deaths are a billion times less likely, that conclusion would be justified. Deaths that do not occur, whether now or in four hundred years, do not matter.

This example illustrates a general point. We ought to discount those predictions that are more likely to be false. Call this a Probabilistic Discount Rate. Predictions about the further future are more likely to be false. So the two kinds of discount rate, temporal and probabilistic, roughly correlate. But they are quite different. It is therefore a mistake to discount for time *rather than* for probability. One objection is that this misstates our moral view. It makes us claim not that more remote bad consequences are less likely, but that they are less important. This is not our real view.

Another objection is that the two discount rates do not always coincide. Predictions about the further future do not decrease in certainty at some constant rate of n percent per year. Indeed, when applied to the further future, many predictions are *more* likely to be true. (Consider the predictions that some policy will have changed, or that certain resources will have been exhausted.) If we discount for time rather than probability we may thus be led to what, even on our own assumptions, are the wrong conclusions.

The Argument That Our Successors Will Be Better Off

It is sometimes claimed that we should discount effects on future generations because they will be better off than we are.[5] When benefits or costs come to people who are better off, there are good reasons for giving them less weight. If we measure these benefits and costs in terms of resources, we can appeal to a nonutilitarian distributive principle. Benefits that are *equally* great, when received by people who are better off, may be plausibly claimed to have less moral importance.

These two arguments, though good, do not justify a social discount rate. The ground for discounting these future benefits is not that they come further in the future, but that they will come to people who will be better off. Once again, we should say what we mean. And the correlation is again imperfect. Some of our successors will not be better off than we are now. When applied to these people, the arguments just given fail to apply.

The Argument from Excessive Sacrifice and from Equality

By bearing costs now, we can give our successors greater benefits. For example, if we reinvest, rather than consume, the resulting benefits may in the end be greater. If we believe that our aim should be to maximize the total sum of benefits, and we give equal weight to benefits in the further future, the optimal rate of saving could be very high. We may seem morally required to choose policies that would impose great sacrifice on the present generation.

If these requirements seem to us excessive, we may again be led, in an attempt to avoid them, to discount effects in the further future. A typical statement runs: We clearly need a discount rate for theoretical reasons. Otherwise any small increase in benefits that extends far into the future might demand any amount of sacrifice in the present, because in time the benefits would outweigh the cost.

The same objections apply. If this is why we adopt a social discount rate, we shall be misstating what we believe. Our belief is not that the importance of future benefits steadily declines. It is rather that no generation can be morally required to make more than certain kinds of sacrifice for the sake of future generations. And this is part of a more general view, which has nothing to do with time. On this view, no one is required to make great sacrifices merely to benefit others. If this is what we believe, this is what should influence our decisions.

If instead we express our view by adopting a social discount rate, we can be led needlessly to implausible conclusions. Suppose that, at the *same* present cost, we could prevent either a minor catastrophe in the nearer future, or a major catastrophe in the further future. Since preventing the major catastrophe would involve no extra cost, the Argument from Excessive Sacrifice fails to apply. But if we take that argument to justify a discount rate, we shall be led to conclude that the greater catastrophe is less worth preventing.

A closely related argument appeals to the claims of equality. If we aim for the greatest net sum of benefits over time, this may require a very unequal distribution between different generations. We may wish to deny that there ought to be such inequality. And we can avoid this conclusion, in some cases, if we discount later benefits. But, as Rawls points out, this is the wrong way to avoid this conclusion.[6] If we believe that such inequality would be unjust, we should not simply aim for the greatest net sum of benefits. We should have a second moral aim: that these benefits be fairly shared between different generations. To our principle of utility we should add a principle about fair distribution. This more accurately states our real view. And it removes our reason for discounting later benefits.

The Argument from Special Relations

Some utilitarians claim that each person should give equal weight to the interests of everyone. This is not what most people believe. According to commonsense morality, we ought to give some weight to the interests of strangers. But there are certain people to whom we either may or should give some kinds of priority. Thus we are morally permitted to give some kinds of priority to our own interests. And there are certain people to whose interests we ought to give some kinds of priority. These are the people to whom we stand in certain special relations. Thus each person ought to give some kinds of priority to the interests of his or her children, parents, pupils, patients, constituents, and fellow citizens.

Such a view naturally applies to the effects of our acts on future generations. Our immediate successors will be our own children. According to common sense, we ought to give to their welfare special weight. And we have similar, if weaker, obligations to our children's children. Similar claims seem plausible at the community level. Most people believe that their government ought to be especially concerned about the interests of its own citizens. It would be natural to claim that it ought to be especially concerned about the future children of its citizens, and, to a lesser degree, about their grandchildren.

Such claims might support a new kind of discount rate. We would be discounting here not for time itself, but for degrees of kinship. But at least these two relations cannot radically diverge. Our grandchildren cannot all be born before all our children. Since the correlation is, here, more secure, we might be tempted to employ a standard discount rate. As before, this would not be justified. For one thing, on any discount rate, more remote effects always count for less. But a discount rate with respect to kinship should at some point cease to apply.[7] We ought to give some weight to the effects of our acts on mere strangers. We ought not to give less weight to effects on our own descendants.

Nor should such a discount rate apply to all kinds of effects. Consider this comparison. Perhaps the United States government ought in general to give priority to the welfare of its own citizens. But this does not apply to the infliction of grave harms. Suppose this government decided to resume atmospheric nuclear tests. If it predicts that the resulting fallout would cause several deaths, should it discount the deaths of aliens? Should it therefore move these tests from Nevada to the South Pacific, so that those killed would not be Americans? It seems clear that, in such a case, the special relations make no moral difference. We should take the same view about the harms that we may impose on our remote successors.

Economic Arguments

We now examine the arguments for discounting that are most popular among economists: the appeal to opportunity costs, and to time preference. Unlike the arguments discussed so far, these arguments do appeal to considerations that are essentially about time. If they were sound, these arguments would provide direct support for the social discount rate. And, unlike the previous arguments, they would provide some guidance on how steep the discount rate should be.[8]

The Argument from Opportunity Costs

It is sometimes better to receive a benefit earlier, since this benefit can then be used to produce further benefits. An investment that yields a return next year will be worth more than the same return arriving in ten years if the earlier return can be profitably reinvested over these ten years. When we add in the extra benefits from this reinvestment, the total sum of benefits will be greater. A similar argument covers certain kinds of cost. The delaying of some benefits involves opportunity costs.

In the language of economics, this argument asserts that the rate of discount should be determined by the marginal rate of transformation between goods today and goods tomorrow in the productive sector of the economy—that is, the marginal product of capital. Positive discounting is justified by an appeal to the positive marginal productivity of capital.

The Argument from Opportunity Costs errs in taking the marginal productivity of capital as exogenous to other social decisions. In fact, the marginal productivity of capital depends on other social decisions, most notably the community's rate of savings. If the rate of savings is determined by how we discount the future, the productivity of capital cannot be invoked as an independent determinant of the discount rate. Instead, the choice of discount rate determines the marginal productivity of capital.

Under the assumptions usually employed by economists, additional increments of capital (additional savings) lower capital's marginal product. Each successive unit of capital invested creates less additional future output than the preceding unit. Consider investments that do not yield returns until the next generation. As long as the marginal rate of return on capital exceeds the intergenerational rate of discount, additional capital should be saved and invested. For instance, if capital yields 5 percent and we are willing to trade off present for future consumption at 4 percent, additional capital should be invested because future returns exceed our rate of discount. Optimality is achieved only when the rate of return on capital equals the discount rate applied to future consumption.

A zero rate of intergenerational discount thus implies the accumulation of capital for intergenerational investments until the marginal product of such capital equals zero. In this case, the marginal rate of return on capital can no longer be used to justify a positive rate of intergenerational discount. At the optimum point suggested by the moral principle of zero discounting of consumption streams, the marginal product of capital is also zero.

It may not be possible, however, for the marginal rate of return on capital to reach zero. The economists' assumption of diminishing marginal productivity could be wrong. Or some other constraint may prevent attainment of a zero marginal rate of return on capital.[9] In this case capital will yield a positive marginal rate of return, whether we like it or not. The Argument from Opportunity Costs may then apply.

Even here, however, the argument fails. Although certain opportunity costs do increase over time, it misrepresents our moral reasoning to treat these opportunity costs in terms of a social discount rate. These costs should be considered directly. If instead we express these costs in terms of a discount rate, we can be led astray.

We may be led, for example, to confuse benefits that will be reinvested with benefits that are merely consumed. When benefits to be consumed are received later, this may involve no opportunity costs. Suppose we are deciding whether to build some airport. Since this airport would destroy a fine stretch of countryside, we would lose the benefit of enjoying this natural beauty. If we do not build the proposed airport, we and our successors would enjoy this benefit in every future year. According to a social discount rate, the benefits in later years count for much less than the benefit next year. How could an appeal to opportunity costs justify this? The benefit received next year—our enjoyment of this natural beauty—cannot be profitably reinvested.

Nor can such an argument apply to those costs that are merely "consumed." Suppose we know that a certain policy carries some risk of causing genetic deformities. The argument cannot show that a genetic deformity next year ought to count ten times as much as a deformity in twenty years. The most that could be claimed is this. We might decide that for each child so affected, the large sum of k dollars would provide adequate compensation. If we were going to provide such compensation, the present cost of ensuring this would be much greater for a deformity caused next year. We would now have to set aside almost the full k dollars. A mere tenth of this sum, if set aside now and profitably invested, might yield in twenty years what would then be equivalent to k dollars. This provides one reason for being less concerned now about deformities in the further future. But the reason is not that such deformities matter less. The reason is that it would now cost us only a tenth as much to ensure that, when such deformities occur, we would be able to provide compensation. This is a crucial difference. Suppose we know that we will not in fact provide compensation. This might be true, for instance, if we would not be able to identify those particular genetic deformities that our policy had caused. This removes our reason for being less concerned now about deformities in later years. If we will not pay compensation for such deformities, it becomes an irrelevant fact that, in the case of later deformities, it would have been cheaper to ensure now that we could have paid compensation. But if this fact has led us to adopt a social discount rate, we may fail to notice when it becomes irrelevant. We may be led to assume that, even when there is no compensation, deformities in twenty years matter only a tenth as much as deformities next year.

The Argument from Transformation

We consider next a variant of the appeal to opportunity costs; examination of this claim further illustrates the problems with that argument. Consider consumption units, which we can either eat now or plant in the ground for a positive return. The Argument from Transformation proceeds as follows:

1. 1.05 units in period two are better than 1 unit in period two;
2. 1 unit in period one can be transformed into 1.05 units in period two.

Therefore,

3. 1 unit in period one is better than 1 unit in period two.

This argument is invalid. The move from (1) and (2) to (3) confuses the two relations "can be transformed into" and "is as good as." It may be possible to transform a frog into a prince, but this does not imply that a frog who stays a frog is as good as a prince.[10] Although 1 unit received in period one can be transformed (through investment) into 1.05 units consumed in period two, 1 unit consumed in period one and 1.05 units consumed in period two are mutually exclusive alternatives, just like the frog and the prince. Transformation may involve an increase, a decrease, or no change in value, but there is no presumption of any initial equivalence in value if the transformation does not take place.

The comparison between receiving a consumption unit in period one and receiving a consumption unit in period two can be broken down into mutually exclusive alternatives. If the first-period consumption unit is received and invested, we receive 1.05 units for period two; this is clearly better than initially receiving only 1 consumption unit for period two. But this dominance relation does not imply that first-period *consumption* (the mutually exclusive alternative to first-period investment) is also better than second-period consumption.

The confusion between the relations "can be transformed into" and "is as good as" is not the only problem with this argument. The argument also ignores the possibility of investing the second-period consumption unit for period *three*. Although 1 consumption unit in period one can yield 1.05 units for the period-two generation, 1 unit in period two could yield 1.05 units in period three for the *next* generation.

For any investment opportunity for period n given by current receipt of a consumption unit, there exists an equivalent investment opportunity for period $n + 1$ given by receipt of a consumption unit one period later. Without some prior argument that consumption units should be discounted across generations, possessing this investment opportunity in period n cannot be considered superior to possessing the same opportunity in period $n + 1$. With a finite horizon, of course, resources in the current period give us one more option than resources in the next period for any decision concerning the *final* period. Nonetheless, current resources are more valuable than future resources only in the special case when current resources are invested and not consumed until the final period of time.

In summary, the opportunity costs determined by the marginal product of capital do indeed structure society's available options, but they do not support a social discount rate.[11] If marginal rates of substitution and marginal rates of transformation do not concur, the marginal rate of substitution should be given priority.

There are other versions of the appeal to opportunity costs, which we cannot consider here. But the central issue is, we believe, simple. When describing the effects of future policies, economists could describe the future benefits and costs in a way that used no discount rate. The arguments that appeal to opportunity costs could be fully stated in these temporally neutral terms. We believe that, on any important policy question, this would be a better, because less misleading, description of the alternatives. It would make it easier to reach the right decision.

The Argument from Positive Time Preference

Another traditional argument for discounting appeals to the fact that most people prefer to receive benefits sooner rather than later. In some cases this preference is clearly rational. By choosing to receive benefits earlier, we sometimes make them greater, or more certain. But many people have a *pure* time preference. They prefer benefits to come earlier even when they know that this will make them smaller; and they postpone costs or burdens even when they know that this will make them greater. We incline to the view that this attitude is irrational.[12]

Even if this attitude is not irrational, it cannot justify an intergenerational discount rate. Perhaps individuals may rationally prefer smaller benefits, because they are in the nearer future. But this argument has no next step. Pure time preference within a single life does not imply pure time preference across different lives. Abstinence from consumption does not involve waiting when consumption is postponed across generations. Such abstention cannot be a meaningful bad for people who are not yet born; in the meantime, nobody is left waiting.

The Argument from Transitivity

It might be suggested that by appealing to the transitivity of the relations "better than" and "as good as" we can bridge the gap between time preference within lives and across lives. The argument might be presented as follows:

1. UPacket40 (1997, John) = UPacket40 (1997, Jim)
2. UPacket40 (1995, John) > UPacket40 (1997, John)
3. UPacket40 (1995, John) > UPacket40 (1997, Jim)

The number following UPacket refers to a quantity of utility, and the information within the parentheses refers to the year the utility is enjoyed and the person who receives the utility. The symbol > means "preferred to," and the symbol = means "as good as."

This argument attempts to derive (1) from utilitarianism, (2) from positive time preference within a single life, and (3) from transitivity. But the conclusion does not follow. The argument is flawed because (1)–(3) contain two different and conflicting notions of utility.

There are two ways of viewing choice among alternatives. Either an individual's ordinal choices always coincide with higher numerical *cardinal* utility for this individual, or they do not.

Consider the first assumption. If the ordinal rankings determined by John's time preference coincide with the rankings offered by a comparison of numerical utilities, claim (2) requires revision. If one utility packet is preferred to another, they cannot both be represented by the same numerical magnitude.[13] The utility packet on the left-hand side of (2) must be assigned a different cardinal number than the utility packet on the left-hand side of (1). It must be worth, not 40, but some higher value, such as 42. (1) and (2) would thus read as follows:

1a. UPacket40 (1997, John) = UPacket40 (1997, Jack)
2a. UPacket42 (1995, John) > UPacket40 (1997, John)
We can then derive:
3a. UPacket42 (1995, John) > UPacket40 (1997, Jack)

But this conclusion does not express a positive discounting of utility. Instead, it simply states that a greater amount of utility now is preferable to a smaller amount of utility later. It does not deny the original claim (3) UPacket40 (1995, John) = UPacket40 (1997, Jack), the claim that rejects the interpersonal discounting of utility.

Next consider the second kind of theory, where cardinal utilities may differ from a person's ordinal choices. John's receipt of the utility packet in 1995 is now valued at 40, rather than 42, as in (2a). When John prefers the utility packet in 1995 to the utility packet in 1997, our theory of utility no longer implies that the preferred packet is worth a greater sum (42) and the inferior packet is worth a lesser sum (40). Instead, we say that both utility packets are worth 40, but that John happens to prefer 40 in 1995 to 40 in 1997.

On this second view, if cardinal utilities and ordinal rankings contradict each other, cardinal utilities are given priority in the social welfare function.[14] In this case, however, the preference relation expressed in (2) no longer expresses a social ranking. Although our approach to utility theory has stipulated that social rankings are derived from cardinal utilities, (2) derives a social ranking from ordinal preferences. If we consistently determine social rankings by cardinal utilities, (2) becomes an indifference relation. The correct sequence of relations would proceed thus:

1b. UPacket40 (1997, John) = UPacket40 (1997, Jim)
2b. UPacket40 (1995, John) = UPacket40 (1997, John)
3b. UPacket40 (1995, John) = UPacket40 (1997, Jim)

The objection to discounting is again confirmed. Transitivity does not allow us to bridge the gap between discounting within a life and discounting across different lives.

The Argument from Time Preference assumes that, because individuals sometimes act cavalierly toward their own future, we ought analogously to discount the utilities of other generations in the future.[15] But if people were like Proust's characters and wished to postpone pleasures into the future, would this imply that benefits for future generations ought to count for more than present benefits?[16]

Altruism and Bequests

We have examined only conflicting interests between different generations; in the above scenarios a fixed quantity of consumption units or utilities are available for distribution. In reality, parents usually possess some degree of altruism for their descendants. The explicit incorporation of altruism into a model of generations, however, does not fundamentally alter the problem or our arguments. We now examine two arguments that suggest that altruism provides grounds against a zero rate of intergenerational discount. One argument suggests that present generations have too little influence over discount rates; the other suggests that present generations acting through family relationships have so much influence over intergenerational allocations that the intergenerational rate of discount chosen in other decision contexts does not matter.

The Argument from Double Counting claims that in the presence of altruism, a zero rate of intergenerational discount places too much weight on the interests of future generations. The interests of future generations are counted as equal to the interests of the present generation because of the zero discount rate; the interests of future generations also receive additional weight through the altruism of the present generation. What this argument calls double counting, however, appears to be a proper counting of interests. If a person benefits from the rescue of his best friend, for instance, it is not double counting to consider as benefits both the value of the life saved and the value of the friendship to the other party.

The Argument from Offsetting Transfers does not challenge the normative validity of a zero rate of discount, but instead challenges its practical significance. As long as generations are linked by a series of altruistic bequest motives, it is argued, any attempt to redistribute resources across generations will be reversed by a change in voluntary intergenerational transfers.[17] Although the use of a zero rate of discount may appear to increase the well-being of future generations, the present generation will offset this effect by decreasing the time, resources, and money devoted to helping descendants.

Assume, for instance, that a father plans to devote $200,000 to his son's upbringing and education. Use of a zero intergenerational rate of discount, however, leads to a policy that takes $10,000 from each member of the father's generation to yield $10,000 (plus epsilon) for each member of the son's generation. Given certain assumptions, it can be shown that the father's utility-maximizing response decreases his transfer to his son by 10,000 to $190,000, undoing the intergenerational redistribution suggested by the zero discount rate. If this argument holds, our choice of discount rate for collective decisions may have little practical significance. Offsetting changes in voluntary intergenerational transfers would allow the present generation to apply whatever rate of discount it chooses to future generations.[18]

The Argument from Offsetting Transfers relies on special assumptions that do not always hold true. First, it assumes that all persons have children, as those without descendants would not be able to perform offsetting voluntary transfers. Second, ex ante voluntary transfers are assumed to exceed the redistributions caused by policy transfers; otherwise no sufficient offsetting adjustment would be possible. Perhaps the most vulnerable assumption, however, is that changes in voluntary intergenerational transfers are costless.

Changes in the size of transfers will not be costless if persons enjoy giving for its own sake. The model of offsetting transfers assumes that parents care only about the size of the transfers their children receive and not about the source of these transfers. According to this argument, parents do not regard a parental gift of $200,000 as preferable to the child receiving all or part of this sum from other parties. But this surely misstates the nature of parental altruism; parents desire their child's welfare but also wish that they are the source of this welfare; that is, they enjoy giving to their children.[19] The parental joy of giving implies that reductions in involuntary intergenerational transfers might have significant costs, and that such reductions might not be used to undo redistributions toward future generations.

The Argument from Offsetting Transfers corrects the idea that any desired intergenerational allocations can always be achieved simply by redistributing wealth. The argument does not, however, show that a social discount rate has no practical consequences.

We have discussed several arguments for the social discount rate. None succeeds. At most, these arguments might justify using such a rate as a crude rule of thumb. But this rule would often go astray. It may often be morally permissible to be less concerned about the more remote effects of our social policies. But this would never be because these effects are more remote. Rather it would be because they are less likely to occur, or would be effects on people who are better off than we are, or because it would be cheaper now to ensure compensation, or it would be for one of the other reasons we have given. All these different reasons need to be stated and judged separately, on their merits. If we bundle them together in a social discount rate, we make ourselves morally blind.

Remoteness in time roughly correlates with a whole range of morally important facts. So does remoteness in space. Those to whom we have the greatest obligations, our own family, often live with us in the same building. We often live close to those to whom we have other special obligations, such as our clients, pupils, or patients. Most of our fellow citizens live closer to us than most aliens. But no one suggests that, because there are such correlations, we should adopt a spatial discount rate. No one thinks that we would be morally justified if we cared less about the long-range effects of our acts, at some rate of n percent per yard. The temporal discount rate is, we believe, as little justified.

When the other arguments do not apply, we ought to be equally concerned about the predictable effects of our acts whether these will occur in one, or a hundred, or a thousand years. This has great importance. Some effects are predictable even in the distant future. Nuclear wastes may be dangerous for thousands of years. And some of our acts have permanent effects. This would be so, for instance, of the destruction of a species, or of much of our environment, or of the irreplaceable parts of our cultural heritage.

Notes

1. Several economists examine the theoretical issues behind choosing a social rate of discount, including Arrow and Kurz, *Public Investment;* Bradford, "Constraints on Government Investment Opportunities"; Mendelsohn, "Choice of Discount Rate for Public Projects"; Warr and Wright, "Isolation Paradox"; Starrett, *Foundation of Public Economics;* Lind et al., eds., *Discounting for Time and Risk in Energy Policy;* and Lind, "Shadow Price of Capital." Economists have devoted little explicit attention to the issue of intergenerational discounting. Two exceptions are Dasgupta and Heal, *Economic Theory and Exhaustible Resources,* and Mueller, "Intergenerational Justice and the Social Discount Rate." Solow, "Economics of Resources or the Resources of Economics," notes in passing that the rate of intergenerational discount should be zero. Cost-benefit studies, however, commonly use positive discount rates without regard for whether benefits and costs are distributed over different generations; see Yang, Dower, and Menefee, *Use of Economic Analysis in Valuing Natural Resource Damages.* Cowen's discussions with economists confirm the nearly unanimous acceptance of a positive intergenerational discount rate. A number of sources examine the philosophical issues

behind intergenerational discounting. See Sikora and Barry, eds., *Obligations to Future Generations;* Parfit, *Reasons and Persons;* and Broome, "Economic Value of Life." In this essay we treat intergenerational discounting as distinct from the problem of intrapersonal discounting, which we do not challenge. Intrapersonal discounting may be more a problem of rationality than of morality.

2. See Holland and Myers, "Trends in Corporate Profitability and Capital Costs."
3. See Rawls, *Theory of Justice,* 296–297.
4. See, e.g., Dasgupta, *Control of Resources.*
5. See, e.g., Mueller, "Intergenerational Justice and the Social Discount Rate."
6. See Rawls, *Theory of Justice,* 297–298.
7. Or, to avoid discontinuity, it should asymptotically approach some horizontal level that is above zero.
8. The references cited at the beginning of note 1 provide various versions of these two arguments.
9. Many investments may yield benefits both within generations and across generations. If informational imperfections prevent the separation of the intragenerational returns from the intergenerational returns, the existence of intragenerational returns, combined with positive discounting within lives, may prevent the attainment of zero rates of return on capital.
10. Nozick, *Anarchy, State, and Utopia,* 64–65, makes a similar point in a different context. If we assert that the relation "can be transformed into" implies "is as good as," we cannot explain voluntary exchange by noting that each person prefers what he or she receives to what he or she gives up.
11. Austrian capital theory as found in Boehm-Bawerk, *History and Critique of Interest Theories,* and in Fetter, *Capital, Interest and Rent,* provides an excellent analysis of the difficulties in using the productivity of capital to determine discount rates.
12. We might, however, defend a person's right to make such choices on grounds of autonomy. Parfit, *Reasons and Persons,* examines the issues surrounding positive time preference.
13. This approach to choice implies that the concept of discounting a given amount of utility is meaningless: utility is what is left over after discounting.
14. If we postulate ordinal and cardinal rankings that do not always coincide, but continue to use ordinal rankings for social rankings, we would in effect revert back to the case where utility is determined by choice. Introducing noncoincident cardinal utilities would serve only a cosmetic function, as these cardinal utilities would not be used to determine social ranking.
15. By combining positive discounting within lives and zero discounting across lives, it may be possible, paradoxically, to increase the value of a stream of benefits simply by deferring these benefits into the future. This result, however, is not disturbing if we accept the premise of positive discounting within a life. Benefits that arrive, say, in twenty years will be enjoyed predominantly by persons who are alive now; these benefits are thus subject to a positive rate of discount for the entire twenty years. In contrast, benefits that arrive in fifty years will be enjoyed predominantly by unborns and will not be discounted for the entire fifty years. Assume, for instance, that the next generation is born in thirty-five years;

benefits arriving in fifty years are thus discounted for only fifteen years and these benefits may be more valuable than the benefits for the current generation in twenty years. However, this reflects the assumption of positive time preference within single lives; making one generation wait fifteen years for their benefits would be less bad than making another generation wait twenty years for their benefits.

16. See Loewenstein, "Anticipation and the Valuation of Delayed Consumption."

17. Examining the use of offsetting transfers as a response to intergenerational redistributions was pioneered by Barro, "Are Government Bonds Net Wealth?" Warr and Wright, "Isolation Paradox," applies Barro's argument to the choice of discount rate.

18. Advocates of the Argument from Offsetting Transfers do not restrict this argument to transfers across adjacent generations. If the present generation is taxed to create benefits for persons seventeen generations later, the present generation will adjust by decreasing transfers to their children, these children will later decrease transfers to their children, and so on, and the resulting chain reaction may restore the initial intergenerational distribution. Such intergenerational linkages are modeled by Barro, "Are Government Bonds Net Wealth?" Barro's reasoning on this point, however, has been challenged by Bernheim and Bagwell, "Is Everything Neutral?"

19. How many parents, for instance, would give up their children for adoption to benevolent millionaires?

VIII

Consequentialism Implies a Zero Rate of Intergenerational Discount

T Y L E R   C O W E N

In chapter 7, Derek Parfit and I examined the arguments used to justify a positive rate of intergenerational discount; we concluded that these arguments do not succeed. Arguments based on positive time preference within lives, positive marginal productivity of capital, the uncertainty of the future, and theories of moral obligation do not suffice to rationalize positive discounting. Costs and benefits borne by future generations should be weighted on an equal par with costs and benefits born by persons in the present.[1]

Here I present an axiomatic argument for a zero intergenerational rate of discount. I use the method of social choice theory by presenting a number of simple axioms and demonstrating the conclusions that necessarily follow. If we consider the axioms reasonable, we must also accept the conclusions. The four axioms that generate a zero rate of intergenerational discount are: (1) Pareto indifference, (2) transitivity of indifference, (3) person neutrality within generations, and (4) well-defined preferences across living in different eras.

The argument for a zero rate of intergenerational discount, however, holds only to the extent that we are consequentialists. I define consequentialism as the set of moral theories that attempts to evaluate and compare outcomes. We might instead evaluate policies in terms of rights and duties. But an intergenerational rate of discount would then become difficult to define, because we would no longer be trading off changes in outcomes at the margin. My framework contains no room for rights and duties, not because I wish to argue for or against consequentialism, but because I wish to show its implications.

I now discuss each axiom in detail. First, Pareto indifference states that two situations are equally good if the same two situations are equally good for all persons involved. In other words, we should be indifferent toward policies that harm no one and benefit no one.[2]

Amartya Sen, among others, has challenged the principle of Pareto indifference by considering situations with equal utilities that differ in some other morally relevant fashion. Persons might be happy, for instance, because they possess base motives, such as enjoying the misfortune of others.[3] Creating happiness through base motives might not be as good, all things considered, as creating an equal amount of happiness through love. We might have ethical grounds for preferring happiness created through love over happiness created through malice, even if the two emotions produce the same amount of utility; Sen stresses the importance of what he calls "non-welfarist" values.

Examples such as Sen's are well-taken exceptions to the principle of Pareto indifference. When I use the Pareto indifference axiom, however, the different situations I am comparing do not differ obviously with respect to non-welfarist values. Persons consume a single homogenous good across different generational eras. Within this context, I simply assume that if a person is subject to an inconvenience and simultaneously compensated for this inconvenience, no one is worse off. Paretian indifference appears an entirely reasonable axiom within the context I consider.

The second axiom, the transitivity of indifference, states that if situation A is equally good as situation B, and B is equally good as situation C, A must be equally good as C. As with the first axiom, the transitivity of indifference need not always hold. Consider the Sorites Paradox. A person may be indifferent between fifty and fifty-one grains of sugar in coffee, indifferent between fifty-one and fifty-two grains, indifferent between ninety-nine and one hundred grains, and so on, but not indifferent between fifty and one hundred grains. Intransitivity arises because of fuzzy preference rankings.[4] Transitive indifference is a bad assumption when imperceptible changes or fuzzy preference rankings are involved, but neither of these factors is present in the issues examined here.

The third axiom, person neutrality within generations, states that a benefit for one person is equally good as the same benefit for another person within the same generation or time period, ceteris paribus. Granting the same benefit to either Jones or Smith is equally good. Similarly, imposing the same cost on either Jones or Smith is equally bad. The ceteris paribus clause rules out such factors as asymmetrically distributed altruism, for example, that other citizens might be happier when Jones gets a benefit than when Smith gets the same benefit. By treating all persons similarly within a time period, the person-neutrality axiom ensures that any resulting asymmetrical treatment of persons is due to their location in time. For the purpose of the following discussion, benefits take the form of cardinal, interpersonally comparable utility.

The fourth axiom is that persons have well-defined preferences across living in different eras. These preferences are well defined if persons would be willing to engage in permanent time travel in exchange for some amount of money or resources. Although persons may prefer living in one era rather than another, a sufficiently large income or endowment differential equalizes their utility in different eras. I also define the concept of era indifference, which applies to a person who requires no net increase or decrease in endowments to switch eras. Persons who are era indifferent do not care when they live, provided they receive the same endowment.[5]

Preferences across eras can be made operational by the following thought experiment. If cryogenic treatments could be used to freeze persons and thaw them out many years in the future (painlessly and risklessly), how much compensation would persons require to undergo such treatments? Unlike traditional uses of cryogenics, these treatments would be applied at the beginning of a person's life, and not at the end in an attempt to avoid or postpone death. Alternatively, we might consider a de novo thought experiment, which gathers all persons at the beginning of time and asks them to define their preferences across eras. Preferences across eras, however, do not require the operationality of any thought experiment or method of time travel; persons need only be able to rank inhabitation of different eras, even if no actual choice is available.

The axioms of Pareto indifference, transitivity, intragenerational person neutrality, and well-defined preferences across eras, taken together, imply a zero rate of intergenerational discount. That is, one additional unit of utility for the current generation is equally good, all things considered, as one additional unit of utility for the future generation. Although both the axioms and the diagrammatical proof are defined across utilities, a similar proof can be constructed across commodities or income as well.

The underlying intuition behind the proof is the following. First, the presence of well-defined preferences across eras implies that we can conduct thought experiments that switch persons and their utility endowments across eras. Of course, if era indifference does not hold, offsetting compensation in terms of endowments is required to preserve social indifference. Intragenerational person neutrality implies that it does not matter which person in a given time period receives a marginal change in utility. Combining these two results with the transitivity of indifference allows the following thought experiment: switch a person (the mover) and his utility forward in time, transfer one unit of utility from the mover to another person in the mover's new generation, and switch the mover back to his initial generation, without the unit he has lost (with compensation for the era switches but not for the lost unit of utility). We are back to where we started, except that the future generation has one additional unit of utility, and the present generation has one unit less.

At each stage in this process, the resulting situation is socially as good as the preceding situation, so social indifference relations are preserved. The initial and final situations differ only with respect to whether the present or future generation receives an additional increment of utility. The derivation of intergenerational neutrality from intragenerational neutrality follows from the extension of individual preference space across eras and the transitivity of indifference relations. Neutrality across generations becomes a natural extension of the traditional consequentialist belief in person neutrality within a single generation.

The above reasoning can be reproduced diagrammatically, where the letter designates a situation or world state, the row indicates the generation or era a person belongs to, and the information in the parentheses indicates a person's identity, material endowment, and utility, in that order. Utility is a function of a person's material endowment and other nonmaterial sources of utility; in the example presented, we are concerned with allocating nonmaterial sources of utility (for example, environmental improvements) across generations. For social rankings, of course, utilities and not material endowments matter.

We wish to compare the two possible outcomes A and E:

A

generation 2   (John: 20, 40)
generation 1   (James: 21, 41)

E

generation 2   (John: 20, 41)
generation 1   (James: 21, 40)

Indifference across these two outcomes implies a zero rate of intergenerational discount for utility, because we would not care if an additional increment of utility was given to the current generation (generation 1) or to the future generation.

Now consider the following comparison between A and B:

A

generation 2		(John: 20, 40)
generation 1	(James: 21, 41)	

B

generation 2	(James: 21 + k, 41)	(John: 20, 40)
generation 1		

Here k may be either positive or negative and is the change in material endowments required to keep James's utility at 41 after switching him to a new era. The existence of a finite k follows from well-defined preferences across eras, and we are indifferent between outcomes A and B because of Pareto indifference.[6] Outcome A, of course, is the outcome that results if generation 1 receives an additional unit of utility.

Now consider outcome C, which takes a unit of utility from James and gives it to John.

C

generation 2	(James: 21 + k, 40)	(John: 20, 41)
generation 1		

We are indifferent between B and C because of intragenerational person neutrality.

Now consider world state D:

D

generation 2		(John: 20, 41)
generation 1	(James: 21 + k + z, 40)	

Here z is the change in material endowments required for James to maintain a level of welfare of 40 after being shifted back to generation 1. The existence of z follows from well-defined preferences across eras, and z may be either positive or negative. Of course, if a person has preferences only across the eras themselves and does not mind the process of switching, then $k + z = 0$.

We are indifferent between C and D because of Pareto indifference.

Transitivity implies that we are indifferent between A and D through the indifference relations with B and C. Now consider world state E again:

$$E$$

generation 2		(John: 20, 41)
generation 1	(James: 21, 40)	

E is equally good as D because of Pareto indifference. That is, James does not care if he receives a given amount of well being through material endowments or directly through utility.

The difference between A and E is the world state that results if we give an additional unit of utility to generation 2 instead of generation 1. Since D has been shown to be equally good as A, and E is equally good as D, transitivity of indifference implies that E is equally good as A, which implies a zero rate of intergenerational discount. We should not care which generation receives an additional increment of utility.[7]

The above proof is not a knockdown argument for a zero rate of discount. A non-consequentialist might simply refuse to accept any of the four axioms outlined above. Some might believe that the allocation of intergenerational resources should be determined by Kantian duties and obligations, for instance, rather than by a comparison of outcomes.

Policy analysts, however, use a consequentialist framework when performing cost-benefit studies. That is, policy analysts try to find the best outcome for society, measured by some standard such as utility, wealth, or Paretian optimality. Rejecting the axioms discussed above implies a rejection of policy analysis as a method, and not merely the rejection of a zero intergenerational rate of discount. The alternative to a zero intergenerational rate of discount, then, is not a positive rate of discount, but an unwillingness to evaluate outcomes by comparing costs and benefits.

Notes

1. See Cowen and Parfit in this volume. References to the relevant literature can be found there.
2. My examples assume that the number and the identity of persons are fixed, thus avoiding the well-known paradoxical results generated by Parfit, *Reasons and Persons*.
3. Sen, *Choice, Welfare, and Measurement*, offers a number of essays critical of Paretianism.

4. Consider another example. The fuzziness of rankings might imply an indifference relation when comparing either Chopin's piano music or Schubert's piano music to Mahler's symphonies. Even given this fuzzy indifference ranking, we might still unequivocally prefer Chopin's piano music to Schubert's.

5. Under pure era indifference, living from 1962 to 1988 is equally good as living from 2062 to 2088, given equivalent endowments. Preferences characterized by pure era indifference exhibit time preference only across intervals when individuals are living or conscious. There may be many reasonable violations of pure era indifference, however. A person may wish to have met Lord Byron or may have an aesthetic preference for belonging to a certain generation. As long as these preferences are not lexicographic, however, an indifference point across eras will still exist: some amount of compensation will induce a person to switch eras.

6. The compensation for switching eras need not actually come from another party; it must only be true that the outcome in which additional income compensates a person for moving is equally as good as the preceding world state. Compensation is treated as manna from heaven, and it does not affect the proof if compensation is not actually available. The series of world states with compensation are only midpoints used for constructing an indifference relation across the feasible world states resulting from the policy choice that gives additional utility either to generation 1 or to generation 2. Whether these midpoints are feasible does not affect the resulting indifference relation between two world states that are feasible. The following analogy illustrates why compensation need not be available for the proof to follow. We might use transitivity to conclude that if preserving the Amazon forest is equally good as irrigating the Sahara and irrigating the Sahara is equally good as preserving Antarctica, then preserving the Amazon is equally good as preserving Antarctica. If it later turns out that irrigating the Sahara is very costly and therefore impossible without manna from heaven (although still valued the same, if it could be achieved without manna), this does not break the indifference relation between preserving the Amazon and preserving Antarctica.

7. Although the above argument portrays each person as inhabiting a single well-defined generation, incorporation of overlapping generations does not affect the proof. The proof does not rule out the existence of other persons whose generations overlap or coincide. The diagrammatical demonstrations assume only that the future will contain people who do not yet exist.

IX

Intergenerational Inequality

LARRY S. TEMKIN

Views about the moral relations between generations may be as varied, and as complex, as views about morality itself. Some see conflicting claims or interests of different generations in utilitarian terms, while others may see the issue in Aristotelian or Kantian terms. Still others may view the issue in Nietzschean, Marxian, Rawlsian, or Nozickian terms. And of course there are other views, including contractualism, relativism, and nihilism.

I am a pluralist. I believe there is a kernel of truth to many moral views, including most of those noted above. Correspondingly, I think the issue of the moral relations between generations is very complex. Indeed, to even present, much less argue for, the many strengths and weaknesses of the relevant moral views lies well beyond the scope of a single chapter. Therefore, this chapter adopts a limited strategy. It focuses on *one* moral ideal, equality, and raises various questions regarding that ideal. Unfortunately, even this limited strategy requires addressing a surprisingly broad set of issues and factors. Moreover, given this limited strategy and the nature of my inquiries, many of my results will themselves be limited or conditional. Still, I believe this chapter serves several purposes. It reveals that various answers might be given to my questions, which have important implications for the conflicting claims or interests of different generations. In addition, in settling certain questions, while raising and leaving others open, this chapter provides direction and helps lay the foundation for future inquiries regarding the complex topic of intergenerational inequality.

Section one addresses the question of how, if at all, population size affects inequality. Section two raises questions regarding the proper unit of egalitarian concern: specifically, whether inequality matters between people's lives taken as a whole, or between different segments of people's lives. As will be seen, the standard answers to these questions are (at best) seriously misleading, and in ways that may have important implications for the moral relations between generations.

A few preliminary comments. As I use the term, an *egalitarian* is anyone who believes equality has *some* value beyond the extent to which it promotes other ideals. Thus an egalitarian need not believe that equality is the only moral ideal, or even the most important ideal. She or he may simply believe that equality is one ideal, among others, worth valuing.

There are many different kinds of inequality. My discussion here will be couched in terms of inequality of *welfare*. This does not significantly affect my claims. Similar questions and considerations could be raised regarding other kinds of inequality.

In some contexts I use the term *equality,* in others *inequality*. For example, I talk about the value or ideal of equality, but about ways of measuring inequality. In some contexts I use both terms. So, for instance, I might note that an egalitarian cares about equality, or alternatively—and equivalently—that an egalitarian cares about inequality. I trust my meaning will be clear whichever usage is employed.

I have argued elsewhere that inequality is a complex notion, with as many as twelve different positions or aspects underlying our egalitarian judgments.[1] Although at several points I state and apply conclusions reached in my earlier work, I do not repeat my arguments for those conclusions here.

Finally, let me add that many of this chapter's considerations and implications could be applied, mutatis mutandis, to nonegalitarian ideals.

Inequality and Population Size

How, if at all, does variation in population size between generations affect inequality? This issue has received little attention; in part because debates regarding the "ideal" size of populations have focused on broadly utilitarian concerns, and in part because the issue is one on which most people have implicitly agreed. This is unfortunate. It is, in fact, a complicated issue that will be resolved, if at all, only with careful deliberation. Indeed, a full exploration of the issue lies well beyond the scope of this chapter. Still, let me begin the task, as the issue has important implications

Figure 9.1

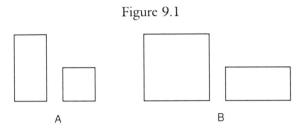

A   B

regarding intergenerational inequality and our obligations toward future generations.

In assessing how, if at all, size variation affects inequality, it will be useful to address a position I shall call the Standard View. Consider figure 9.1. As drawn, A's and B's better- and worse-off groups are at the same levels but B's groups are twice as large as A's. In terms of *inequality*, many would judge A and B equivalent. As they might put it, since the *pattern* of inequality is identical in A and B there is nothing to choose between them; the "mere" fact that B is larger than A is irrelevant to how they compare regarding inequality.

The judgment that A and B are equivalent expresses the Standard View, which asserts that proportional variations in the number of better off and worse off do not affect inequality (P). According to the Standard View, size is not itself relevant to inequality. Variations in size will matter only insofar as they affect inequality's pattern, for example, by altering the better off's and worse off's levels or the ratios between them.

Each of the economists' statistical measures of inequality implies P.[2] Moreover, although the statistical measures have been criticized for being invariant if the better off's and worse off's *levels* vary proportionally,[3] they have not, to my knowledge, been criticized for being invariant if the better off's and worse off's *numbers* vary proportionally. Given the economists' scrutiny of the statistical measures, this suggests that proportional variation in terms of numbers as opposed to levels is widely accepted as unobjectionable. I think, then, that the Standard View is appropriately named.

P has great plausibility and widespread appeal. In fact, I suspect most would regard it as obvious and uncontroversial. It is not. Despite its intuitive attraction, P stands in need of argument rarely, if ever, offered. This is not to say that P must be rejected. Rather, one must seriously consider under what circumstances, or to what extent, it should be accepted, rejected, or modified.

Strong considerations can be adduced on both sides of the position.

Let me next indicate some of these considerations, without pursuing all of their many interesting implications and complications. I begin by considering some of the reasons for accepting P, with its implication that A and B are equivalent. Though the reader may already be convinced of P's truth, I ask that he or she bear with me in what follows, as it is important for setting up, and for balancing against, the rest of this section. (Unless context determines otherwise, comparisons between A and B refer to figure 9.1, and how the situations depicted there compare *regarding inequality*. Nothing is implied about how A and B compare either in terms of other specific ideals or *all things considered*.)

In "Inequality" I argued that one important aspect of inequality is concerned with *social* rather than natural inequalities, where the judgment that one society is better or worse than another regarding inequality will be a judgment about the principles and institutions of those societies responsible for (social) inequality. Such a judgment would be, as it were, a judgment about the "character" of the societies. Thus just as we would not regard one judge who solicited and accepted bribes in every case as less corrupt than another who did the same, merely because he or she had fewer cases, so we would not regard one society as less unjust than another with identical principles and institutions merely because—being located in a less densely populated area—it had fewer members unjustly affected.

It is easy to see how such an aspect might support P's plausibility. Suppose representatives of America's worse off met with administration officials to complain about inequality. Surely they would not be consoled—indeed, would be completely unmoved—by assurances that the population size was proportionally changing. After all, the worse off's representatives presumably want the government to *do* something about America's inequality. They want to see changes in the inheritance and tax laws, the judicial process, the educational and vocational systems, and so on. In other words, in meeting with administration officials their concern is with the principles and institutions governing society. Clearly, this concern is not addressed by the assurances in question.

One can see, then, how a concern for social equality might support the judgment that A and B are equivalent on the implicit assumption that A and B differ solely in size—that is, that they are alike in all other relevant respects, including their principles and institutions. More generally, I think the preceding helps explain P's widespread appeal. Many economists and others who have endorsed P have been mainly concerned with social justice. Their interest has been in determining whether a society seeking equality should pattern its principles and institutions after those of Britain, Russia, America, or some other model altogether. Given their concerns, there is good reason to accept P.

Two comments. First, the assumption that A and B are alike except in size is necessary if one wants to conclude—based on a concern about social inequality—that they are equivalent regarding inequality. For example, it might be that A's principles and institutions are much better (or worse) than B's, but that the gaps between A's and B's better off and worse off are the same due to other, natural circumstances. In such a case, a concern for social equality would support P, but not the judgment that A and B are equivalent.

Second, the concern about social inequality is a legitimate and important egalitarian concern. Hence there is some reason for accepting P. However, this does not settle the issue of how size variations affect inequality. After all, the concern for social equality is not the only significant aspect of the egalitarian's concern and, as will be seen, other considerations suggest a different conclusion.

A second aspect of inequality supporting P is one that judges inequality in terms of "gratuitousness." As I argued in "Inequality," on this aspect a situation's inequality will be gratuitous, and hence bad, insofar as the "costs" of a redistribution of the sources of welfare would be relatively small, and the "gains" relatively large. Thus a situation where just a few are well-off and the vast majority are badly off would be much less objectionable than one where just a few are badly off and the vast majority are well-off, since in the former situation, unlike the latter, a redistribution of the sources of welfare would presumably involve a tremendous loss in the quality of life for some, with virtually no gain for those thus "benefited." Such a position supports P, since if the pattern of inequality is identical in two societies, so that their only difference is that one is proportionally bigger, then the relative costs and gains of a redistribution of the sources of welfare to the better off and worse off should be the same in the two societies. Correspondingly, their inequality will seem equally gratuitous, and hence equally objectionable.

Two other positions or aspects of inequality that support at least P's spirit, and hence its intuitive plausibility, are the maximin principle of equality combined with the relative to the average view of complaints (MP & AVE) and the maximun principle of equality combined with the relative to the best-off person view of complaints (MP & BOP).[4] Roughly, according to MP & AVE and MP & BOP, comparisons between two societies regarding inequality will depend on how much those societies' worst-off members have to "complain" about regarding inequality, where this will depend on how they fare relative to the average and the best-off persons in their societies. Basically, then, one society's inequality will be worse than another's if its gaps between the average or best-off person and the worst off are larger. Since the size of the gaps between the average or best-off person and the worst off would not be affected by proportional variation in a society's population, such positions intuitively support P.

There is another way of thinking that may support P. To take a non-egalitarian example, suppose there were four societies, F, G, H, and I, such that those in F were susceptible to measles, those in G and H were susceptible to polio, and those in I were susceptible to AIDS. There is a straightforward sense in which one might judge that regarding illnesses G and H were equivalent to each other, worse than F, and better than I. Such judgments might be simply, and strictly, judgments about the *kinds* of illnesses obtaining in the societies. Correspondingly, they would be independent of the societies' sizes or, for that matter, of the prevalence of the respective diseases within each society. That is, such judgments would be independent of both the absolute numbers and the percentages of those afflicted with the diseases.

Analogously, suppose there were four societies, F, G, H, and I, whose only inequalities were due to birth defects. Specifically, suppose that the only inequalities were between those born with a limp and those born without one (in F), between those born deaf and those born with hearing (in G and H), and between those born blind and those born sighted (in I). As before, in a straightforward sense someone who cared about natural inequality might judge that regarding inequality G and H were equivalent to each other, worse than F, and better than I.[5] Such judgments might be simply, and strictly, judgments about the *kinds* of inequality obtaining in the societies. They would be independent of the societies' sizes, or even of the prevalence of the inequality within each society. That is, they would be independent of both the absolute numbers and the percentages of the societies who were worse off relative to the better off. Clearly, then, such judgments would support P, on the assumption that "mere" proportional variations in the number of better and worse off would not affect the kind of inequalities obtaining in a society—at least not in the sense described.

There is still another way of thinking that may support P. Consider again our nonegalitarian example involving G and H, whose members were susceptible to polio. Although, as we have seen, there is one sense in which one might judge that regarding illnesses G and H were equivalent to each other, in another sense one might judge that regarding illnesses G was worse than H, for example, if most in G were afflicted by illness but few in H were. More particularly, from a health standpoint, one might judge G more dangerous or worse than H if, say, 80 percent of G's population were seriously ill, while only 20 percent of H's were, and this would be so even if in absolute terms more people might be seriously ill in H than in G due to H's being a larger society.

The preceding suggests a sense in which our judgment about how to compare two societies regarding illnesses (or, alternatively, in terms of their citizens' health) may depend on the societies' *patterns* of illnesses in terms of both the kind and the prevalence of their illnesses—that is, on the *relative* rather than absolute numbers of those afflicted by illness. Similar reasoning suggests that our judgment about how to compare two societies regarding inequality may depend in one sense on the societies' patterns of inequality in terms of both the kinds of inequalities obtaining (in the sense indicated above) and the extent to which the inequalities are pervasive (that is, the relative numbers of "victims" of inequality in each society). Thus in our earlier example, where G and H both involve inequality between the deaf and those who hear, there is a sense in which we might not regard G and H as equivalent regarding inequality if, say, 80 percent of G were deaf, while only 20 percent of H were, but we would regard them as equivalent if the same percentage were deaf in each society. Moreover, this would be so regardless of the absolute numbers who were deaf. So even if more people were worse off than others through no fault of their own in H than in G—because H was larger—there is *a* sense in which we might regard H's inequality as equivalent or even preferable to G's depending on the relative number of deaf in the two societies.

The view I have been discussing has different implications than the previous one in cases where size variations are not proportional—specifically, where a society's *kinds* of inequality remain constant, but the numbers of better off and worse off change disproportionately so that the relative numbers of better off and worse off vary. However, as should be clear, the implications are the same for cases where size variations are proportional. Hence this view also supports P.

I have noted six positions that support P, or at least the judgment that proportional variations do not significantly affect inequality. The first position concerns only social inequality. The others may concern both social and natural inequality. I have not claimed that each position is equally plausible. But each represents an intelligible way of judging inequality that cannot simply be dismissed. Moreover, however exhausting, my discussion is not necessarily exhaustive. Other positions may also support P. In sum, it is not surprising that P has been widely accepted. It is intuitively appealing and supported by a number of intelligible and plausible positions.

Already convinced of P's truth, many readers may regard the foregoing results as insignificant, even if more or less accurate and plausible. However, it is important to be aware of the arguments supporting P because there are also strong reasons for rejecting P. In fact, I think that ultimately P is *not* plausible as an *all things* considered egalitarian judgment. Hence insofar as P is plausible it needs to be seriously revised or limited in scope along the lines implicitly suggested by the foregoing arguments. Although I cannot hope to fully defend this claim here, let me next offer some considerations supporting that view.

It is often observed that equality is an essentially distributive principle, and I readily grant that egalitarians are concerned with distributions and not merely with totals—with *who* has what, rather than with *how much* there is. Nevertheless, I believe the egalitarian's concern is not so much essentially distributive as essentially comparative. The egalitarian has no intrinsic concern with how much people have; his or her concern is with how much people have *relative to others,* with some having less while others have more. More bluntly, I believe the ultimate intuition underlying egalitarianism is that it is bad (unjust or unfair) for some to be worse off than others through no fault of their own. It is this intuition— at the heart of the egalitarian's position—that underlies my objections to P.

Consider again figure 9.1. Even if one grants that in a certain sense the kind of inequality is no worse in B than in A, and even if one grants (the more controversial claim) that in a certain sense the pattern or distribution of complaints is no worse in B than in A, it is crucial to bear in mind *why* the egalitarian cares about kinds of inequality or patterns and distributions in the first place. If, as I have suggested, it is because the egalitarian regards it as bad for some to be worse off than others through no fault of their own, then there is good reason to regard B as worse than A. After all, to paraphrase the basic insight of the utilitarians, more of the bad is worse than less of the bad, and in the end, there is more of what the egalitarian regards as bad in B than in A.

One plausible position or aspect of inequality that would judge B's inequality worse than A's would combine an *additive principle of equality* with a *relative to all those better off view of complaints*. Roughly, an additive principle (AP) measures inequality in a situation by adding up the "complaints" of all those in that situation who have a complaint regarding inequality, and a relative to all those better off view of complaints (ATBO) measures the size of someone's complaint regarding inequality by comparing how she fares relative to all those better off. AP and ATBO reflect, respectively, the plausible views that if it really is bad for one person to be worse off than another through no fault of his or her own, it would be even worse for two people to be in such a position, and that if it is bad to be worse off than one person through no fault of one's own, it would be even worse to be worse off than two. In accordance with these views, then, B's inequality is worse than A's, and I fail to see why these views should be ignored, revised, or supplemented to avoid this result. After all, not only are B's worse off at the same level as A's, and not only are the gaps between the better off and the worse off just as great in B as in A, but in B there are twice as many in the position of being worse off than others through no fault of their own, and there are twice as many who are better off than they are.

One can see how an additive principle of equality combined with a relative to all those better off view of complaints would oppose P. According to such a position, proportional increases in a society's population would worsen inequality, as the result would be *more* people with *larger* complaints regarding inequality. Let me add, without argument, that other views might also combine with the views in question to oppose P. Specifically, an additive principle of equality might also plausibly combine with either a relative to the best-off person view of complaints or a relative to the average view of complaints to oppose the positions in question. So, too, a relative to all those better-off view of complaints might plausibly combine with either a maximin principle of equality or a weighted additive principle of equality to oppose the positions in question.[6]

Let me put the objection to P another way. Suppose there were two equally deserving people, Tim and John, whose positions improved as if Fate were steadily apportioning welfare according to an unwavering rule: one for Tim, ten for John. So when Tim was at level 1, John would be at level 10, when Tim was at level 100, John would be at level 1,000, and when Tim was at level 1,000, John would be at level 10,000. I believe that as time passed the situation would be worsening regarding inequality. After all, if Tim and John really were equally deserving, then other things equal even one allocation of welfare in accordance with a rule like "one for Tim, ten for John" would be somewhat unfair; and if one such allocation would be bad, surely two would be worse, three would be worse still, and so on.[7] Analogous reasoning might support the judgment that B is worse than A, as well as the more general judgment that proportional increases in population worsen inequality.

Suppose there are a million people in each group of A, two million in each group of B, and that the better off and worse off are at levels 2,000 and 1,000, respectively. Suppose, also, that each of the better off is named John, and each of the worse off Tim. Then in each world it is as if Fate has apportioned welfare in accordance with an unwavering rule (R): if there are two equally deserving people named John and Tim, give 2,000 units to John and 1,000 units to Tim. But now, if the people really were equally deserving, it would be bad for Fate to allocate welfare in accordance with R even once, worse to use R twice, and still worse to employ R three or more times. In other words, since it really is bad for welfare to be apportioned in accordance with R, the more times R is followed, the worse it is (unless later uses rectify earlier ones). Moreover, this is so whether R is repeatedly applied to the same individuals, or to different individuals.[8] But if this is right, then it would seem that B is worse than A, since in B it is as if R has been applied two million times, whereas in A it is as if R has been applied one million times.

Again, the point here can be ultimately couched in terms of the basic intuition underlying egalitarianism. I claim that the inequality between Tim1 and John1 will offend egalitarians because they regard it as bad for one person to be worse off than another through no fault of his or her own. But if it really is bad for Tim1 to be worse off than John1, then it should for the same reason be bad for Tim2 to be worse off than John2, and thus it should be even worse if, in addition to Tim1 being worse off than John1, Tim2 is worse off than John2. Extended, this reasoning leads straightforwardly to the judgments that B is worse than A and that proportional increases in population worsen inequality.

One way to put my point is that, in general, numbers count; this is true in most spheres of life, and morality is no exception.[9]

Consider again our earlier example of two societies, G and H, both of whose members were susceptible to polio. We saw that there is a sense in which we might judge G and H equivalent regarding illness, regardless of their respective sizes or even of the prevalence of polio within each society. Such a judgment would be based strictly on the *kinds* of illness in the societies—and, by analogy, we saw that a similar kind of judgment might be made regarding inequality. We also saw that in another sense we might judge that G was worse than H regarding illness, for example, if most of G's population was afflicted by illness but few in H's population were. Such a judgment would be a judgment about both the kind of illness in the societies and the relative prevalence of the illness—and again, by analogy, we saw that a similar kind of judgment might be made regarding inequality. But clearly, in yet *another* sense, and a crucially important one, we would judge the situation regarding illness to be worse in H than in G if there were *more* people with polio in H than in G. Such a judgment would reflect the view that, from one perspective at least, it would be better if all illness were eradicated in H rather than in G. Here, too, a similar kind of judgment might be made regarding inequality.

Suppose, for example, that G were the size of Haiti, and H the size of China. If 80 percent of G suffered from polio and 10 percent of H, then as we have seen there is a sense in which we might judge G and H equivalent, and another sense in which we might judge G worse than H. Still, as suggested above, there is a third sense in which we would judge H worse than G. After all, whereas in G four million would be ill, in H a hundred million would be ill. Given the choice between the eradication of all polio in G and the eradication of all polio in H, few would think we ought to flip a coin. Most would say that here, as elsewhere, numbers count, that other things being equal it is better to eradicate more illness rather than less.

I think similar considerations apply in the case of equality. If 80 percent of G and 10 percent of H were worse off than the better off by a certain amount, then as we have seen there is a sense in which we might judge G and H equivalent regarding inequality, and another sense in which we might judge G worse than H. Still, there is a third sense in which we should judge H worse than G. After all, whereas in G four million would be worse off than one million, in H more than a hundred million would be worse off than more than nine hundred million. Given the choice between eradicating all of G's inequality or all of H's, we ought not to flip a coin. Here, as elsewhere, numbers count.

Some will insist that equality is not bad in the same way illness is. More generally, they will insist that equality and utility are different *kinds* of moral ideals and that the two ideals can, and should, be treated differently. According to this view, that numbers count regarding utility is completely irrelevant to—that is, suggests *nothing* about—whether numbers count regarding equality. I sympathize with this view, which is why I have mainly tried to motivate my claims by appealing to elements internal to

Figure 9.2

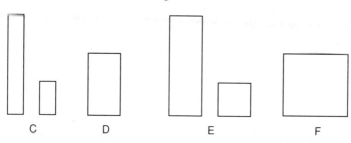

C   D   E   F

egalitarianism, for example, by showing how my claims reflect both the basic intuition underlying egalitarianism and particular aspects of inequality. Still, I am not sure that ultimately our moral ideals are isolated from one another in the way suggested. Depending on how moral ideals combine to yield all things considered judgments, at least some may need to share certain formal or structural features if we are to avoid unacceptable implications.

Consider figure 9.2. C represents an unequal society, D a perfectly equal society with less total utility. E and F are just like C and D, respectively, except they are twice as large. Looking at C and D, many would judge that D is better than C all things considered. They would judge the slight loss of utility in moving from C to D regrettable, but outweighed by the substantial gain in equality. Similarly, looking at E and F, many would judge that F is better than E all things considered. Again, they would judge the loss of utility in moving from E to F regrettable, but outweighed by the gain in equality. More important, few if any would approve a redistribution between the better off and the worse off in C so as to bring about D while opposing redistribution between the better off and the worse off in E so as to bring about F. That is, most would agree that *if* moving from C to D were desirable, then moving from E to F would also be desirable.

The foregoing claims may seem obvious and uninteresting, but they have important implications. Depending on how one thinks moral ideals combine to yield all things considered judgments, they can imply that if numbers count for utility, they must also count for equality. Suppose one thinks that the move from C to D is only a slight improvement all things considered, because the gain in equality is just *barely* enough to outweigh the attendant loss in utility.[10] Then it looks as if F would be *worse* than E if numbers count for utility but not for equality. After all, E and F are twice as large as C and D. This means that the loss in utility in moving from E to F will be twice as great as the loss in utility in moving from C to D, and hence, on the view in question, that the move from E to F will be much worse than the move from C to D regarding utility. Yet if numbers don't count for equality or, more specifically, if we accept P—the view that proportional increases do not affect inequality—then the gain in equality in moving from E to F will be exactly the same as the gain in equality in moving from C to D. But then it looks as if the gain in equality in moving from E to F *won't* be sufficient to outweigh the attendant loss in utility, since by hypothesis the gain in question is *barely* enough to outweigh a loss in utility that is only half as large. In sum, if moving from E to F is significantly worse than moving from C to D regarding utility, and no better regarding equality, then it is easy to see that all things considered moving from E to F could be undesirable even if moving from C to D were desirable.[11] But this, of course, is contrary to the "obvious and uninteresting" view noted above.

The preceding considerations suggest that perhaps different moral ideals cannot be fully and adequately characterized in isolation from one another. Specifically, a plausible and coherent account of the role moral ideals play in relation to one another and to our all things considered judgments may require that at least some ideals share certain formal or structural features. Thus if we want to hold on to the view that numbers count regarding utility, we may also have to be prepared to hold that numbers count regarding equality.

The foregoing result may be surprising, but I do not find it perplexing or disturbing. I accept the view that if moving from C to D were desirable, so too would be moving from E to F. I also accept the view that in an important sense moving from E to F would be worse than moving from C to D regarding utility. This leads me to believe there is an important sense in which moving from E to F would be better than moving from C to D regarding inequality. But, of course, this implies that E is worse than C regarding inequality, which in turn implies that there is reason to reject P and the judgment that A and B in figure 9.1 are equivalent regarding inequality.

Some people may continue to resist the conclusion that there is reason to reject P. The most natural way of resisting is to adopt *average* views regarding both utility and equality. According to an average view of utility, one society will be better than another regarding utility if the average level of utility is higher in one society than in the other. Similarly, on an average view of equality one society will be better than another regarding equality if the average level of equality is higher in one society than in the other—or, as I prefer to put it, if the average level of "complaint" that people have regarding inequality is smaller in one society than in the other.

Many find an average view of utility independently plausible and appealing. Many also find an average view of equality independently plausible and appealing. For example, many economists measure a society's inequality by adding up the gaps between the better off and the worse off (in one way or another) and then dividing that number by the society's size. In essence, such an approach can be seen as measuring the average level of inequality (or the average level of "complaint" regarding inequality). Surely, the prevalence of such approaches is no accident. Such measures are formulated to yield judgments about average levels of inequality precisely because many economists (and others) find it plausible to believe that one society will be better than another regarding inequality if the average level of inequality is smaller in one than in the other.[12]

Clearly, an average view of equality will support P. In addition, an average view of equality will combine with an average view of utility to support the intuitively plausible judgment about figure 9.2 that if moving from C to D were desirable, then moving from E to F would also be desirable. After all, the fact that E and F are twice the size of C and D will not affect how they compare in terms of average utility or equality. Correspondingly, the moves from E to F and C to D will involve the same size losses and gains in terms of average utility and equality.

Although average views have a fair amount of initial appeal, *at most* they offer further reasons for accepting P. They do not, I think, undermine the significant considerations for opposing that view. In any event, I think average views should be rejected. Let me explain why.

My first objection is to the average view of equality—specifically, to measuring inequality by dividing the total amount of a society's inequality by its size. To illustrate my objection it will be helpful to first consider a different position; one that is wildly implausible and which nobody advocates. I present it because I think its shortcomings are obvious and telling, and because I think that on reflection the average view of equality involves—though less starkly and hence less obviously—a similar shortcoming.

I believe that inequality matters more at low levels than at high levels in the following sense. A gap of 100 units between the best-off person and the worst-off person will matter more if the worst-off person is very poorly off, say at level 100, than if the worst-off person is very well off, say at level 100,000. One way of capturing such a view would be to measure inequality by measuring the gap between the best-off person and the worst-off person and then dividing that number by the level of the best-off person, where the larger the resultant number the worse the inequality. In the example suggested, the inequality in the first case would be $(200 - 100)/200 = 1/2$, whereas the inequality in the second case would be $(100,100 - 100,000)/100,100 = .000999$. Since $1/2 > .000999$, such an approach for measuring inequality, let us call it M, yields the intuitively plausible conclusion that the inequality between someone at level 100 and someone at level 200 is worse than that between someone at level 100,000 and someone at level 100,100.

Despite yielding the "correct" judgment regarding the above example, I think M is not a plausible way of capturing the view that inequality matters more at low levels than high levels. To see this, consider the following conversation between John and Tom. It concerns the transformation of C into D, where, for simplicity, C and D are two-person worlds. In C, Bob is at level 100 and Bill is at level 10,000, whereas in D, Bob is at level 100 and Bill is at level 100,000.

J: Poor Bob. He's so unlucky. It was bad enough when he was 9,900 units worse off than Bill through no fault of his own. Now he is 99,900 units worse off. I thought he had a great deal to complain about before, but compared to what he has to complain about *now* that seems trivial. The inequality *was* bad, now it's *outrageous*.

T: Calm down John. Although it's true the gap between Bob and Bill is now much larger than it was, you seem to be forgetting or ignoring the fact that Bill is now *much* better off. Before, Bill had only 10,000 units, now he has 100,000. Bearing this in mind, surely you can see that while Bob has a *bit* more to complain about now than he did before, he doesn't have too much more to complain about (before he had a complaint of .99, now he has just the slightly larger complaint of .999).

J: You can't *possibly* be serious! *Of course* I'm not forgetting or ignoring the fact that Bill is now much better off. It is *that very fact* that makes Bob's situation so much worse regarding inequality. You seem to think that somehow Bill's being better off mitigates the effect of the much larger gap between Bob and Bill. That's absurd! In the absence of an accompanying improvement in Bob's position, there is *no way* that an improvement in *Bill's* position could contribute—even partially or indirectly—to a lessening of Bob's complaint. To the

Figure 9.3

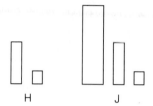

H   J

contrary, the vast improvement in Bill's position greatly and unequivocally increases Bob's complaint.

Suffice it to say, I side with John. It isn't, contrary to what M seems to
imply, that the adverse effects of Bill's improvement always outweigh
(though only slightly) the positive effects of that improvement. Rather,
there *are* no positive effects from Bill's improvement regarding inequality.
This is because there is *no* respect in which Bob fares better relative to
Bill in D than in C. The point here can be summed up as follows. M
measures inequality as if *even regarding inequality* there is a positive or
partially redeeming feature of the best-off person becoming even better
off (even in the absence of related gains to the worse off). Since this isn't
so, M seems inappropriate and implausible.

Bearing the inadequacy and implausibility of M in mind, let me return
now to the average view of inequality, according to which inequality
could be measured by dividing a society's total amount of inequality by
its population size. Suppose we came across a world, T, where some are
worse off than others. Suppose our initial observations reveal T to be
sharply divided into two groups, but that later we discover a third group,
larger and even better off than the rest, living a short distance away. So
our first picture of T resembles H, our revised picture resembles J (see
figure 9.3). How would the realization that T resembles J and not H
alter our view of T's inequality?

I claim that the presence of the third group clearly and unequivocally
worsens T's inequality. It is not as if, regarding inequality, the negative
features of the third group outweigh the positive ones. Rather, just as
there would be no positive effects from Bill's improvement in the above
example, so there would be no positive effects from the presence of the
third group on T's inequality.

What positive effects could there be? Presumably, we find T's inequality
objectionable even before discovering the third group's presence. And

presumably this is because we consider it bad for one group to be worse off than the other through no fault of its members. So then how could the discovery of a third group better off than the other two in any way mitigate T's inequality? Surely the presence of an even better off group could serve only to aggravate those features of T to which we originally objected.

The worse off in J fare just as badly relative to the group we had thought was best off as they did before we discovered the third group. It just turns out that in *addition* to being worse off than *that* group, there is another group they are even worse off than. Clearly, this can in no way make J's inequality less offensive than H's. But neither does the fact that the group we had thought was best off turns out not to be best off after all. This could only make the inequality seem even worse, since they, too, turn out to be worse off than others through no fault of their own.

The only other candidate for a feature in J not present in H that might mitigate J's inequality is the status of the third group itself. However, I fail to see how the existence of a group better off than anyone else, and hence with nothing to complain about regarding inequality, could in any way lessen the complaints of those less fortunate or otherwise ameliorate their world's inequality. This seems no more plausible than the contention that the seriousness of the larger gap between Bob and Bill, which results from the improvement in Bill's position, can be partially offset by Bill's now being much better off than he was before. To the contrary, it is precisely because Bill is much better off that Bob fares comparatively worse than he did before, and hence that the inequality is worse. Similarly, it is precisely because the third group is better off than the others that the two previously known groups fare even worse relative to the other members of their world than had been realized, and hence that T's inequality is worse than we first thought.

The upshot is that the economists' method of dividing the total amount of a society's inequality by the society's size is inappropriate and implausible. Such a method fails to properly reflect the unequivocal manner in which the presence of the third group worsens T's inequality, since the presence of that group would increase both the numerator and the denominator of the formula expressing that method. Thus, the problem with such a method isn't so much that it sometimes yields the wrong answer, but that even when it yields the right answer it measures inequality as if, even regarding inequality, there were a positive or a partially redeeming feature to one group being better off than all the others.

Average views also face other, better-known, shortcomings (see figure

Figure 9.4

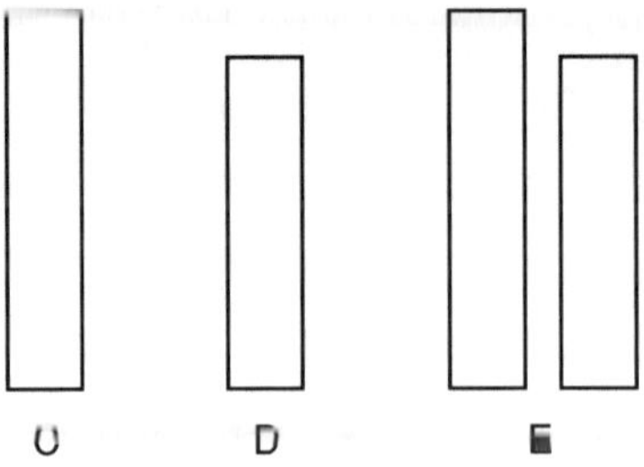

9.4). Let D represent a world where everyone is better off than today's best off, C a world where everyone is even better off, though not by a lot, and E a universe containing both C and D. Derek Parfit has argued that all things considered, E is not worse than C.[13] I think he is right. However, even if he is not, this much seems clear: it would be most implausible to contend that E's having a lower average level of utility than C gives one reason to maintain that E is worse than C. E does have a lower average level of utility. But this is so because E includes D *as well as* C, and it is difficult to see how the *mere addition* of a group of people, all of whom have lives that are exceedingly rich and who in no way lessen the quality of life for C's people, could *worsen* the situation solely by lowering the average level of utility.[14]

I am not denying that there may be plausible (even if not conclusive) reasons for ranking E worse than C; perhaps because E's worse off fare worse than C's do, or because E is unequal while C is not. Surely, however, the mere fact that E's average utility is lower than C's is not itself such a reason.

Let me be clear about the implications of the foregoing for the conflict between average utilitarianism (AVU) and total utilitarianism (TU). In claiming that E's lower average utility is not itself a reason to prefer C to E, I am not claiming that AVU is implausible as a moral theory (though I think it is), or even that it is less plausible than TU. However, I am implying that AVU lacks TU's intrinsic appeal. Let me explain.

I believe that the ultimate bedrock intuition underlying utilitarianism is that more of the good is better than less of the good. This is an extremely powerful intuition and one that supports TU. Thus it is no coincidence that the greatest and strongest advocates of utilitarianism— Bentham, Mill, and Sidgwick—were total utilitarians. Those men were pure utilitarians. They believed that in the end utility is all that matters— that all other ideals, such as liberty, justice, and equality, have value only because, and to the extent that, they promote utility. But clearly, if the bedrock intuition of utilitarianism is that more of the good is better than less of the good, then insofar as one is a utilitarian (that is, concerned strictly with utility), one will be, as each of those men was, a total utilitarian.

Average utilitarians might, of course, try to deny this. They might claim that AVU has just as much intrinsic appeal as TU. However, I fail to see the kind of powerful intuition(s) underlying AVU that clearly underlies TU. Thus even in cases where TU seems most implausible—because, unlike the pure utilitarian, one rejects the view that utility is all that matters— one can always feel the pull of TU, the force of the claim that more of the good is better than less of the good. The same cannot be said for AVU. In cases where AVU seems most implausible—for instance, when it implies that a world where a few are exceedingly well-off would be better than a world where many are just as well-off and others are almost, though not quite, as well-off—it seems completely devoid of intrinsic appeal. So the problem with AVU is not just that in such cases it yields an implausible judgment as to which world is better, rather, there is simply no force to the average utilitarian claim as to *why* the one world is better. Yes, it has a higher average level of utility. So what?

I think, then, that insofar as one is a utilitarian one should be a total utilitarian. As indicated above, however, it does not follow that TU is more plausible than AVU all things considered. Since utility is not all that matters, it could be that AVU's judgments correspond to our all things considered judgments more adequately than TU's. Whether this is so (and I doubt that it is), AVU is perhaps best regarded not as a principle reflecting our utilitarian intuitions but rather as a compromise of sorts between those intuitions and others. Not surprisingly, it is not the best such compromise that we could find.[15]

Similar remarks can be made about negative utilitarianism. The negative utilitarian believes both that disutility is bad and that disutility is all that matters. Naturally, I believe that the negative utilitarian is wrong in thinking that disutility is all that matters. But that is not my present concern. My present concern is to point out that insofar as one is a negative utilitarian one should be a total negative utilitarian and not an average negative utilitarian.

Consider again figure 9.4. This time, let D represent a world where there is tremendous disutility. In fact, imagine that each person in D is worse off than any person who has ever lived, well below the level at which life ceases to be worth living. Let C be a world where everyone

Figure 9.5

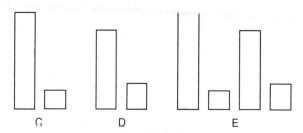

C   D   E

is even worse off—though not by a lot—and E the universe containing both C and D. Surely negative utilitarians would want to say that D represents a terrible situation, and C an even worse one. But then it seems clear that negative utilitarians would also want to say that E is worse than C, since in E there is far more of what negative utilitarians regard as bad than there is in C.[16]

Of course, average negative utilitarians might try to resist this conclusion. They might contend that negative utilitarians should be concerned with the average amount of disutility, and that as such E would be better than C. But this seems implausible. Why should E's lower average level of disutility make E more palatable to someone concerned about disutility, when the only reason it *has* that lower average is that it contains D *as well as* C? How could the mere addition of such a group really improve the situation, especially in the eyes of those who think that disutility is bad and that disutility is all that matters? I think it could not.

Again, as with regular utilitarianism, average negative utilitarianism might accord better with our all things considered judgments than total negative utilitarianism does (though I think this is most unlikely, and that neither would fare very well). Still, once one considers what it is that makes one a negative utilitarian in the first place—that is, once one gets clear on the basic intuitions underlying negative utilitarianism—it becomes evident that insofar as one is a negative utilitarian, average negative utilitarianism has nothing to commend it.

It should now be even clearer why egalitarians should reject measures of inequality that focus on a situation's average inequality (see figure 9.5). Let D represent a world where the gap between the better off and the worse off is very large, C a world where the gap between the better off and the worse off is even larger, and E the universe containing both. Two things seem clear. First, on certain aspects of inequality, for example the additive principle and the relative to the best-off person view of complaints, E's average level of inequality is lower than C's. Second, that fact alone is not *itself* reason to think that E is better than C regarding inequality. Suppose, for instance, that D's inequality is worse than the most extreme inequality on earth today. Since egalitarians regard inequality as bad, naturally they would regard D's situation as very bad. But the question then can be forcefully asked: how could the mere fact that on certain aspects E's average level of inequality is lower than C's make E more palatable to someone concerned about inequality, when the only reason it *has* that lower average is that it contains D *as well as* C?

Again, I am not claiming anything about how E and C compare all things considered. For that matter, I am not even claiming that there is no reason for *egalitarians* to prefer E to C. What I am claiming is that (1) given that egalitarians regard inequality as bad, that (2) egalitarians will thus regard both C and D as very bad, and that (3) E involves the *mere addition* of D to C, surely it is implausible to contend that egalitarians would find E's inequality preferable to C's insofar as, and simply because, on certain aspects it has a lower average level of inequality.

Here as elsewhere one must begin by focusing on what egalitarians care about if one wants to determine how E and C compare regarding inequality. Having done this one will see, I think, that although in accordance with certain egalitarian intuitions E would be better than C, in accordance with others (in fact most) E would be worse. So, for instance, E would be worse according to the intuitions underlying the additive principle and the relative to the best-off person view of complaints. This is because those intuitions reflect the egalitarian's concern for how *each* person compares to the best-off person. More particularly, they reflect the views that (1) it is bad for one person to be worse off than another through no fault of his or her own, (2) the size of someone's complaint depends on how that person fares relative to the best-off person, and (3) it is worse if in addition to *one* person being worse off than another through no fault of his or her own, there are others who are *also* in such a position.

Ultimately, then, an average view is no more plausible for egalitarianism than for utilitarianism or negative utilitarianism. One cannot defend P by invoking an average view of inequality and combining it with an average view of utility for cases like those depicted in figure 9.2.

It should now be clear why, at the beginning of this section, I stated that the issue of how variations in population size affect inequality is a complicated one that can only be resolved with careful deliberation. Even if some of the specific claims of this section are controversial, I hope I have convinced the reader that the Standard View can no longer be assumed without argument and probably needs to be revised or replaced.

Let me close this section with the following observation. Any answer to the question of how, if at all, variations in population size affect inequality will have significant practical implications regarding intergenerational inequality and obligations toward other generations. It will be relevant to whether we should strive for increases or decreases in the size of the better and worse-off groups of future generations (as well as in their levels). Moreover, this will be relevant both for our assessment of the inequality within the future generations themselves, and for our assessment of the inequality between the future generations and other generations. I trust this point is evident, and that its importance for the egalitarian needs no elaboration or defense.

Inequality and a Question about Scope

In this section, I want to consider an issue Dennis McKerlie raised in a fascinating article on equality and time.[17] Roughly, the issue concerns whether the proper unit of egalitarian concern should be people's lives taken as a whole, or selected portions of their lives.[18]

Most people implicitly assume that insofar as one is an egalitarian one should be what McKerlie calls a *complete lives* egalitarian. As its name suggests, on a complete lives view the proper units of egalitarian concern are the complete lives of individuals. Thus, according to a complete lives view, an egalitarian should be concerned about A's being worse off than B to the extent, and only to the extent, that A's life, taken as a complete whole, is worse than B's, taken as a complete whole.

McKerlie points out, correctly, that although complete lives egalitarianism is commonly accepted, it is only one of a number of views an egalitarian might adopt regarding the proper units of egalitarian concern. Other views include what McKerlie calls *simultaneous segments* egalitarianism and *corresponding segments* egalitarianism. Basically, a simultaneous segments egalitarian would divide history into a series of temporal stages, say, twenty years each, and measure inequality in terms of the inequalities obtaining between people's lives within the same temporal stages; while a corresponding segments egalitarian would divide each person's life into a series of stages, for example, childhood, early adulthood, middle age, and old age, and measure inequality in terms of the inequalities between

Figure 9.6

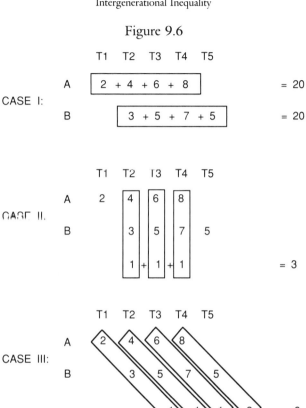

the comparable stages of people's lives. These views may be illustrated diagrammatically.

In figure 9.6, T1–T5 are temporal segments of twenty years each. A and B are two people, each of whom lives eighty years and whose lives are divided into four twenty-year segments. The numbers next to A and B represent how well they fare during the different segments of their lives, which correspond to the temporal segments T1–T5. Since A lives from T1 through T4, there is no number for A under T5.[19] Similarly, since B—born twenty years later than A—lives from T2 through T5, there is no number for B under T1. Obviously, our diagram implicitly makes a large number of simplifying assumptions, for example, that we can assign a number corresponding to the quality, or utility, in each segment of someone's life. For the purposes of discussion, we shall also assume a simple additive model for measuring quality of life, according to which the overall quality, or utility, of someone's life is a direct additive function of the utility of that person's life's segments.[20] Though unrealistic and implausible, our simplifying assumptions merely enable us to illuminate the views under discussion in a clear straightforward way. They do not affect the substance of our conclusions.

Supposing that a score of 2 represents a very poor quality of life and a score of 8 a very high quality of life, figure 9.6 indicates that the quality of A's life was very poor during the first segment of her life and very high during the last segment of her life, and that each segment of her life was better than the previous one. No segment of B's life was either as poor or as good, respectively, as the first and last segments of A's life, but the overall quality of A's and B's lives were equivalent.[11] During each temporal segment they were contemporaries (T2–T4) B was worse off than A. Moreover, although B was better off during the first three segments of her life than A was during the corresponding segments of her life, B was worse off during the fourth segment of her life than A was during the corresponding segment of her life. Most important, for our present purposes, figure 9.6 illustrates the three approaches discussed above for measuring the inequality between A and B. Specifically, Cases I, II, and III illustrate how one might compare A and B regarding inequality in terms of, respectively, complete lives, simultaneous segments, and corresponding segments egalitarianism. On complete lives egalitarianism there would be no objectionable inequality between A and B, since their lives are equivalent in overall quality. On both simultaneous and corresponding segments egalitarianism there would be objectionable inequality between A and B, corresponding, respectively, to the extent of the differences in quality between the simultaneous and corresponding segments of their lives. Specifically, on simultaneous segments egalitarianism there would be a total of three units of inequality between A and B, and on corresponding segments egalitarianism there would be a total of six units of inequality between A and B.

I believe each of the three views regarding the proper unit of egalitarian concern may seem plausible in some cases, and implausible in others. In illustrating this, let me begin with an example intended to cast doubt on the adequacy of the standard view, complete lives egalitarianism. This is a hypothetical conversation between the Devil and God pertaining to God's treatment of two of his servants, Job1 and Job2.

D: I see you have finally seen the dark.

G: What do you mean?

D: I am talking about your treatment of Job1 and Job2, whom I have been watching, with amazement, for forty years now. So far as I can tell, Job1 and Job2 are equally deserving in every relevant way imaginable, yet Job1's life has been filled with all the blessings life can bestow and Job2 is utterly wretched. Thus while Job1 has complete inner peace, accompanied by the total fulfillment of his desires and plans, Job2 is a penniless beggar sleeping fitfully in the streets, whose plans and desires are constantly frustrated.

G (somewhat impatiently): I know the condition of my faithful servants Job1 and Job2, and they *are* equally deserving! So what? Exactly what is it about their condition you find so disturbing?

D: Nothing. That's the point! I have obviously misunderstood and underestimated you. I thought you would have treated both like Job1. And, simpleton that I am, I would have treated both like Job2. But what you have done is create a situation *dripping* with injustice by treating two equally deserving people so *grossly* unequally . . . it really is *exquisitely* devilish.

G: Bah! You once again display your limited powers. The situation is not "dripping" with injustice, because the "gross" inequality you see is a mere temporary phenomenon, a misleading appearance that arises because you see only a part of the picture. If, like me, you saw the whole picture, you would realize that Job1's and Job2's situations will be reversed during the second half of their lives, so that in fact the overall quality of their lives, taken as a whole, will be *completely* equal.

D (grinning broadly, knowing he's won): Bravo! You really *are* the Master. I couldn't have given a better answer myself.

God's treatment of Job1 and Job2 exemplifies what McKerlie called "changing places egalitarianism." Like McKerlie (and the Devil!), I reject the implication of whole lives egalitarianism. That is, that in a situation involving differential treatments of equally deserving people—no matter how significant, sustained, widespread, systematic, and even perverse those differing treatments are—there can be no egalitarian objection as long as the roles of the equally deserving people are interchanged so that each receives an equivalent share of the treatments meted out. In addition to whatever other objections one might have to God's treatment of Job1 and Job2, I find the first forty years of inequality between Job1 and Job2

Figure 9.7

		T1	T2	T3	T4		
	A	8 + 8 + 2 + 2					= 20
CASE IV:							
	B	2 + 2 + 8 + 8					= 20

		T1	T2	T3	T4		
	A	5 + 5 + 5 + 5					= 20
CASE V:							
	B	5 + 5 + 5 + 5					= 20

objectionable. I think it is unfair or unjust for Job2 to be so much worse off than Job1 through no fault of his own, and my objection to the unequal situation does not disappear (though it is, to some extent, altered)[22] when I learn that Job1 will subsequently be worse off than Job2 to an equivalent degree.

That Job1 will be much worse off than Job2 during the second half of their lives is not irrelevant to my assessment of the inequality obtaining between them during the first half of their lives (see below), but neither does the later inequality simply cancel out or remove the objectionable character of the earlier inequality. I think *both* periods of inequality are objectionable, whether considered separately or together. In sum, even looking at the whole picture I think God's treatment of Job1 and Job2 could be criticized on egalitarian grounds, and I think it is a shortcoming of the whole lives view that it is unable to accommodate this.

Some object to examples involving God. But there are analogous examples of changing places egalitarianism that would be wholly social in character and origin. A caste system involving systematic and substantial biases toward, and differential treatment of, the members of different castes might be objectionable on egalitarian grounds *even if* the demographic composition of the castes periodically changed so that each person was a member of each caste and the overall quality of each life was equivalent.[23]

Let me illustrate the point I have been making (see figure 9.7; recall that 2 represents a very poor quality of life, and 8 a very high quality of life). On the complete lives view, in Case IV it doesn't matter that B, through no fault of his own, was significantly worse off than A for half

Figure 9.8

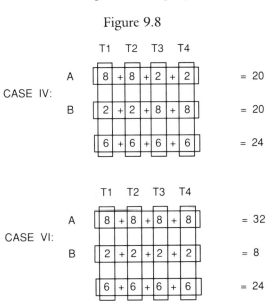

his life. Nor does it matter that A, through no fault of his own, was significantly worse off than B for half his life. All that matters, on the complete lives view, is that taken as a complete whole the overall quality of the two halves of A's and B's lives was the same. Thus on complete lives egalitarianism there is no reason to prefer Case V to Case IV, and this is so even though throughout their lives A and B were perfectly equal in Case V and significantly unequal in Case IV. This conclusion is hard to accept.

Clearly, both a simultaneous segments view and a corresponding segments view would judge Case IV's inequality worse than Case V's. Measuring A and B's inequality as a function of the inequality between their simultaneous and corresponding segments, the two views will be extensionally equivalent for cases like IV and V.[24] Measuring inequality along the lines suggested by figure 9.6, on each view Case V would receive a perfect score of 0 and Case IV a (relatively high) score of 24.

Should the whole lives view be rejected entirely and replaced by some combination of the simultaneous and corresponding segments views? I think not. Each of the other views also has implausible implications. Indeed, in some cases the judgments of the simultaneous and corresponding segments views seem less plausible than the judgment yielded by the whole lives view (see figure 9.8). According to both the simultaneous and the corresponding segments view, Case IV's inequality will be as bad as Case VI's. On the whole lives view, Case VI's inequality will be worse than Case IV's. Even if one believes Case IV's inequality is objectionable, it is hard to believe that it is *just* as objectionable as Case VI's. However bad it may be for one person to be much worse off than another half his life, and much better off the other half, it seems far worse for one person to be much worse off than the other for his entire life.

Consider the following. Suppose one were forced to choose between two severe caste systems, the only difference between them being that people in the first would occupy but one caste their entire lives, and people in the second would occupy each caste equally over the course of their lives. As objectionable as both caste systems might be, surely most egalitarians would prefer the second to the first. Although any caste system that distributes undeserved benefits and burdens so that some live like kings while others live like paupers would be objectionable, it would be more objectionable if the same people always received benefits and others always received burdens, than if all shared, in turn, both benefits and burdens.

On both simultaneous and corresponding segments views, how two people have compared in the past is *completely* irrelevant to whether it would be better for one of them to be better off than the other in the future. This seems implausible, and to the extent it does the whole lives view may seem attractive. But note that it is not obvious how an egalitarian should count past inequalities between contemporaries.

Suppose that for the first half of their lives A has been the beneficiary and B the victim of a severe caste system such that, on our scale, they have been at levels 8 and 2, respectively. Other things being equal, should an egalitarian favor retaining the severe caste system but reversing A's and B's places within it, so that for the second half of their lives they would be at levels 2 and 8, respectively? This is what a whole lives view would seem to imply, since the overall quality of A's and B's lives would then be equal. Or should the egalitarian favor removing the caste system entirely, so that for the second half of their lives both A and B would be at level 5? This is what the simultaneous and corresponding segments views would seem to imply, since it would minimize the overall extent of any inequality between the relevant segments of A's and B's lives. Such a position has an intuitively attractive purity. If an inegalitarian system is truly objectionable, shouldn't an egalitarian clearly and unequivocally oppose and seek to dismantle it, rather than favor its perpetuation with a different set of victims? But of course purity is not

Figure 9.9

		T1	T2	T3	T4
	A	8	8	2	2
CASE IV:					
	B	2	2	8	8

		T1	T2	T3	T4	T5	T6
	A	8	8	2	2		
CASE VII:							
	B			2	2	8	8

always a virtue in the complex world of morality. And it has long been recognized that an egalitarian may have to permit, and even require, certain inequalities—say, present, short-term, or income inequalities— to reduce or remove other more objectionable inequalities—say, future, long-term, or welfare inequalities. Or should the egalitarian support a system that would favor B over A during the second half of their lives, but not as strongly as the original caste system favored A over B? Perhaps B should be raised to level 6 or 7, and A reduced to level 4 or 3. Such a position might appear to be a plausible compromise, favoring the amelioration of inegalitarian systems without simply ignoring how people have compared in the past.

As with other questions raised in this chapter, several answers are possible to the question of how one should count past inequalities between contemporaries. Different answers may seem plausible depending on one's views regarding the proper unit of egalitarian concern, and of course, conversely, one's views regarding the proper unit of egalitarian concern may in turn be influenced by the plausibility of the answers they yield.

I have considered several examples where simultaneous and corresponding segments egalitarianism would be extensionally equivalent. But they are different views, which will yield different judgments about many cases. Thus, granting that there are cases where the whole lives view seems implausible, one still needs to determine whether one is being influenced by the simultaneous segments view or the corresponding segments view or both (or some other view[s] entirely). Toward this end, consider figure 9.9. Case IV is familiar from figures 9.7 and 9.8. As seen earlier, the simultaneous and corresponding segments views agree with each other, and oppose the whole lives view, in judging Case IV's inequality objectionable. Case VII is just like Case IV, except that B was born forty years later. Does this make no difference, some difference, or all the difference regarding whether there is objectionable inequality between A and B?

Cases IV and VII would be judged equivalent on the whole lives view. Both would be perfect regarding inequality. Cases IV and VII would also be judged equivalent on the corresponding segments view. Both would be equally objectionable. Cases IV and VII would be judged differently on the simultaneous segments view. Whereas Case IV's inequality would be considered objectionable, Case VII would be deemed perfect regarding inequality. This suggests the following. If one thinks that Cases IV and VII are both objectionable regarding inequality, and *equally* so, one probably accepts the corresponding segments view and completely rejects the simultaneous segments view. If one thinks that Cases IV and VII are both objectionable, but that Case IV's inequality is worse, one is probably influenced by both the corresponding and the simultaneous segments view. If one thinks that Case IV is objectionable, but that Case VII is not, one probably accepts the simultaneous segments view and completely rejects the corresponding segments view.[25]

I have discussed three views regarding the proper unit of egalitarian concern.[26] Variations of these views are possible, as their spirit might be interpreted or their details developed in ways other than those suggested here. Entirely different views may also be possible. The point of my discussion has not been to provide a definitive and exhaustive account of the proper unit of egalitarian concern. Nor has it been to establish that the standard complete lives view is less plausible than a simultaneous or a corresponding segments view, much less that a complete lives view should be rejected in favor of one or both of the other views. Rather, it has been to suggest that there is no simple, clear, or obvious account to be given. Several views may seem plausible, each of which faces numerous complexities and problems (including many not even touched on here).[27] Moreover, as my discussion of figures 9.6 through 9.9 indicates, whatever view (or combination of views) one ultimately adopts regarding the proper unit of egalitarian concern will have important implications regarding the nature, extent, and significance of intergenerational inequalities.

Let me conclude this section with two observations regarding the practical significance of our results. First, on a simultaneous segments view inequality matters only between contemporaries, that is, between the simultaneous segments of overlapping generations. Correspondingly, inequality will matter within, but not between, past, present, and future (nonoverlapping) generations. So, for example, to the extent that a simultaneous segments view seems plausible, vast consumption of the world's resources would be objectionable if, other things being equal, it had an adverse effect on inequality within the present generation or within some other generation, but it would not be objectionable if its effect was "merely" to leave the present generation much better off than either past or future ones.

Second, different views about the proper unit of egalitarian concern may have direct implications for the moral desirability of transfers between overlapping generations, for example, between the young and the old. Do we think the elderly are better off than the young? Even if they are financially better off, is this enough to offset losses in hearing, eyesight, memory, health, and loved ones? If not, then insofar as a position like simultaneous segments egalitarianism is plausible, someone who cares about equality of welfare will favor transfers from the young to the old. On either the whole lives view or the corresponding segments view, however, even if we think today's elderly are significantly worse off than today's young, that by itself will tell us nothing about the moral desirability of transfers between the young and the old. To the contrary, both views might support transfers from the elderly to the young, even if the elderly are currently much worse off than the young. Clearly, on the whole lives view the relevant question regarding the moral desirability of transfers between the young and the old will not be how the two groups compare now, but how they compare over the course of their lives. Similarly, on the corresponding segments view the relevant question will not be how today's elderly compare to today's young, but rather, to put it roughly, how today's elderly compare to tomorrow's elderly and how today's young compare to yesterday's young.

One can see, then, how an egalitarian view about the desirability of exchanges between the young and the old will depend on both the proper unit of egalitarian concern and empirical facts about how the young and old compare with respect to that concern. If more than one view is plausible regarding the proper unit of egalitarian concern, then several egalitarian reasons may be relevant to the desirability of exchanges between young and old. And these reasons may or may not support the same conclusion.

This section also has other interesting implications for such topics as transitivity and temporal neutrality. Though I cannot pursue these issues here, I hope to return to them on another occasion.

For much of human history the topic of obligations toward other generations remained largely unexplored. The biblical injunction to "be fruitful and multiply" represented the principal, if not sole, obligation people recognized toward other generations. Limits on the earth's capacity to sustain succeeding generations at increasingly high levels had not yet been reached. Correspondingly, people saw increases in population size as wholly good and were blissfully unaware of the serious possibility of intergenerational conflicts of interest.

This rosy picture drastically changed, of course, thanks in no small part to the gloomy Malthusian predictions of the "inevitable" catastrophic consequences of unrestrained population growth—predictions that gave economics its apt moniker "the dismal science." Malthus's predictions, together with a deteriorating environment and other events, forced a rethinking of the naive view that larger populations are always preferable to smaller ones. Now, the nature of our obligations toward future generations is a matter of earnest debate.

Unfortunately, but not surprisingly, most debates about obligations toward other generations have involved the "ideal" size of future generations and have focused on broadly utilitarian concerns. People have wondered under what circumstances having more people would be better than having fewer. Will this be true when there is more *total* utility, or when there is more *average* utility? Will it be true if there is no one for whom the larger population would be worse, or if each person in the larger population is better off than each person in the smaller population, or, perhaps, if for each person in the smaller population there is a corresponding person in the larger population who is better off (though others in the larger population may be worse off than those in the smaller population, making the larger population's average lower than the smaller population's)?

Such questions have preoccupied contemporary philosophers regarding our obligations toward other generations. And they are as significant as they are vexing. But other vexing questions also need addressing, including questions about justice and equality, and they are as important and fundamental as the ideals they concern.

In this chapter I have raised several questions relevant to intergenerational inequality, questions about whether size affects inequality and about the proper unit of egalitarian concern. I have argued that certain widely held views on these topics need serious revision and that my questions do not admit of obvious or easy answers. More specifically, I have shown that to answer my questions a number of complex, difficult, and often conflicting considerations will need to be assessed.

The issue of obligations between generations cannot be fully resolved—or resolved in any plausible way—in the absence of a careful and sustained inquiry into the topic of intergenerational justice. Moreover, an adequate account of intergenerational justice will require as one of its central components a thoughtful and systematic treatment of the topic of intergenerational inequality. Nothing remotely resembling such a treatment has been afforded to date. Until it is, our understanding of the nature and extent of our obligations toward other generations will be incomplete and woefully inadequate. Indeed, I believe our current understanding of such issues will require major practical and theoretical revisions in the light of a satisfactory account of intergenerational inequality.

Notes

1. Temkin, "Inequality."
2. These include the range, the relative mean deviation, the variance, the coefficient of variation, the standard deviation of the logarithm, and the gini coefficient. For useful discussion of the statistical measures, see Sen, *On Economic Inequality.* See also my *Inequality.*
3. A measure that is invariant if the levels of the better off and worse off increase proportionally would say, for example, that a situation where the better- and worse-off groups were at levels 100 and 10, respectively, was equivalent regarding inequality to one where the better- and worse-off groups were at levels 1,000 and 100, respectively. Such measures are sometimes referred to as "mean-independent," or, technically, as "invariant under affine transformations." In *Inequality,* I argue that mean-independence is not a desirable feature for a measure of inequality.
4. These aspects, like the other aspects of inequality discussed in this chapter, are more fully presented—and defended—in "Inequality" and *Inequality.*
5. I here assume that the inequality between the blind and the sighted is worse than that between the deaf and those with hearing, which in turn is worse than that between those who limp and those who don't. Anyone denying this assumption should revise the example accordingly.
6. The positions mentioned here are characterized and defended in "Inequality" as well as in *Inequality.*
7. This is not to say that I believe two applications of the rule are necessarily twice as bad as one, only that two are *worse* than one.
8. I am not claiming that both kinds of repeated applications would be equally bad, just that both would be bad.

9. John Taurek explicitly denies that numbers should count in his rich and widely discussed article "Should the Numbers Count?" Others who raise serious questions about whether numbers count in all cases include Bernard Williams and Elizabeth Anscombe. See the concluding comments of "2. The structure of consequentialism," in Williams's "A Critique of Utilitarianism," and Anscombe's "Modern Moral Philosophy."

Despite such writings, most people accept the view that numbers count in the moral realm, and I think they are right in doing so (even though I also think there are good reasons to believe that numbers probably do not count in the simple additive way most have implicitly assumed). Other things being equal, more pains are worse than fewer pains, more infringements of liberty are worse than fewer infringements of liberty, more injustices or inequalities are worse than fewer injustices or inequalities. Even deontologists can accept such claims, though they deny that we ought, morally, to always maximize the good or minimize the bad.

10. If this doesn't seem plausible for C and D as drawn, imagine them redrawn (along with E and F) so that it would seem plausible. That is, imagine the level of those in D lowered (or raised?) further, so that the loss of utility in moving from C would be greater than that suggested by figure 9.2—indeed, just enough so that the loss in utility would be barely outweighed by the gain in equality. I presume, of course, that someone who genuinely cares about both equality and utility will want to permit *some* losses regarding either of the ideals in exchange for "sufficient" gains regarding the other.

11. This argument is powerful, but not conclusive. David Aman has pointed out that one could avoid its implications by adopting a multiplicative function for moral ideals rather than an additive one. For example, instead of adding together numbers representing how good situations are regarding utility and equality in order to arrive at one's all things considered judgment, one might multiply the relevant numbers. Though such a move accommodates what many would (at least initially) want to say about the particular situations in question, I am not sure it can be independently motivated or ultimately defended. Prima facie, at least, it strikes me as odd, implausible, and ad hoc to contend that how good a situation is all things considered will depend on, among other things, how good it is regarding utility *times* how good it is regarding equality. Nonetheless, the suggestion is worth pursuing since there are serious difficulties with the more natural and intuitively appealing additive approach.

12. There is some logical tension between the claim made here and my earlier observation that many economists may be primarily concerned about social inequality. The tension is reduced, however, if one adds the implicit psychological assumption that a society's average level of inequality is generally correlated with the society's principles and institutions affecting inequality.

13. See Parfit's discussion "The Mere Addition Paradox" (esp. pp. 158–159), in "Future Generations."

14. Thus far the argument is taken straight from Parfit. Moreover, I follow Parfit's presentation when I advocate analogous positions in the ensuing discussion.

15. The best such compromise won't be found by looking for a simple method, like AVU, which just happens to correspond to our considered judgments. Instead, we must first get clear about the ideals we value, next come up with a measure for each ideal, and then decide how much to weight them. Only then would we be in a position to devise a (no doubt complex and partially incomplete) measure that plausibly combined each of our ideals, according each its due weight. As the preceding discussion suggests, such a measure would, I think, give weight to TU, but not to AVU.

16. This example closely parallels Parfit's example of Hell Three in *Reasons and Persons*, 422. I wrote this several years before the publication of Parfit's book, but he and I have had many discussions about these topics, and I am afraid I no longer remember whether I developed this example independently of Parfit or in collaboration with him, or whether here, as so often elsewhere, I am simply indebted to him for bringing this point to my attention.

17. McKerlie, "Equality and Time."

18. Many would regard this as a false dichotomy. They would insist that the proper unit of egalitarian concern is *society*. This holistic—as opposed to individualistic—view of equality is widely held, but I think it is deeply mistaken and shall not consider it in this chapter. My reasons for rejecting a holistic view of equality in favor of an individualistic one are given in my forthcoming book, *Inequality*.

19. One might think a zero should appear rather than nothing where nonexistence is involved. Doing so would not affect our subsequent discussion regarding whole lives or corresponding segments egalitarianism, but would make a difference regarding simultaneous segments egalitarianism. However, I think putting a zero where nonexistence is involved would strongly conflict with the spirit of simultaneous segments egalitarianism and yield highly implausible implications. Hence I shall not pursue this line in this chapter. Those who think there *should* be a zero instead of nothing where nonexistence is involved obviously would need to revise my discussion accordingly.

20. For example, if like A, the "scores" of the segments of someone's life are 2, 4, 6, and 8, the score corresponding to the overall quality of that life is 20, and the overall quality of that life is equivalent to that of someone whose four segments received, respectively, scores of 5, 5, 5, and 5, or for that matter, 8, 6, 4, and 2. Now, in fact, I think the simple additive model is seriously deficient and that the sequence 2, 4, 6, 8 is much preferable to the sequence 8, 6, 4, 2, even if the total amount of utility in the two lives is identical. But in this chapter I want to leave aside any possible objections to the additive model for assessing the overall quality of someone's life. To be sure, doing this runs a certain risk, since some of the intuitions and judgments discussed below may be influenced by one's views regarding the limitations of the additive model. Still, assuming a simple additive model greatly facilitates the discussion, and with care we should be able to prevent our simplifying assumption from leading us astray. More particularly, it should be apparent that the conclusions I shall be arguing for could be reached even by adopting a more complex and realistic view regarding how best to judge the overall quality of a life.

21. Recall that for the sake of this chapter I am assuming a simple additive view, where the overall quality of someone's life will be a straightforward additive function of the quality of the different segments of that person's life. So for both A and B the score representing the overall quality of their lives is 20. (See note 20.)

22. The importance of this qualification will become clearer below.

23. This point is reminiscent of one made by John Schaar in "Equality of Opportunity and Beyond." Schaar argued that complete equality of opportunity might succeed in altering the demographic composition of society's groups—, for example, more blacks and women might be doctors and more white males might be garbage collectors—yet do little or nothing to alter the basic social and economic inequalities between doctors and garbage collectors that many find objectionable.

24. This follows from our earlier assumptions about what is to count as simultaneous and corresponding segments in our examples.

25. Note that, depending on their clarity and certainty, one's judgments about examples like figure 9.9 might be indicative of a number of positions one might hold. If one thinks that Cases IV and VII are clearly and unequivocally perfect regarding inequality, for example, one probably accepts the whole lives view and completely rejects the other two views. If one thinks that Cases IV and VII are clearly and unequivocally objectionable regarding inequality, one probably accepts the corresponding segments view and completely rejects the others. If one thinks that Case IV is clearly and unequivocally objectionable regarding inequality, but that Case VII is clearly and unequivocally perfect regarding inequality, one probably accepts the simultaneous segments view and completely rejects the others. If one thinks there is *no* difference between Cases IV and VII regarding inequality but is ambivalent about them—in the sense that one feels pulled toward thinking both that their inequalities are perfect and that they are objectionable— one probably attaches some weight to both the complete lives and corresponding segments views, but no weight to the simultaneous segments view. If one thinks that Case IV is clearly and unequivocally objectionable regarding inequality but is ambivalent about Case VII, one probably attaches some weight to both the simultaneous and the corresponding segments view, but no weight to the complete lives view. If one thinks that Case VII is clearly and unequivocally perfect regarding inequality but is ambivalent about Case IV, one probably attaches some weight to both the complete lives and the simultaneous segments view, but no weight to the corresponding segments view. Finally, if one thinks that Cases IV and VII are not equivalent regarding inequality and that neither is clearly and unequivocally perfect or clearly and unequivocally objectionable, this may be because one is influenced by all three of the different views regarding the proper unit of egalitarian concern.

26. It is perhaps worth stressing that the three views I have discussed are completely independent of one another in the sense that each of their judgments may be in agreement or disagreement, depending on the particular case in question. Thus, depending on the situations, all three of the views may concur in their judgments,

any two of the views may concur with each other and oppose the third, or all three may disagree.

27. In "Inequality" I discussed numerous complexities involved in the notion of inequality. In that article I implicitly assumed a whole lives view, but most of the questions and issues raised there would apply, mutatis mutandis, to simultaneous or corresponding segments views. For example, according to a simultaneous segments view, should one determine the size of someone's complaint during a given segment of her life by comparing the quality of her life during that segment to the quality of the person who is best off during that segment, or to the average quality of life during that segment, or to the quality of life of each of the others who are better off than she during that segment? Similarly, in assessing how bad the inequality during a temporal segment is, should one adopt something like a maximin principle, an additive principle, or a weighted additive principle of equality? (See "Inequality" for a characterization of these different views and principles, and the considerations that might be adduced in their favor.) In addition to the problems and complexities raised in "Inequality," it is not clear on the simultaneous and corresponding segments views what grounds are to be employed for arriving at "appropriate" segments for comparison. Selecting certain segments will produce wildly implausible implications, but other segments may seem arbitrary and ad hoc. Also, as McKerlie notes, advocates of the different views will need to consider the problem of quality versus quantity for lives or segments of unequal duration.

X

Generations, Justice, and the Future of Collective Action

DAVID THOMSON

Modern welfare states have evolved a mythology for themselves that is about to unravel. A blinkered, protective, and self-justifying complex of values, beliefs, ideologies, records, and analytical approaches has served for half a century to keep us from recognizing the highly inequitable and unsustainable character of much of what has been going on. The people at large, in my own country of New Zealand anyway, are beginning to recognize the hollowness, the injustice, the "living on borrowed time" of it all—well before most scholars of the subject. There seems to me to be a real danger of scholars' being sidelined by fast-moving events, of being regarded as perpetrators of the myths that have allowed late-twentieth-century welfare states to assume dangerously unbalanced proportions. In this essay the use of contentious terms is deliberate. I want to set a provocative tone, to emphasize that if we are to grasp what is agitating our society, we must be prepared to think afresh in difficult and painful areas. Generation is an emotional and divisive issue, and we shall have to grapple with it.

In the 1990s and beyond, the meaning and achievement of social policy in contemporary societies may well come in for a bitter reconsideration, perhaps resentful reconsideration. Populations will come to recognize that collective action for welfare has not worked as they had supposed it would. What will have to be discussed, I believe, is something hitherto unthinkable for most: does such collective action have a future? More specifically, can we expect a continuation into the twenty-first century of the pooling of resources and risks that has come to be known in the late twentieth century as the welfare state? Perhaps not, and for reasons that go much deeper than those being currently considered.

These remarks will read rather differently on the two sides of the Atlantic. In North America, perhaps because the post–World War Two Baby Boom was much larger and more sustained than elsewhere, the concepts of generations and their conflicts are relatively familiar (see, for example, Easterlin 1980; Foner 1984). In Europe, by contrast, the notion of generation as a powerful social divider and dynamic has never gained much currency. But even in the North American literature generation remains a peripheral rather than a central social variable, a concept to which one refers lightly, erratically, often dismissively. That is what is being confronted here. Generation, in the sense of a birth cohort or a group defined by having been born in the same era, is being moved to the heart of social analysis.

My discussion begins with two pieces of social ground clearing, without which no progress can be made. First, I show that our understanding of how the welfare states came about—and hence of how they might proceed—is grossly inadequate and does not accord with the facts. The histories that have been fashioned have narrowed our vision, inhibited our judgments, and kept us from seeing what is taking place. Second, I consider the true nature of our collective action, since the greatest confusion seems to exist on this subject. In general we have mistaken a minor function of collective action—moving resources toward the poor—for a primary one and so created a vast industry of welfare scholarship, which is, for the most part, irrelevant because premised on a mistake. (Throughout this essay the term *welfare* is used in its broader and more benign European sense rather than in the somewhat pejorative North American one, though the differences between the two are fast fading.) Beyond that, I explore the widening gulf between what welfare states have done and what their participants thought they would do, which was to help them save for the future. Finally, I consider whether populations will tolerate this manifest failure to shift resources equitably across time or between generations.

The Welfare State: New or Old?

Like a good many others, I suspect that we are entering an era of radical reconsideration of the obligations, rights, and duties of individuals and collectivity. However, my reasons are not the familiar ones associated with the moral traditionalist, the libertarian, the demographic doomsayer,

David Thomson

or the economic forecaster. They are based on the observations of a historian of welfare policies and practices in a number of countries and across several centuries of recent history. That study has taught a central lesson: the account of the evolution of social policy that is widely accepted still, and more important, that has served as a major underpinning of the expansive social-spending policies of the later twentieth century, is badly mistaken (Thomson 1986, 1991).

This orthodox history is excessively, almost laughably Whiggish, as the historians call it—simplistic, progressive, teleological, and determinist. It enshrines the welfare state as the ultimate goal toward which humankind has been groping. The tale is one of inexorable advance. From the grim Dark Ages, when individuals and families fended for themselves while the collectivity looked on with indifference, we have climbed toward the welfare state in which individuals increasingly share their resources for the uplift of all (see, for example, Ashford 1986; Bruce 1968; Flora and Heidenheimer 1983; Fraser 1984; Guest 1985; Patterson 1981). In turn, this faith has bolstered the belief that the expanding welfare state is historically inevitable, proper, and right; that ever-greater pooling and redistributing of resources through political action must be desirable since they are in line with a progressive evolution; and that any questioning of this is hopelessly or maliciously reactionary, because flying in the face of history's known and indubitable course. Such a view once saved us all from much critical thinking but it will do so no longer, for that orthodoxy is being exposed as wrong. Reassessment has proceeded further in Britain than elsewhere as scholars of various eras rediscover the continuities in ideas and practices between our own period and former times (Gordon 1988; Laslett 1984, 1989; Macfarlane 1978, 1987; Smith 1984, 1986, 1988; Snell and Millar 1987; Thomson 1986, 1989).

We should draw a number of key lessons from this. First, it is not clear that public funding of education, health, income support, and the like is necessarily rooted in the arrival of modern industrial society, or even that redistributions for these purposes on twentieth-century scales have not been seen before. For example, we can make estimates for England over the past two centuries and more of such things as the numbers of elderly pensioners and of single-parent families maintained by the community, the values of their pensions, and the fractions of national or regional income being expended on welfare activities of various sorts. In other words, the historian can ask the questions we pose in measuring the performances of contemporary welfare states—and the answers are surprising.

In early nineteenth-century England many communities invested as large a fraction of their resources in "public welfare activities" as did mid-twentieth-century nations. Moreover, poorer rural communities did a great deal more in this line than did wealthier urban and industrial ones. During the 1820s and 1830s this expenditure was everywhere cut sharply, often to just one-third of its former peak levels. Yet even so, what remained was considerable. For instance, in the mid-nineteenth century a majority of all elderly persons throughout England received regular cash pensions, paid not by their relatives but by local communities that acknowledged their legitimate claims on the resources of the collectivity. In rural areas, where most of the elderly lived, three-quarters and more were pensioners, in urban communities somewhat less (Thomson 1981). A few tens of thousands were assisted by the central government on account of former military or civil service, but two-thirds of all elderly women and one-half of men were maintained by the Poor Law on weekly allowances funded by a local property tax.

Furthermore, these poor law pensions—for that is what they were called by all involved—had a contemporary worth, relative to the resources of the nonelderly, in excess of that of state pensions in the twentieth century. Others among the aged received community support in various forms: a minority of the nonpensioners remained in employment and substantial fractions held private incomes. Families were not required by law or custom to make payments to their elders or to share homes with them, and this was by no means new to the nineteenth century (Macfarlane 1987; Thomson 1984a, 1984b). In short, large-scale collective action in the welfare arena is a development neither of the past century nor of industrial societies.

Second, the historian learns that changes and reversals in ideology, policy, and practice come about rapidly. The situation described above obtained in the period 1840–1870; that is, when the values of self-help and the Victorian virtues of family responsibility associated with Samuel Smiles were supposedly at their height. But from 1870 a rapid shift took place, being the very opposite of the move toward greater communal action that historians have detected in the last quarter of the nineteenth century as they search for the origins of the modern welfare state. These signs of the future, so favored by historians, were insignificant to contemporaries by contrast with a much more powerful retreat from collective action and responsibility.

A wide-ranging attack on community support for the aged and others was launched, together with a companion crusade to force families to take up obligations once accepted and now being discarded by the collectivity. By 1890 the proportion receiving pensions was barely one-third of mid-century levels, the relative value of payments had been halved, and the conditions for securing and retaining an allowance had been made much more rigorous and demeaning in a myriad little ways. The corollary was that families were made to bear duties toward their aged on a scale not seen during the previous century. The lesson for the welfare historian is unmistakable: major changes occur over very short spans of time.

Third, the experiences of generations are distinctive and contradictory. Late-nineteenth-century Poor Law administrators made their cutbacks through what we might now call attrition or natural wastage. Pension lists were closed, no more names were added, and numbers and costs dwindled as the elderly population concerned was diminished by deaths. Whereas two-thirds of those reaching their late sixties in the 1850s and 1860s had been granted pensions, few of the group reaching old age just twenty years later were. Membership in a particular generation or birth cohort—the accident of birth—was more critical in determining how old age would be spent than were many of the more familiar social variables with which scholars conjure.

This points to a larger issue: a weak handling of time, by historians no less than others. Our grasp of the temporal and its impact remains rudimentary in the extreme. In most social analyses, time consists of a string of discrete, finite, and unrelated moments. Too often the consequences of the passage of time are assessed by selecting two or more such moments, many years apart, and comparing the situations at those points. All of us know this to be wrong. People exist through time, at all moments and not just at a selected few, and in doing so they accumulate experiences and expectations, memories and prejudices, faiths and fears. Beyond that, it does matter which particular segments of historical time individuals have occupied, just as it did for those generations of aging English men and women. We acquire many of our most important and distinctive traits by inhabiting specific fragments of time—and yet an acknowledgment of this seldom impinges on our intellectual inquiries. The assessment of what can be called generation-specific or cohort-specific experiences, the experiences accumulated as a result of being born in a particular era, is still largely ignored. But we are perhaps not going to get away with this much longer. Populations sensing serious generational inequity will not allow it.

A fourth lesson must be the striking absence of the expected progressive sweep to the changes under scrutiny. Instead, two things stand out. The first is a regular course of major reassessments every thirty or forty years. Across the past two centuries of British history a number of dates have long been accepted by historians as pivotal: the 1750s, 1790s, 1830s, 1870s, 1900s, 1940s, and now the 1980s and 1990s. Behind this pattern lies a larger, more leisurely, and rather cyclical one. The nineteenth century was marked by movement away from collective social activity toward individual responsibility, our own century by the reverse, and historians of earlier centuries are now hinting at similar long-term cycles. The evidence for a clear advance toward the modern welfare state is poor.

What might drive these movements is unclear. I believe the dynamic force is something internal, something inherent and intrinsic to the welfare issues themselves and the ways communities try to resolve them, rather than being simply an external product of the emergence of industrial society, of the economists' long-wave cycle, of the experiences of economic expansion or demographic contraction, or of something else. The communities I study appear to hold to, and they do so equally strongly over long periods of time, a mass of conflicting and poorly articulated goals. The jumbled and contradictory motives behind their collective activities include the following, and the list is neither all-inclusive nor arranged in any priority order. There is a good neighbor motive, or the desire to save people from destitution and to assist the unfortunate to lead fuller lives; a development motive, embodying a wish to use the society's resources for the enhancement of all; a risk prevention motive, which aims to protect individuals against major declines in personal circumstances; an internal security motive, seeking to avoid disorder by alleviating disruptive distress; a control motive, to regulate troublesome or unattractive behaviors; a moral motive, rewarding some approved forms of living and punishing others; and a productive motive, encouraging enterprise and the work ethic. The requirements of some of these are in obvious contradiction to those of others, and the result is tension, instability, experimentation, and flux, as a society repeatedly sorts through its options and decides to give the ascendancy for a time to one mix of priorities, now to another. Determining which goals should be given preeminence is in large part reactive to whatever has gone before, and not something propelled inexorably by an underlying "thrust of history."

These reinterpretations are at an early stage, and alternatives to the progressive orthodoxy must remain speculative for the present. But the central point should be clear nevertheless. A fresh look at the past widens

David Thomson

our comprehension of the present and the future. Because a certain view of the past has dominated hitherto, many possibilities have seemed closed off and unthinkable, for example, that modern populations might call a halt to ever-expanding redistributive policies, might collapse programs already in force, might even question the essential worth or validity of collective social action. All of these things are happening in the 1990s as nations once again sort through their social priorities and walk away from the enthusiasms of a previous era—indeed, as they will for themselves what seemed impossible just a few years ago. We are not going to understand the choices being made if we insist that the late-twentieth-century state represents a kind of social nirvana toward which the human species has struggled for eons, and from which neither going back nor beyond is conceivable. A critical review of all beliefs rooted in the simpleminded teleology that we have constructed for ourselves has become imperative.

Saving the Poor or Ourselves?

The second piece of ground clearing concerns the nature of our collective actions. For fifty years and more the prevailing view has been that redistributions are between rich and poor, haves and have-nots—or at least that this is what was intended. While study built around this belief has grown immense, it seldom involves a fundamental questioning of assumptions. This will not do, for the purposes of redistributive action have been misconceived by their students, and most of our measurements and debates thus miss the point. Theoretical economists and philosophers among others have long appreciated the very different nature of welfare actions, but this understanding remains to be taken on board by a wider intellectual community (Burbidge 1987; Samuelson 1958; Sikora and Barry 1978).

The issue might be presented this way. At the outset, as nations created their "new" welfare states in the 1940s and 1950s in particular, the purposes of this massive pooling and political redistribution were unclear. Large numbers agreed, in the wake of depression and war, that market distributions of resources had failed in too many ways, and that a superimposed corrective political redistribution was desirable. But what were to be its bases? One was clearly humanitarian, the desire to move resources from rich to poor, and this motive provided much of the Christian-Socialist ideology and rhetoric of welfare programs. Another motive, often more muted and less likely to inspire oratorical flourish, was based on savings, or risk prevention. This derived from the evident fact that individuals go through income cycles during their lives, with phases of relative surplus alternating with comparative deficit. Greater security and well-being lay in spreading individuals' private resources more evenly across time, and the overlapping of the surplus phases of some citizens with the deficit phases of others offered the means to this end. Where private institutions had failed to secure a workable transfer, public institutions might succeed.

Two possible surpluses thus presented themselves for redistribution: the excess riches of a wealthy few and the smaller transitory life-cycle accumulations of the many. Redistribution in the humanitarian mode would mean the permanent alienation of resources through political action. Wealthier citizens would hand over substantial portions of their incomes, with no expectation of a return other than the possible satisfaction of living in a safer, more attractive, and perhaps more productive community. The savings model, by contrast, presupposed only a temporary alienation of private resources. Individuals at all income levels would in effect lend their current surpluses to people who were much like themselves, except for being in a passing life phase of deficit. Resources would flow back and forward across time as individuals aged and passed through successive phases of relative abundance and need: the structure of affluence would remain largely unaltered.

In the early years there was confusion as to which redistributive model was to operate, and if both, which would predominate. Forty years later there need be no confusion in the mind of the historian. Populations everywhere have sorted out a balance between the two, although we have in large part still failed to recognize this. For the first ten or so years the humanitarian drive was strong, and the gap between richest and poorest narrowed measurably. But the savings motive soon triumphed and has remained preeminent as populations have gone on enlarging their collective actions in the belief—ultimately and badly mistaken, as I shall argue—that they were involved in only a temporary lending of private income. Those who continue to analyze redistribution in the belief that permanent alienation and reallocation were to be its basis have missed a crucial point in modern history.

That savings rather than humanitarianism would dominate should not have surprised anyone. A major difficulty in sustaining humanitarian programs was that they could never retain their initial electoral attractiveness. A limited degree of direct redistribution from richest to poorest might be welcomed, if it perhaps brought some arrogant or

ostentatiously wealthy people to heel, or removed some of the ugliest
and most socially disruptive effects of poverty, or helped repair the
ravages of depression and war. But if pressed too far the Robin Hood
approach held few promises and many more threats for the majority.
Their hopes for personal advancement would be thwarted in a level-
ing world, and they might find themselves deemed "rich" and hence
eligible to be drained. A welfare state on the savings model held
much more appeal. It would represent a daring experiment in mass
insurance based on enlightened self interest. It might include an element of altruism; those in deficit throughout life as a result of market
allocations could be granted some assistance. The prime purpose of
collective action, however, would always be to help those with some
surpluses move them forward through time.

The triumph of the savings motive soon became evident in various
ways. One, measures of the gap between rich and poor, have made it
clear that the gulf has widened in many societies in recent decades
(Jones 1983; Levy 1987; Thomson 1991; Townsend 1979). A second has been the very structure of the redistributive mechanisms that
were established, with their limited means to move resources between
persons in the same life phase. A third has been the public reaction to
these two, for the realities of increasing inequality in wealth have not
been hidden from modern populations. Since the early 1960s they
have been faced with a steady stream of reports demonstrating first
the persistence, then the regrowth of poverty and inequality. But exposure to this information has provoked remarkably little reaction.
Electorates everywhere have remained untroubled. The failure to redistribute affluence and life chances between rich and poor have produced rhetoric and hand wringing, but little of substance. Quite
simply, expanding collective activity and the moving of resources from
rich to poor do not go together.

It is time to acknowledge the significance of these countertrends.
Modern citizenries are saying something important about why they
have welfare states. It is not for humanitarian reasons alone, or even
primarily. Permanent, continuous redistribution from richer to poorer
persons is not what they want, or will tolerate. Their welfare states
are mechanisms for saving, for putting private resources out on loan
for a time to people older or younger than themselves. And so long
as they believe that welfare states work to this end, populations have
been willing to place growing amounts of their income in the pool
for redistribution by state action.

The Welfare Gamble

This raises a further range of questions. In particular, what are the expectations of successive generations as they play their part in these exchanges? how well are they being met? and what might they do as they come to appreciate the failure of their welfare states in this regard? These questions will be the focus of the rest of this chapter. The welfare states may not have moved far toward equality of rich and poor, but this has mattered little to their populations because it is deemed ultimately irrelevant. Those same populations will treat the failure to move resources fairly between generations with no such equanimity.

Operating a welfare state as a savings or insurance institution raises immediate difficulties. How is the citizen to be induced to go along with a huge pooling of resources, putting money and hopes in a political process of redistribution over which each can exercise minimal control? This commitment involves an enormous personal gamble, and the standard image of the welfare state as provider of cradle to grave insulation against risk misrepresents the situation badly. The citizen may face few chances of sudden or catastrophic change in material fortunes. But this security is acquired by assuming heavy risk of another sort—the risk that one will not get value for money, that a lifetime of contributions will not produce a return commensurate with the private consumption forgone, that promises of future benefit will not be honored.

The welfare states have followed two paths here. The paths are distinct in theory, although in practice all states have fudged and blurred the boundaries to produce messy and ultimately dangerous mixes of the two. The first course is to issue an explicit contract of social insurance between individual and state, whereby the citizen is provided with an agreed cover against specified risks in return for a stated premium; the second is simply to presuppose that an unspoken contract exists. Societies pursuing the social insurance ideal should establish social security funds, record regular contributions from each citizen, and make later payments on the basis of those lifetime savings according to a predetermined scale. But in practice nothing of the sort has occurred. Good insurance principles are nowhere observed—only the fiction of an explicit contract is maintained (Burbidge 1987; Creedy and Disney 1985).

For one thing, many people do not have lifetime earnings sufficient to pay the membership premiums, and major exceptions to true insurance rules have always had to be allowed. Second, populations have proven unwilling to pay during their working lives the contributions necessary to sustain the lifetime benefits that they expect to receive. Political rather than actuarial considerations determine contribution rates. In numerous instances governments have knowingly and deliberately established "partially funded" (the euphemism for underfunded) schemes of social insurance, whereby subsidization of present employees and employers by those who come later is presupposed from the outset. It may be excellent politics, but it isn't insurance.

Moreover, like contributions, repayments are being fixed according to current political dictates, usually in relation to earnings at the end of the working life. The actual amount invested by the individual is largely immaterial: the fact of having participated in the scheme is what counts. In other words, governments are proving unwilling or unable to quash the rising demands of the aging members of social insurance funds. The formulas for calculating benefits have been tampered with repeatedly during the past twenty years, and rising inflation in the 1970s and 1980s provided a convenient occasion for discarding contractual links between amounts paid in by and those paid out to individuals. What populations wanted and have insisted on was the security of an explicit insurance contract, and the right to have its terms altered or overridden by later political action if that should suit better.

Growing subsidization of insurance funds by subsequent generations is the result, and all governments plan to intensify this in coming years. The same applies to most private superannuation schemes as well (Burbidge 1987; Council of Economic Advisers to the U.S. President 1985; Coward 1974; Health and Welfare Canada 1986). Various subterfuges have been employed here while maintaining the pretense of insurance. Increased direct cross-subsidization of insurance funds from general taxation is now common; employer contributions have been increased; and the invested funds of these schemes have been earning large sums through high interest rates, property trading, and the like—all ways of drawing income from the present working population toward the earlier born. Most important, rates of contribution required of individuals have been increased substantially. That is, the percentage of earnings taken from the average worker under social insurance has often doubled or trebled in the past twenty years, as with National Insurance contributions in Britain. This means that the young worker of today can expect across a lifetime to invest several times as large a fraction of earnings in these insurance programs as did current beneficiaries, but without the promise of any better rate of return in the end.

In short, the explicit contract of social insurance is a fiction. Behind an actuarial facade a gross disregard for insurance considerations has evolved, and many nations are now abandoning the charade. New Zealand dropped all notions of funding, insurance, and personal record twenty-five years ago. Both contributions and benefits are determined by the political processes of the moment, explicit contracts of insurance notwithstanding, and the sooner this is admitted, the sooner honest and clear thinking will enter social policy debate.

This leads back to the earlier question: why do individuals go along with it all, in societies that have abandoned the insurance fiction and in those where the falseness of it is becoming obvious to everyone? This is something hitherto little discussed. Whereas explicit contracts of social insurance have been closely debated, amended, and discarded, their ultimate underpinnings have been neglected. I predict we will find ourselves talking a great deal about these matters before long.

The essential core of a modern welfare state is simple and readily comprehensible to all; I shall call it the implicit welfare contract between generations. An individual belongs to a welfare state and tolerates the risky and expensive pooling of resources this has come to entail because he or she believes that an inherent, unspoken agreement binds persons of all ages and generations, including those yet to be born. An insurance company could expect few clients if its policy read, "Your premiums will be $10,000 a year, but we haven't a clue what your eventual return might be." A welfare state offering the same "policy" could anticipate no more support: some assurance has to be forthcoming to make the enormous risks of membership worth the gamble.

The implicit welfare contract between generations is that assurance. The guarantees it offers are something we all assume to exist, if almost never talk about. But this makes them no less compelling or crucial as the cement that bonds citizens in a modern state. At the contract's heart are the twin concepts of consistency and reciprocity. That is, individuals must have faith that others are obliged to behave toward them in certain ways, and that they will do so according to agreed on and stable procedures. Each carries the expectation of like beliefs and behaviors on the part of fellow citizens of all ages. (I am here using the term *reciprocity* in a slightly unconventional sense. There is little expectation of reciprocity between individual and individual, much more between individual and collectivity.) A simple statement of this critical trust might run: "I make my surpluses available to others today, and am happy to continue doing so, in the firm belief that in time, when I am in a similar position to those I now assist, others will in turn make their surpluses available to me, in comparable manner and amount." We have emphasized that consistency and reciprocity, or the obligations to respond in like manner and degree, are the key elements of this compact between generations. Only on this basis can individuals have faith that their current surpluses are being appropriated temporarily by the collectivity and not simply being stripped away forever—for this, I hold, a modern population will not vote.

A welfare state without such an assumed agreement is unthinkable, and the contract's significance, together with the dangers of ignoring these assumptions, will be very evident if we consider simple analogies. An immediate one might be a sports game. Imagine what would happen if members of one team started demanding and being granted changes to the rules during a game, for example, insisting that their team score three points when passing halfway but that the opposition lose six for doing exactly the same thing. Consistency is imperative. A closer parallel perhaps is the group of friends who drink together regularly in a hotel. One option in buying drinks is that each fend for himself or herself, drinking expensively when flush with funds and going without when the money dwindles: those short of cash must sit and watch companions continue to drink. A more sociable and quite familiar alternative is for the friends to form a collective and pool their resources—to set up a system of "shouting," with each taking a turn to buy drinks for everyone. (I am aware that this is to abuse the much more complex notion of shouting.) This provides for a degree of sharing as well as simplicity and convenience, with those short of money this week perhaps being carried until next, or those always low on income being subsidized by their more affluent colleagues.

Such a group would have to decide how to coordinate its efforts. It could create a fund, with everyone paying in agreed amounts and a treasurer recording the consumption of each individual. In practice few would bother with this insurance path. Much more common would be the assumption of an implicit contract, an unspoken agreement simply to abide by certain rules. These might never need to be spelled out, and yet all would understand them. They would recognize, too, the threat to the group and to the whole pooling agreement if some members started to abuse the trust and bend the rules, perhaps by demanding expensive whiskeys when others were shouting and insisting on mineral water for everyone when they themselves were paying, or by disappearing outside for a time when it came their turn to pay, only to return and take up drinking again once that duty had been avoided. Moreover, the tensions generated and the foreshortened life of the group can well be envisaged if it became apparent that it was always the same individuals who were evading the responsibilities that went along with the benefits of group membership. A return to individual purchase would soon follow, or at least a return to a strict system of accounting. And the anger and mistrust engendered would ensure that a pooling of resources based simply on faith in an unspoken agreement would not be tried again for a long time.

This is precisely the dilemma of the welfare states at the end of the twentieth century. The agreements have not been observed, the trust not honored. A generational analysis of their histories suggests two strong trends. The first is inconsistency; the rules of the game are changing constantly. Housing subsidies in place for one generation when young are not available to their successors in identical circumstances. Tax reliefs for dependents, home purchase, job training costs, and other expenses particular to certain life phases are offered in some years but not in others. Free health and education services are provided to some generations of parents but not to those who follow, and social security benefits rise and shrink in size.

Second, this perpetual reshaping of the welfare states has not been random or patternless. Instead, certain generations are emerging as persistent winners as they find the prizes and penalties of membership reshaped in step with their own aging interests. In the process two distinct welfare states have been created within each national one; no doubt others will soon find more than two. These are not the welfare states of the middle classes and the poor, as it has become fashionable to insist. They are those of the welfare generation, the initiator generation of young adults for whom the postwar welfare states were created primarily, and of their successors. The first welfare state has been one of large lifetime benefits and few contributions, the second the necessary antithesis. Membership is determined by date of birth, and passing from one state to the other is not permitted. In short, neither consistency nor reciprocity, the essentials of a sustainable welfare contract, have been apparent in practice, although populations have until now been kept from recognizing this because of the insistence on talking about the welfare state as if it operated in the humanitarian mode.

Creating the Two Welfare States

These claims cannot be detailed in a short essay. Each modern nation, for its own historical, political, and demographic reasons, has evolved a particular regime of prizes and penalties and has altered them over time according to its own preferences. And yet common patterns are discernible. Political economists long ago speculated that the welfare states might behave like the childish chain letter (Samuelson 1958), benefiting the instigators at the expense of their successors and running just as long as the supply of the gullible lasted. What the historian is noting here, forty years on, is how disturbingly apt that premonition was.

In the following paragraphs I want to give a sense of how far-reaching the inconsistent experiences of successive generations are proving. One approach is to amass examples, culled from the secondary literature of numerous societies. This is not difficult, and one's card index soon bulges. The evidence of enhanced provisions for the elderly of today, shrinking family allowances for their successors, rising youth poverty, falling public investments in housing for young families, and much more is readily to hand, from nation after nation. I have indicated something of this elsewhere (Thomson 1989) and will not crowd the present text with extensive lists.

Such a cataloging of parallels, however, still leaves the issue at a superficial level. What matters to the individual is not simply that these developments are occurring, but that he or she is enmeshed in all of them simultaneously. The effects of each are compounding rather than discrete, one adding to the other to create distinctive generational experiences. This cumulative impact can be traced only through close local studies, and the experiences of New Zealand are offered here as an illustration of what one such inquiry reveals. My initial work on companion studies in various parts of the English-speaking world suggests that comparable trends are present everywhere. As a case study of a much larger process, New Zealand does possess several merits. The country expanded its social welfare programs early, thus giving time to reveal their longer-term flaws. All taxation and social security is administered at a single national level, making the interaction of programs relatively easy to trace and comprehend. New Zealand has had little truck with social insurance pretensions, and so perhaps reveals the intergenerational play of pooling and redistribution more openly and nakedly than most. And it is a modest social spender by international standards, neither at the top end among the northern European nations nor in the laggardly North American league.

During the early decades of the twentieth century New Zealand introduced a number of low-slung safety nets for selected groups among the poor—pensions for the elderly, widows, invalids, and miners and from the mid-1920s a limited program of family allowances. These measures complemented a free primary education system and the subsidized health and welfare services established late in the previous century. Most New Zealanders ventured little to belong to this minimal welfare state: by 1929, for instance, less than 20 percent of the working population paid any income tax. But the 1930s soon taught how limited a cover against risk this purchased the citizen, and from 1935 a new Labour government began to erect the modern welfare state.

The new expanded welfare and taxation programs of the 1930s and 1940s were given a peculiar twist for several reasons —the need for nation building following depression and war, the fears of population decline, the desire to reward soldiers and their contemporaries, the shape of existing public welfare programs, and the demands of selling a new concept of collective action to a population grown wary of state mismanagement and inaction in the 1920s and 1930s. It was a twist shared widely elsewhere (Flora and Heidenheimer 1981). Existing programs for the aged were enhanced, but most of the new effort and expenditure went into creating a youth state, a welfare state designed to benefit young adults and their children ahead of others. Spending on education and child health and welfare programs rapidly overtook all state spending on the older half of the population. A new family allowance, granted to all who cared for children regardless of income level, absorbed as great a portion of the total national income as did the old-age pension scheme. Annual public investments in housing for young families absorbed a further 2 to 3 percent of GDP (Gross Domestic Product) throughout the 1950s and 1960s, as much once again as the whole of public expenditure on social security for the aged (Thomson 1991).

Meanwhile, the new tax regime was shaped to steer costs well away from the young. The bulk of the increased funding needed was generated through direct income taxation, and exemptions for children and non-earning spouses ensured that the middle aged paid most, younger adults very little. A young man of average earnings in his twenties or thirties, supporting a nonearning spouse and just two children through the 1940s, 1950s, and 1960s, enjoyed a nil "effective" tax rate. That is, his income tax exemptions, together with the two cash family benefits received on account of his children, equaled his total income tax demand. Since marriage and raising children were nearly universal among that generation of young adults, fewer than one in ten young married women held paid employment, and the average family had closer to four children than two, the majority of young adults in that era faced an even more favorable prospect—a highly negative effective income tax rate for at least half of their working lives. A calculation for the whole generation, taking everyone aged twenty-five to thirty-four in 1950, for example, and following them through the 1950s and 1960s, suggests an overall annual effective income tax rate of just 2 to 3 percent of gross income. "Effective" does not, of course, take into account the major returns to this group in other forms—free health and education services, housing grants, and the like. A more elaborate calculation of lifetime contributions and benefits, counting all taxes and all public expenditures, suggests that those who were young adults in the 1940s, 1950s, and 1960s, as a generation, ultimately will collect around four times as much from the welfare state as they will contribute to it.

The effect was to create the first welfare generation, consisting of those reaching adulthood between about 1945 and the end of the 1960s—a generation soon in heavy and lasting debt to the collectivity. This in turn established powerful expectations concerning the purpose of collective action. The implicit contract of consistency and reciprocity presupposes that resources will flow back and forth between persons in various life phases. It also presupposes that the direction and scale of the flows will be reasonably stable over long periods of time, that the rules of the game will not be tampered with. But the contract does not determine the purpose or direction of those flows, only that once set, the movement must remain consistent. One community might make its prime beneficiaries those meeting the heavy costs of child raising; another could target the needs of the aged. Each would be free to set its own priorities and need not choose arrangements that were equitable or just at any one moment; justice lies in consistency over time, in everyone getting a turn at being both beneficiary and contributor. What could not be contemplated was a rapid remodeling of priorities once the exchange was well under way and major benefits had been drawn. New Zealand, like many other societies, made a choice for youth, thus establishing the expectation that each generation in turn would agree to accept large benefits when young and repay them when older by passing on to successors a range of benefits comparable to those they themselves had enjoyed.

This exchange between generations is predicated on a peaceful cession of place. It will work only if generations are willing to change roles as they age, to step aside and let others take up the benefits, to move from being major consumers of public services and grants to major contributors. But this is precisely what the original beneficiaries have not proven willing or able to do, in New Zealand and elsewhere. The key test of transition was failed in the 1960s and 1970s, as the initial welfare generation ceased in large numbers to have any further use for a youth-favoring state and faced the prospect for the first time in their lives of paying heavily for their participation in these intergenerational transfers. Instead of making the required cession of place, the first welfare generation has seen the nature and purpose of the exchange revised. Since the end of the 1960s youth-sponsoring programs have been diminished or abolished altogether; investment of public funds in programs for the middle aged and the elderly has expanded rapidly; and taxation has been redirected away from the middle aged on to the young. Thus were the two welfare states for successive generations formed.

Behind this "capture" of the welfare agenda are factors too complex to explore here (Thomson 1989, 1991). They have something but not much to do with a deliberate defrauding of subsequent generations and with the painting of the initiator generations as especially deserving of unusually generous provisions throughout life because of the depression, or the war, or some such. They have much more to do with the limitations inherent in democratic processes of government, which do not allow the vague interests of future voters to be weighed nearly as readily as those of current ones. They have still more to do with the unrealistic expectations born of the peculiar treatment given to the first welfare generation in early adult life, and with the favorable economic circumstances of the 1950s and 1960s.

Crucial, too, has been the unwillingness of populations (and of their political and intellectual leaders) to consider the fragile nature of welfare exchanges between generations. The terms of lifelong membership in a welfare state, or the needs for give and take, restraint, and responsibility that this imposes were nowhere spelled out or debated. And beyond lie larger and more deeply troubling issues. The very nature of the contemporary welfare state—an anonymous pooling, rather like a giant and compulsory chain letter, where no one is allowed to know what anyone else is putting in or taking out over time—will lead perhaps inexorably to mounting demands for instant rather than delayed benefit, for minimal long-term investment, and for the shifting of costs ever further into the future. The worst laws of the common are brought into play.

The following are just some of the more obvious steps in this process of redesign. First, social security programs have been refashioned. Everywhere in the past twenty years state pensions for the aged have been enhanced in various ways. In New Zealand the age for full entitlement has been lowered to sixty years for all; assets and means testing has been eliminated; all contributions records have been scrapped; and require-

David Thomson

ments to retire before receiving benefits have been abolished. Most important, the value of the pension has been raised sharply in relation to wages and is now indexed to the cost of living or movements in earnings, whichever is more favorable to the aged.

In the meantime, universal allowances to the young have been cut, and the family benefit eroded to insignificance. During the past thirty years its value has increased by 300 percent in unadjusted dollar terms, while prices have gone up by 700 percent and gross earnings by 800 percent; the basic old-age pension has increased by no less than 1,600 percent (1,200 percent net of taxation). In 1951 old-age pensions absorbed 2.8 percent of GDP, family benefits 2.2 percent; by 1986 these percentages were 7.4 and 0.6, respectively. Demographic changes explain only a small fraction of this movement; conversely, the movement may explain rather more about demographic changes in the past fifty years, but that subject must be left aside here. The reversal in priorities has been both stark and symbolic of a wider trend in social security, as unemployment payments for the young shrink, early retirement provisions grow, and so on.

In spending on public services a companion reversal of purpose is evident. Educational spending has in many nations dropped faster than the falling numbers of the young might warrant, and New Zealand has shared in this. Resources within the public health service (New Zealand operates a scheme much like the British National Health Service) have been channeled increasingly into areas of prime interest to the older half of the population. But it is in housing that the most dramatic changes have taken place, and it is no surprise that in a nation of overwhelming private home ownership this is the public expenditure of perhaps least continuing interest to those past age forty.

Within the past twenty years investment in public rental housing in New Zealand, most of which goes to young adults, has been cut to around one-tenth of its 1950s and 1960s levels when measured as a fraction of GDP. More important, because it affects many more people, has been the virtual ending of cheap state loan assistance to young buyers, this having been the standard route to private home ownership in the three decades preceding the early 1970s. Free grants and low-interest mortgages then met most of the costs of buying a house, and no capital gains taxes or mortgage revisions returned to the collectivity any of the subsequent profits accruing to private homeowners. Since the mid-1970s the state has abdicated this function, and public investment in private ownership is now around one-fifth or less of what it was twenty years ago in real terms. A similar withdrawal from sponsorship of new private businesses has also taken place.

Taxation moves have complemented these processes. Because of a variety of taxation reforms and changes in employment practices, together with demographic shifts, a substantial portion of all taxes is now paid by adults in their twenties and thirties, where formerly this group paid very little. Tax deductibility for all individual contributions to private superannuation schemes was ended recently, after having been in place for forty years to benefit the now aging members of the earlier working population. Income tax exemptions for dependents dwindled for many years, and in the 1980s disappeared altogether. High marginal tax rates have been eliminated during the past decade, with consequences much more beneficial to older workers than to younger ones since the highest incomes are earned by those over age forty. Thirty years ago the self-employed and companies paid around one-third of all direct taxes: they now pay a small fraction, and because older persons predominate heavily in these categories, the effect once again has been to shift more of the tax burden toward the young.

Some estimates can be made of the impact on successive generations. For the young adults of the 1950s and 1960s, taken as a whole, the effective income tax rate was around 2 percent of income; for the same age group twenty years later it was 20 percent. A lifetime's direct and indirect tax contributions, measured as a fraction of earnings, seem likely to be five or more times as great for the later born. This remains true, moreover, at all income levels or classes. The "value" of a child has dropped dramatically. In the 1950s two small children were worth almost as much as an old-age pension, in that they brought in tax reliefs and cash allowances to their parents, regardless of income, the equivalent of the weekly pension of an elderly person. This was more than five times the worth of children to parents in the 1980s. Buying a first home now absorbs four to five times as large a fraction of after-tax income as did buying an identical house for an identical person born twenty years earlier, after changes in house prices, incomes, taxes, social security grants, state housing subsidies, interest rates, and the like are all taken into account. Services once free—education for children through postgraduate levels, health, and many more—are charged to the later born as they were not to their predecessors, and the intention is to extend this further. Plans to collapse public provision for those reaching old age in the twenty-first century—that is, those suffering all these unfavorable

tendencies at the present moment—have been announced. The two welfare states of the different generations are incompatible, with each barely
recognizable to an inhabitant of the other.

The revision of social priorities in public spending and revenue gathering has been striking, but this must not be mistaken for the whole of
the change. The powers of the state have been used in many further ways
to advance the interests of some generations at the expense of others.
For example, the conditions under which money is borrowed and lent
have been revised radically. Up to the 1970s investment policies in New
Zealand were overshadowed by reactions to depression and war: borrowers (almost invariably young) had to be protected against lenders
(almost invariably older). Interest rates, mortgage terms, and the like
were all controlled by statute and regulation, and governments used their
powers to borrow and lend at subsidized rates to undercut and so force
down any private competition. Exchange controls ensured that lenders
could not move their money out of the country in search of a better deal,
and the effects were low returns to investors alongside mounting gains
for borrowers.

In the past fifteen years these priorities have been inverted. Most financial controls have been removed, and the government has ceased to
compete with the private lending sector. The interests of the lender are
now the express concern of governments. Whereas economic development and social betterment for all were once seen to lie in restraining
investors and helping borrowers, they are now seen as best served by
letting lenders do what they choose. Mortgage agencies alter interest
terms frequently and at will, without consultation with borrowers, so as
to maintain a continuing high rate of real return to investors—behavior
that was not permitted by law or social consensus just twenty years ago.
The rightness of these changes need not concern us here, but issues of
consistency and reciprocity must. Those who benefited most under the
former regime of control are now those who, having aged into another
phase of life, also stand to gain most from the new freedoms for investors.
The advantages of one set of intergenerational exchange arrangements
are not being passed on to successors as they must be if generational
resources are to be temporarily borrowed rather than permanently
alienated.

Employment policies advance this process further: in the language of
the nursery, the fairy godmother of one generation becomes the vindictive
stepmother of the next. During the 1950s and 1960s New Zealand
governments actively promoted employment opportunity, by manipu-

lating rates of immigration and stimulating housing and public works construction to produce "over-full employment." More important, from the late 1930s to the 1970s governments imposed heavy import controls with the deliberate purpose of enhancing the employments of New Zealand workers. These efforts kept the welfare generation from experiencing unemployment or the threat of losing a job, while promotion prospects for young adults were good and real earnings rose rapidly. But from the early 1970s rationing of jobs has been ever more necessary, and it is clear now to the historian that in the face of this the society made a decision of unpremeditated but immense significance. If employment was to be limited, top priority would be given to protecting the lifetime employments of the young adults of the 1940s, 1950s, and 1960s, now in middle age.

The means to this end have been many and varied. Union powers fostered during the years of over-full employment were used to protect existing workers ahead of potential ones, by enforcing "last-on-first-off" practices. Lifetime employment contracts were issued in government and many private employments. Expanded redundancy laws and agreements rendered it difficult and expensive to dispense with older workers, while making firms reluctant to take on many young ones. Above all, a widespread acceptance that this was right and proper, that the middle aged had to be protected and that their unemployment could not be tolerated, ensured a particular distribution of employment chances and rewards. The consequences have been minimal unemployment and early retirement among those in their forties and fifties, alongside heavy youth unemployment. Around one-half of all unemployment in the 1970s and 1980s has been endured by persons under age twenty-five. Career promotions have been slower for those entering employment in the past twenty years, and earnings of younger workers have fallen relative to those of older ones. In the 1950s and 1960s, for instance, men in their early twenties who were employed full-time earned on average at least 75 percent as much as those in their forties did. By the mid-1980s, the figure for the equivalent younger group was something like 60 percent; those over age forty suffered no such retreat.

This distribution of employment must be called particular because it is not inevitable or natural, as many will comfort themselves by arguing. Contrasts here with the Great Depression of the 1930s are fascinating. In that earlier instance of economic difficulty the society responded by putting the interests of younger adults ahead of those of older ones. Unemployment was concentrated most heavily among older workers, and not the young. Old-age pensions were cut. Mortgage interest rates on both housing and business loans were altered by the government: interest rates on private mortgages were ordered down, arrears of interest and principal were waived, and capital and mortgage valuations were lowered by court order (Thomson and Macdonald 1987). Older lenders protested loudly but to no avail—the needs of the young were deemed greater than those of the old. But faced with similar needs to ration resources today, our priorities are the reverse. The comparisons give the lie to those who insist that societies have little choice in these matters, that such things are determined by demographic accident or the blind machinations of the market (see, for example, Easterlin 1987).

In government financing, too, the experiences of the generations are moving farther apart. Since the early 1960s New Zealand governments have spent more than their regular income, and they have responded to the growing imbalances in various ways. One we have noted already— the altered collection of taxes. They are also charging for a wide range of services once free to the public and plan to do a great deal more of this in future in education, health, housing, and elsewhere. The effect, inevitably, is to make the lifelong welfare state of one generation, those who have lived their working lives in a world of free public services, quite unlike that of their successors.

But most important, governments in the 1970s and 1980s have borrowed, building up substantial debts to foreign and internal lenders. These must inevitably have very different meanings for those too old to have to contemplate repaying the debts but not too old to enjoy the immediate benefits, and for those who are younger and face repayment of debt incurred by predecessors. The standard justification for this borrowing has been that it is for development, for vital investment that will enrich the futures of all. Official statistics do not bear this out, however. In the past fifteen years investments in lasting capital assets (new water schemes, sewerage reticulation, energy generation, highways, and the like) by public and private investors alike have been falling steadily as a fraction of GDP, while both borrowing and taxation have mounted.

Lowered investment in human capital parallels this. The causes of the dramatic fall in fertility during the past quarter-century are too complex to be considered here, though they may be related intricately to this larger refashioning of social priorities. But the consequences of these twin declines in investment fall unevenly on successive generations. One immediate effect of fewer births has been reduced competition between older and younger dependents for shares of the income and attention of working-age adults, which has permitted the diversion of resources to aging. The likely future costs of these low human investments—a heavily aged population, intensified competition for portions of the income of a shrinking pool of the young, the need to make the capital and environmental reinvestments that were avoided in the late twentieth century—again mean very different things to those who will and will not live far into the next century. In terms of what they deliver currently the welfare states of successive generations stand far apart. But the future prospects they can offer their citizens is where their greatest differences lie.

A Future for Collective Action?

As they proceed through the 1990s Western societies will face a number of difficult ethical and social policy questions, only a few of which can be raised here. At the outset we will experience the shock and dismay of recognizing a fiction. For twenty years or so the exchanges between successive generations have been going badly awry—just how badly will emerge only gradually, as populations absorb the enormity and the implications of it all. Resources have been flowing permanently rather than temporarily from one generation to another. There neither will nor can be a substantial return from the pooling of resources to the young adults of today, at any stage in their lives. The welfare state for them is now and must remain an ever-deepening drain.

But while the exchanges have been breaking down for decades we have contrived not to notice. I suspect that we did not want to, or to contemplate what might follow. We blamed the economy, and said things would come right one day. We blamed demography, attributing the mounting misfortunes and disadvantages of the young to their oversupply. In other words, we have pleaded circumstances beyond anybody's control or responsibility. We have kept repeating the rhetoric of humanitarianism to mask redistributions of a very different kind. Most of all, we have held out the hope to the younger half of our populations that things would improve, that their present travails were but passing, that the agreed exchanges would in the end work.

That faith is dying fast, and with it many of the remaining props of the current generational exchanges and of the whole welfare state enterprise. Those in their twenties and thirties are coming to realize that there will be no future for them comparable to that they are providing for their predecessors; and moreover, that there is no intention even to try to provide it. Governments are in effect telling them so, in all of their policy proposals: there will never again be job security, or free public services, or cheap houses, or heavy subsidies for superannuation savings, or low retirement ages, or generous state pensions. No longer is it seen as the task of government to supply these for future generations. Demography now makes these cuts and changes unavoidable, and the point is increasingly widely recognized and discussed. What is not realized, even so, is that the alternative to which everyone instinctively turns, that of private saving, faces exactly the same demographic limits as does any state program. And through all this, the message runs, the disfavored generations are to continue to pay the high taxes needed to fund the welfare state of their predecessors. It is not easy to see how the faith and hope that form the heart of a generational exchange can survive.

A peculiar timing will make our reassessments especially fraught in the 1990s. At least two distinct issues will be run together and confused (Daniels 1988, 1989). One will be old age, and the duties of the young toward the old. The other will be the failure of generational exchanges between the first welfare generation and others, and the question of what might be done to correct this. Those reaching old age now and in the next two decades, and so expecting and depending on large additional transfers of funds from their successors, will be the very group who have failed most to play a full part in these exchanges. All of us will be torn by conflicting notions of justice and desert; as elderly people, the old may deserve to be treated indulgently, as members of the welfare generation perhaps not. It is a pity, but now inevitable, that our discussions of social policy will revolve around the elderly.

Reactions to the analysis outlined here are likely to follow two interweaving courses. The first will be to disbelieve some parts, to question others, to deny more; the second to consider some of the larger implications. In a book-length study of New Zealand I anticipate and address a range of these likely queries. Some objections arise from ignorance, others from anger, and more from special pleading of extenuating circumstances. But many have much more substance, and sadly, can be given no time here.

Beyond the objections lie larger issues to do with implications. One is that much of our social policy research and debate has been unacceptably flabby. We have blithely assumed that the welfare state experiment would simply continue, regardless of how we abused it, because history taught that it was here to stay. One senses this assumption of irrevocability underlying current attempts by governments to amend social policy. The

welfare state of those now young is to be further tampered with and
shrunk ahead of them as they move through life; more young women
are to take up dual careers at home and in the taxpaying workforce so
as to keep enlarging the pool of resources available for redistribution;
and the taxes of the young are to continue flowing to their predecessors.
Few question why this will happen: why the young will continue in their
designated roles, uncomplaining and unconcerned for their own futures,
regardless of how much the terms of the exchange keep moving against
them. It is assumed that they will simply play the hand dealt them by
life—"history" allows them no other option. This is not so. But until
now we believed that the alternatives were unthinkable.

We have not faced seriously the question, When does the risk of being
a member of a welfare collective come to outweigh the advantages? For
forty years we have acted as though there was no such question; the
benefits of membership for the initiator generations were so great and
so obvious to all that the query made no sense. But will a population
accept a welfare compact that simply returns to them their own money
spread across a lifetime? Or will they pool only when the return doubles,
trebles, quadruples, or multiplies their investment by some larger figure?
Is getting back a fraction of one's investment enough to keep a generation
paying a lifetime of contributions? At what point might they say "enough,
let us halt this, and all try our luck at private saving; we cannot do worse
than under the present arrangements"? The issue can be put still more
bluntly. Why should the young adults of the 1990s and beyond feel
bound to pay for the welfare state of their predecessors? What bonds,
what obligations, what contract requires this of them? What possible
moral basis could such an exchange have? Why would they not argue
that there now is no contract between generations, because it has been
voided by the behavior of their elders? Such questions have not been
part of the currency of welfare debates, but they will be.

One rather cynical argument I have heard in New Zealand is that young
adults of today have nowhere to go. If they call for the immediate dis-
mantling of the intergenerational exchanges they will recover none of
their lost investment and will stand alone in their own old age. It is, so
this thinking goes, in their interests to put up with a bad deal, and in
turn to exploit those who follow them as ruthlessly as they can. This is
an argument with little merit or charm. I cannot comprehend a welfare
state based on deliberate, calculated, and acknowledged exploitation of
successors. The whole enterprise must be rooted in trust and good faith
between generations, and seems possible only so long as these last. More-

over, the suggestion presumes a calculating foresight and sense of long-term strategy not evident in modern populations. Why would a generation choose to go on paying high taxes based on the calculation that this would somehow entitle it to extort from those who follow later, instead of making the much simpler decision to end the whole exchange arrangement at once?

Much closer scrutiny of entitlements, dues, and duties can be expected in the years ahead. At present, claims of a right to an old-age pension or some other public service pass largely without challenge, but the legitimacy of such assertions is going to be looked at intensely. A variety of rights will be insisted on by the aging welfare generation. One will be the right of the insured holder of an explicit contract of social insurance—an actuarial right that will stand no searching attention. A second right will be that of the lifetime taxpayers, those who have paid their dues and are now claiming just returns. Lifetime contributions and benefits will not bear such inspection either and should not be pressed by those wanting to substantiate a claim to a retirement pension in the 1990s. An argument based on those grounds could well be an argument for major flows from old to young.

A third right, that of the aged who are poor to redistributions from their successors, will also disintegrate. This has been a potent argument for giving to the aged for some time, since their poverty relative to the young has been obvious. It no longer applies, now that redistributions toward the aged are flows toward generations of greater overall affluence from those of less. Few have yet recognized the significance of this development during the 1980s; for the first time in history, studies in North America, Europe, and Australasia are showing that the elderly on average are receiving more income, spending more, and saving more than those in their twenties and thirties, when responsibilities for dependent children are taken into account (Clark 1984; Council of Economic Advisers to the U.S. President 1985; Fiegehen 1986; Harrington 1984; Levy 1987; Thomson 1991). This has come about despite the rise in the numbers of young women with paid employment, the fall in the number of children with whom younger adults must share their resources, and the sharp decline in employment among those over sixty.

Moreover, this disparity will increase rapidly in the 1990s, with the aged becoming increasingly more prosperous relative to the young, even if governments should act now to curtail social security spending and the like. The elderly population of the 1980s consisted for the most part of the young adults of the 1920s and 1930s, and not of the welfare generation, who as they enter old age in the next few years will carry with them assets quite unlike those of their less favored predecessors. Again, a standard argument about rights has been turned on its head by recent developments—rights based on poverty might now demand a flow from old to young.

A fourth right to be voiced is that of the aged to a share of the rising general affluence of the community. According to this argument, even though in terms of insurance, past taxes, and the like the aged may not be entitled to much, they should nevertheless partake in any general rise in living standards. But has there been such an improvement? Studies of the incomes and expenditures of generations rather than of the population as a whole point to significant groups among the young who have enjoyed no rise in purchasing power for many years (see, for example, Levy 1987). In New Zealand, for instance, the median single-income two-child family has faced at least a 20 percent fall in real purchasing power during the past twenty years, whereas the elderly have experienced a 100 percent rise. Further, it may be questioned in what senses the apparent rising affluence of the young in recent decades has been real. Much of it derives from the increase in young female employment and the decrease in the numbers of children. Had young adults not modified their behaviors in these ways their current incomes would look very poor indeed compared with those of older persons or viewed in terms of real purchasing power.

There is, too, a larger question here concerning what constitutes affluence. Is a generation that can take skiing holidays but is not investing in children or other future goods truly affluent? According to conventional measures and thinking it is, but this must be debatable. It may be that the purchase of international travel and compact disc players by the young, while seemingly evidence of an affluence not available to predecessors and of which the aged should be granted a share, is not a sign of growing real income so much as of the reverse—the inability to afford more expensive items like housing, or space, or children. The argument that a rise in general living standards has occurred in the past twenty years and so must be shared with the aged also has to be questioned. It is not apparent that the affluence of the young has in fact risen in the past two decades, once we look beyond the most obvious baubles of the yuppies. And if this is so, then the reverse of the argument that the elderly deserve more as general living standards rise must apply equally.

A fifth right will be asserted—I have heard it already. It is that contributions take many forms other than taxation, that members of the welfare generation have made these, and that these other contributions somehow right all apparent imbalances. The details of this claim are never spelled out, but the other contributions hinted at are homemaking, raising children, voluntary community work, and the like. This point has some substance—generational contributions can be made in many forms. But these are also being made by other generations born both before and after the welfare generation: to claim loosely that putting nonmonetary items on the generational scales resolves everything will not do.

One further right will be voiced widely, that of the children of the Depression and the survivors of the war to special treatment. It has been suggested to me that I have been naïve in my assessment of the purposes of intergenerational exchange. The welfare state, I am told, was never intended as more than a one-generation phenomenon, a reward or catch up for those who felt deprived by their youthful experiences in the 1920s, 1930s, and 1940s and who believed that their successors therefore owed them something. The whole exchange arrangement, the implication runs, was never intended to be fair between generations or sustainable for more than a few decades. It was, in short, to be the classic chain letter. In this sense the welfare state can perhaps be said to have worked well. The only concern now is that younger generations have wised up to the ruse a little too soon and may endanger the exchanges planned for the "unlucky" generation in their old age.

My reaction is that this looks rather too much like a desperate ex post facto justification. There is little evidence that in the 1940s and 1950s the concept of the welfare state was ever sold to populations on these terms, or that they understood its purposes to be simply this despite all the rhetoric to the contrary, or that they would have put their faith in something so nakedly exploitative. On the other hand, as an argument for special treatment it will be advanced, wrapped in less cynicism or intellectual gloss, by many of the current aged. It is a dangerous one that they should avoid. There is no obvious reason why young voters in the 1990s and beyond will feel sympathy for large claims to assistance on the basis of events that may have occurred decades before they were born.

Nor is it evident—even if pleading the Depression or the war is admitted—how much is owed. Have not the housing subsidies, the free health, the negative effective income taxes and more already discharged this debt? How much is required? It would remain, too, an open question just which generations deserved this special treatment most. Why is the claim of the children of the Depression stronger than that of the children of the First World War, or that of the adults of the 1920s and 1930s? There was no push by the welfare generation to give their elders special treatment. Beyond that, such special pleading strips the welfare exchanges of much of their moral pretension. It says that there has been no lasting contract of exchange, of consistency or reciprocity. Each generation is on its own, out simply for what it can get. Do collective intergenerational exchanges have a future when reduced to this?

We return in the end to rights conferred by participation in the implicit contract, and the claims of the aged in the 1990s do not look sound on this ground either. Disputes over justice and equity, rights and obligations will take many forms in the wake of the withering of the welfare consensus, and it remains an open question whether the current experiment in large-scale transfers between generations will survive. I hope it can. I am deeply suspicious of the values of the New Right and aware as a historian that previous retreats from collective action have resulted in new tensions and distress. But our generational inequities have advanced to such an extent that I am no longer convinced that a vital sense of trust now bonds the young to the old, sufficient to carry existing exchange arrangements far into the future. Despair at ever being able to make the exchanges work fairly may tempt us to put an end to all collective welfare actions. We must work hard if we want to avoid this option.

Bibliography

Ackerman, Bruce. 1981. *Social Justice in the Liberal State*. New Haven: Yale University Press.

Anscombe, G. E. M. 1958. "Modern Moral Philosophy." *Philosophy* 33 (124): 1–19.

Aquinas, Saint Thomas. 1964. *Summa Theologica*. Latin text and English translation. New York: McGraw-Hill.

Arrow, Kenneth, and Mordecai Kurz. 1970. *Public Investment, the Rate of Return and Optimal Fiscal Policy*. Washington, D.C.: Resources for the Future.

Ashcraft, Richard. 1986. *Revolutionary Politics and Locke's Two Treatises of Government*. Princeton: Princeton University Press.

Ashford, Douglas E. 1986. *The Emergence of Welfare States*. Oxford: Basil Blackwell.

Atiyah, Patrick. 1981. *Promises, Morals, and Law*. Oxford: Clarendon Press.

Barro, Robert. 1974. "Are Government Bonds Net Wealth?" *Journal of Political Economy* 82: 1095–1117.

Barry, Brian. 1989. *Democracy, Power and Justice: Essays in Political Theory*. Oxford: Clarendon Press.

Becker, Gary S. 1974. "A Theory of Social Interactions." *Journal of Political Economy* 82: 1063–1093.

Bengston, Vern L., et al. 1985. "Generations, Cohorts and Relations between Age-Groups." In Robert H. Binstock and Ethal Shanas, eds., *Handbook of Aging and the Social Sciences*. 2d ed. New York: Van Nostrand Reinhold.

Bennett, Jonathan. 1978. "On Maximizing Happiness." In R. I. Sikora and Brian Barry, eds., *Obligations to Future Generations*, 61–73. Philadelphia: Temple University Press.

Bernheim, Douglas, and Kyle Bagwell. 1988. "Is Everything Neutral?" *Journal of Political Economy* 96: 308–338.

Bittker, Boris. 1973. *The Case for Black Reparations*. New York: Random House.

Boehm-Bawerk, Eugene. 1959. *History and Critique of Interest Theories*. South Holland, Ill.: Libertarian Press.

Bradford, David F. 1975. "Constraints on Government Investment Opportunities and the Choice of Discount Rate." *American Economic Review* 65: 887–899.

Braudel, Fernand. 1979. *The Wheels of Commerce*. Translated from the French by S. Reynolds. New York: Harper and Row.

Broome, John. 1985. "The Economic Value of Life." *Economica* 52: 281–294.

Bruce, Maurice. 1968. *The Coming of the Welfare State*. London: B. T. Batsford.

Buchanan, James M., Robert D. Tollison, and Gordon Tullock, eds. 1980. *Toward a Theory of the Rent-Seeking Society*. College Station: Texas A&M University.

Burbidge, John. 1987. *Social Security in Canada: An Economic Appraisal*. Canadian Tax Foundation Paper no. 79. Toronto.

Burke, Edmund. 1790. *Reflections on the Revolution in France.* London: J. Dodsley.

Clark, Robert L. 1984. *Inflation and the Economic Well-being of the Elderly.* Baltimore: Johns Hopkins University Press.

Coons, John E., and Stephen Sugarman. 1978. *Education by Choice: The Case for Family Control.* Berkeley: University of California Press.

Council of Economic Advisers to the U.S. President. 1985. *Annual Economic Report of the President.* Transmitted to the Congress, February 1985. Washington, D.C.

Coward, L. 1974. *Mercer Handbook of Canadian Pension and Welfare Plans.* Toronto: CCH Canadian.

Creedy, John, and Richard Disney. 1985. *Social Insurance in Transition: An Economic Analysis.* Oxford: Clarendon Press.

Daniels, Norman. 1985. *Am I My Father's Keeper?* Oxford: Oxford University Press.

———. 1988. *Am I My Parents' Keeper? An Essay on Justice between the Young and the Old.* New York: Oxford University Press.

———. 1989. "Justice and Transfers between Generations." In Paul Johnson, Christopher Conrad, and David Thomson, eds., *Workers versus Pensioners: Intergenerational Justice in an Ageing World,* 57–79. Manchester: Manchester University Press.

Dasgupta, Partha. 1982. *The Control of Resources.* Cambridge: Harvard University Press.

Dasgupta, Partha, and G. M. Heal. 1979. *Economic Theory and Exhaustible Resources.* Cambridge: Cambridge University Press.

Davis, Lawrence. 1976. "Comments on Nozick's Entitlement Theory." *Journal of Philosophy* 73: 836–844.

Deacon, Robert J., and M. Bruce Johnson, eds. 1985. *Forestlands: Public and Private.* San Francisco: Pacific Institute for Public Policy Research.

Dunn, John. 1984. *Locke.* Oxford: Oxford University Press.

Easterbrook and Fischel. 1985. "Limited Liability and the Corporation." *University of Chicago Law Review* 52: 89–118.

Easterlin, Richard A. 1980. *Birth and Fortune.* New York: Basic Books.

———. 1987. "The New Age Structure of Poverty in America: Permanent or Transient?" *Population and Development Review* 13: 195–208.

Eisner, Robert. 1986. *How Real Is the Deficit?* New York: Free Press.

Epstein, Richard A. 1975. "Unconscionability: A Critical Reappraisal." *Journal of Law and Economics* 18: 293–315.

———. 1984. "Toward a Revitalization of the Contract Clause." *University of Chicago Law Review* 51: 703–751.

———. 1985. *Takings.* Cambridge: Harvard University Press.

———. 1986. "Past and Present: The Temporal Dimension in Property Law." *Washington University Law Quarterly* 64: 667–722.

Feinberg, Joel. 1975. "Rawls and Intuitionism." In Norman Daniels, ed., *Reading Rawls: Critical Studies of* A Theory of Justice. New York: Basic Books.

———. 1985. *The Moral Limits of the Criminal Law.* New York: Oxford University Press.

Fetter, Frank. 1977. *Capital, Interest, and Rent.* Kansas City, Kan.: Sheed, Andrews, and McMeel.

Fiegehen, C. 1986. "Incomes after Retirement." In *Social Trends* 16. London: Her Majesty's Stationery Office.

Filmer, Sir Robert. 1949. *Observations upon Aristotle's Politiques Touching Forms of Government* (1652). In Peter Laslett, ed., *Political Works of Sir Robert Filmer.*

Fishkin, James. 1979. *Tyranny and Legitimacy.* Baltimore: Johns Hopkins University Press.

———. 1982. "Justice between Generations: The Dilemma of Future Interests." *Bowling Green Studies in Applied Philosophy* 4: 24–33.

———. 1983. *Justice, Equal Opportunity, and the Family.* New Haven: Yale University Press.

———. 1984. *Beyond Subjective Morality.* New Haven: Yale University Press.

Fiss, Owen. 1977. "Groups and the Equal Protection Clause." In Marshall Cohen, Thomas Nagel, and Thomas Scanlon, eds., *Equality and Preferential Treatment.* Princeton: Princeton University Press.

Flora, Peter, and Arnold Heidenheimer, eds. 1981. *The Development of Welfare States in Europe and North America.* New Brunswick, N.J.: Transaction Books.

Flowers, Marilyn R. 1987. "Rent Seeking and Rent Dissipation: A Critical View." *Cato Journal* 7: 431–440.

Foner, Nancy. 1984. *Ages in Conflict: A Cross-cultural Perspective on Inequality between Old and Young.* New York: Columbia University Press.

Fourastié, Jean. *The Causes of Wealth.* Trans. Theodore Caplan. New York: Free Press, 1960.

Fraser, Derek. 1984. *The Evolution of the British Welfare State.* London: Macmillan.

Fried, Charles. 1981. *Contract as Promise.* Cambridge: Harvard University Press.

Golding, Martin P. 1968. "Ethical Issues in Biological Engineering." *U.C.L.A. Law Review* 15: 443–479.

———. 1972. "Obligations to Future Generations." *Monist* 56: 85–99.

Gordon, C. 1988. *The Myth of Family Care? The Elderly in the Early 1930s.* STICERD Welfare State Programme no. 29.

Griffin, James. 1987. *Well-being.* Oxford: Clarendon Press.

Guest, D. 1985. *The Emergence of Social Security in Canada.* Vancouver: University of British Columbia Press.

Hamilton, W. D. 1964. "The Genetical Theory of Social Behavior." *Journal of Theoretical Biology* 7.

Hammel, E. A., K. W. Wachter, and C. K. McDaniel. 1981. "The Chickens Come Home to Roost: The Kin of the Aged in 2000." In S. B. Kiesler, J. N. Morgan, and V. C. Oppenheimer, eds., *Aging and Social Change.* New York: Academic Press.

Hardin, Russell. 1982. *Collective Action.* Baltimore: Johns Hopkins University Press.

Hare, R. M. 1975. "Abortion and the Golden Rule." *Philosophy and Public Affairs* 4: 201–222.

Harrington, Michael. 1984. *The New American Poverty.* New York: Firethorn Press.

Hayman, Ronald. 1982. *Kafka: A Biography.* New York: Oxford University Press.

Health and Welfare Canada. 1986. *Overview: The Income Security Programmes of Health and Welfare Canada.* Ottawa.

Hilton, George W. 1966. "The Consistency of the Interstate Commerce Act." *Journal of Law and Economics* 9: 87–113.

Holland, D. M., and S. Myers. 1979. "Trends in Corporate Profitability and Capital Costs." In R. Lindsay, ed., *The Nation's Capital Needs*, 103–189. New York: Committee for Economic Development.

Hooker, Richard. 1676. *The Works of that Learned and Judicious Divine, Mr. Richard Hooker: in Eight Books of Ecclesiastical Polity*. London: Printed by R. White, for Rob. Scot, Tho. Basset, John Wright and Rich. Chiswel.

Jencks, Christopher. 1979. *Who Gets Ahead? The Determinants of Economic Success in America*. New York: Basic Books.

Jones, M. 1983. *The Australian Welfare State*. Sydney: George Allen and Unwin.

Koestler, Arthur. 1941. *Darkness at Noon*. Translated by Daphne Hardy. New York: Macmillan.

Laslett, Peter. 1967. "Social Contract." In Paul Edwards, ed., *The Encyclopedia of Philosophy*. New York: Macmillan.

———. 1979. "The Conversation between the Generations." In Peter Laslett and James Fishkin, eds., *Philosophy, Politics and Society, Fifth Series*, 36–56. New Haven: Yale University Press. Originally published in 1972 in *The Proper Study: Royal Institute of Philosophy Lectures, Vol. 4, 1969–70*, edited by G. N. A. Vesey.

———. 1984. "The Significance of the Past in the Study of Ageing." *Ageing and Society* 4: 379–390.

———. 1985. Review of *The Works of Thomas Robert Malthus*, ed. E. A. Wrigley and D. Souden. *Population Studies* 42: 321–325.

———. 1987. "The Character of Family History, Its Limitations and the Conditions for Its Proper Pursuit." *Journal of Family History* 12: 263–284.

———. 1989. *A Fresh Map of Life: The Emergence of the Third Age*. London; paperback, Cambridge: Harvard University Press, 1991.

Laslett, Peter, and John R. Harrison, eds., 1965. *The Library of John Locke*. Oxford: Oxford University Press.

Laslett, Peter, and J. E. Smith. 1988. "La parente en chiffres." *Annales*, ESC 43: 1–25.

Levin, Michael E. 1980. "Reverse Discrimination, Shackled Runners, and Personal Identity." *Philosophical Studies* 37: 139–149.

Levy, F. 1987. *Dollars and Dreams: The Changing American Income Distribution*. New York: Russell Sage Foundation for the National Committee for Research on the 1980 Census.

Lind, Robert. 1986. "The Shadow Price of Capital: Implications for the Opportunity Cost of Public Programs, the Burden of the Debt, and Tax Reform." In Walter Heller, Ross Starr, and David Starrett, eds., *Essays in Honor of Kenneth J. Arrow, volume 1*, 189–212. London: Cambridge University Press.

Lind, Robert, et al., eds. 1982. *Discounting for Time and Risk in Energy Policy* (Washington, D.C.: Resources for the Future.

Locke, John. [1689] 1989. *Two Treatises of Government: A Critical Edition with an Introduction and Apparatus Criticus by Peter Laslett*. Cambridge: Cambridge University Press.

————. *Essays on the Law of Nature*. [1676]. 1958. The Latin text with a translation, introduction, and notes, together with transcripts of Locke's shorthand in his journal for 1676. Ed. W. von Leyden. Reprinted from corrected sheets of 1st ed. (1954). Oxford: Clarendon Press.

Loewenstein, George. 1987. "Anticipation and the Valuation of Delayed Consumption." *Economic Journal* 97: 666–684.

Lomasky, Loren E. 1987. *Persons, Rights, and the Moral Community*. New York: Oxford University Press.

Lyons, David. 1977. "The New Indian Claims and the Original Rights to Land." *Social Theory and Practice* 4: 249–272.

Macdonald, Margaret. 1951. "The Language of Political Theory" (1941). In Anthony Flew, ed., *Essays on Logic and Language*, no. 9. Oxford: Basil Blackwell.

Macfarlane, Alan. 1978. *The Origins of English Individualism*. Oxford: Basil Blackwell.

————. 1987. *The Culture of Capitalism*. Oxford: Basil Blackwell.

Machan, Tibor R., ed. 1987. *The Main Debate: Communism versus Capitalism*. New York: Random House.

Mack, Eric. 1987. "In Defense of 'Unbridled' Freedom of Contract." In Tibor R. Machan, ed., *The Main Debate: Communism versus Capitalism*, 425–438. New York: Random House.

McKerlie, Dennis. 1989. "Equality and Time." *Ethics* 99: 475–491.

Mackie, J. L. 1967. "Fallacies." In *The Encyclopedia of Philosophy*, vol. 3.

Macneil, Ian R. 1974. "The Many Futures of Contracts." In *Southern California Law Review* 47: 691–816.

Malthus, T. R. 1802. *An Essay on Population*. 2d ed. London.

Mannheim, Karl. 1952. "The Problem of Generations" (1928). *Essays on the Sociology of Knowledge*. Ed. Paul Kecskemeti: New York: Oxford University Press.

Mendelsohn, R. 1981. "The Choice of Discount Rate for Public Projects." *American Economic Review* 71: 239–241.

Mill, John Stuart. 1962. "On Liberty." In *Utilitarianism*. Ed. Mary Warnock. New York: New American Library. Originally published London: Parker, 1859.

Mueller, Dennis. 1974. "Intergenerational Justice and the Social Discount Rate." *Theory and Decision* 5: 263–273.

Nagel, Thomas. 1979. *Mortal Questions*. Cambridge: Cambridge University Press.

Narveson, Jan. 1967. "Utilitarianism and New Generations." *Mind* 76 (301): 62–72.

Nozick, Robert. 1974. *Anarchy, State, and Utopia*. New York: Basic Books.

Osberg, Lars. 1981. *Economic Equality in Canada*. Toronto: Butterworths.

Parfit, Derek. 1982. "Future Generations: Further Problems." *Philosophy and Public Affairs* 11: 113–172.

————. 1984. *Reasons and Persons*. Oxford: Oxford University Press.

Patterson, James T. 1981. *America's Struggle against Poverty: 1900–1980*. Cambridge: Harvard University Press.

Pitkin, Hanna. 1972. "Obligation and Consent." In Peter Laslett, W. G. Runciman, and Quentin Skinner, eds., *Philosophy, Politics and Society, Fourth Series*, 45–85. Oxford: Basil Blackwell.

Rawls, John. 1971. *A Theory of Justice*. Cambridge: Harvard University Press.

Rousseau, Jean Jacques. [1755] 1984. *Discours sur l'origine et les fundements de l'iné-galité parmi les hommes: A Discourse on Inequality*. Translated with an introduction and notes by Maurice Cranston. Harmondsworth, Middlesex: Penguin.

Rowley, Charles K., and Alan T. Peacock. 1975. *Welfare Economics: A Liberal Restatement*. London: Martin Robertson.

Samuelson, J. Paul. 1958. "An Exact Consumption-Loan Model of Interest, with or without the Social Contrivance of Money." *Journal of Political Economy* 66: 467–482.

Schaar, John H. 1967. "Equality of Opportunity and Beyond." In J. Roland Pennock and John W. Chapman, eds., *Nomos IX Equality*, 228–250. New York. Atherton Press.

Schwartz, Thomas. 1978. "Obligations to Posterity." In R. I. Sikora and Brian Barry, eds., *Obligations to Future Generations*, 3–13. Philadelphia: Temple University Press.

Sen, Amartya. 1973. *On Economic Inequality*. Oxford: Clarendon Press.

———. 1982. *Choice, Welfare, and Measurement*. Cambridge: MIT Press.

Sharp, Andrew. 1990. *Justice and the Maori*. Auckland: Oxford University Press.

Sher, George. 1975. "Justifying Reverse Discrimination in Employment." *Philosophy and Public Affairs* 4: 159–179.

———. 1979a. "Compensation and Transworld Personal Identity." *Monist* 62: 378–391.

———. 1979b. "Effort, Ability, and Personal Desert." *Philosophy and Public Affairs* 8: 361–376.

Sidgwick, Henry. 1874. *The Methods of Ethics*. London: Macmillan.

———. 1891. *The Elements of Politics*. London: Macmillan.

Sikora, R. I., and Brian Barry, eds. 1978. *Obligations to Future Generations*. Philadelphia: Temple University Press.

Simon, Herbert A. 1961. *Models of Man, Social and Rational*. New York: John Wiley.

Singer, Peter. 1979. *Practical Ethics*. Cambridge: Cambridge University Press.

Smith, R. M. 1984. "The Structured Dependence of the Elderly in the Middle Ages and Thereafter." *Ageing and Society* 4: 409–428.

———. 1986. "Transfer Incomes, Risk and Security: The Roles of the Family and the Collectivity in Recent Theories of Fertility Change." In David Coleman and Roger Schofield, eds., *The State of Population Theory*. Oxford: Basil Blackwell.

———. 1988. "Welfare and Management of Demographic Uncertainty." In M. Keynes, D. Coleman, and N. Dimsdale, eds., *The Political Economy of Health and Welfare*. London: Macmillan.

Snell, K., and J. Millar. 1987. "Lone-Parent Families and the Welfare State: Past and Present." *Continuity and Change* 2: 387–422.

Solow, Robert. 1974. "The Economics of Resources or the Resources of Economics." *American Economic Review* 64: 1–14.

Sommerville, Johann P., ed. 1991. *Patriarcha and Other Writings*. Cambridge: Cambridge University Press.

Starrett, David A. 1988. *Foundation of Public Economics*. Cambridge: Cambridge University Press.

Taurek, John. 1977. "Should the Numbers Count?" *Philosophy and Public Affairs* 6: 293–316.

Teichgraeber, Richard, III. 1986. *"Free Trade" and Moral Philosophy*. Durham: Duke University Press.

Temkin, Larry S. 1986. "Inequality." *Philosophy and Public Affairs* 15: 99–121.

———. 1992. *Inequality*. New York: Oxford University Press.

Thomson, David. 1981. "Provision for the Elderly in England: 1834–1908." Ph.D. diss., University of Cambridge.

———. 1984a. "The Decline of Social Welfare: Falling State Support for the Elderly since Early Victorian Times." *Ageing and Society* 4: 451 101.

———. 1984b. " 'I Am Not My Father's Keeper': Families and the Elderly in Nineteenth Century England." *Law and History Review* 2: 265–286.

———. 1986. "Welfare and the Historians." In Lloyd Bonfield, Richard Smith, and Keith Wrightson, eds., *The World We Have Gained*, 355–378. Oxford: Basil Blackwell.

———. 1989. "The Welfare State and Generation Conflict: Winners and Losers." In Paul Johnson, Christopher Conrad, and David Thomson, eds., *Workers versus Pensioners: Intergenerational Justice in an Ageing World*, 33–51. Manchester: Manchester University Press.

———. 1991. *Selfish Generations? The Ageing of New Zealand's Welfare State*. Wellington, N.Z.: Bridget Williams Books.

Thomson, David, and B. Macdonald. 1987. "Mortgage Relief, Farm Finance and Rural Depression in New Zealand in the 1930s." *New Zealand Journal of History*, 21: 228–250.

Townsend, Peter. 1979. *Poverty in the United Kingdom*. Harmondsworth, Middlesex: Penguin.

Tuck, Richard. 1979. *Natural Rights Theories*. Cambridge: Cambridge University Press.

Warr, Peter, and Brian Wright. 1981. "The Isolation Paradox and the Discount Rate for Benefit-Cost Analysis." *Quarterly Journal of Economics* 95: 129–145.

Wheeler, Samuel C. 1980. "Natural Property Rights as Body Rights." *Nous* 16: 272–289.

Williams, Bernard. 1962. "The Idea of Equality." In Peter Laslett and W. S. Runciman, eds., *Philosophy, Politics and Society, Second Series*, 110–131. Oxford: Basil Blackwell.

———. 1973. "A Critique of Utilitarianism." In J. J. C. Smart and Bernard Williams, *Utilitarianism For and Against*, 77–150. Cambridge: Cambridge University Press.

Williams, Stephen F. 1978. "Running Out: The Problem of Exhaustible Resources." *Journal of Legal Studies* 7: 165–199.

Woodward, C. Vann. 1987. Review of *Unfree Labor: American Slavery and Russian Serfdom*, by Peter Kolchin. *New York Review of Books* 34, no. 18 (November 19).

Yang, Edward J., Roger C. Dower, and Mark Menefee. 1984. *The Use of Economic Analysis in Valuing Natural Resource Damages*. Washington, D.C.: Environmental Law Institute.